CARCERAL CITIZENS

CARCERAL CITIZENS

Labor and Confinement in Puerto Rico

· CAROLINE M. PARKER ·

THE UNIVERSITY OF CHICAGO PRESS · CHICAGO & LONDON

The University of Chicago Press, Chicago 60637
The University of Chicago Press, Ltd., London
© 2024 by Caroline M. Parker
Published 2024
Printed in the United States of America

33 32 31 30 29 28 27 26 25 24   1 2 3 4 5

ISBN-13: 978-0-226-83621-8 (cloth)
ISBN-13: 978-0-226-83623-2 (paper)
ISBN-13: 978-0-226-83622-5 (e-book)
DOI: https://doi.org/10.7208/chicago/9780226836225.001.0001

Library of Congress Cataloging-in-Publication Data

Names: Parker, Caroline M., author.
Title: Carceral citizens : labor and confinement in Puerto Rico / Caroline M. Parker.
Description: Chicago : The University of Chicago Press, 2024. | Includes bibliographical references and index.
Identifiers: LCCN 2024018756 | ISBN 9780226836218 (cloth) | ISBN 9780226836232 (paperback) | ISBN 9780226836225 (ebook)
Subjects: LCSH: Correctional institutions—Puerto Rico. | Rehabilitation centers—Puerto Rico. | Faith-based human services—Puerto Rico.
Classification: LCC HV9572 .P37 2024 | DDC 365/.97295—dc23/eng/20240517
LC record available at https://lccn.loc.gov/2024018756

The relationship between slavery and race,
race and unfreedom, unfreedom and labor is
one that we constantly try to untangle.
At our peril we ignore it. But also at our peril,
we make it too simplistic.

· RUTH WILSON GILMORE ·

· CONTENTS ·

· INTRODUCTION ·

Rocky, a veteran drug trafficker, had finally found a home: "Here is the place where I am needed."

Having finished his chores, Rocky stood next to me on the terrace, smoking a cigarette and gazing out at the green dappled mountains. Below us, men in paint-spotted overalls were taking a break in the sun. The balcony had just been painted; the grass had just been mown. The men were taking a well-earned rest. "Right now, I am blessed. I have a home, a job, a family, and I have thirty-two men who really want to change." With these words Rocky gestured to a lifetime of experience that had led him to where he was that morning in 2016: at La Casita, a reeducation program for men in Puerto Rico's rural interior. Like most of Puerto Rico's "therapeutic communities," La Casita was a nonprofit organization grounded in self-help (*auto-ayuda-mutua*). Its founder and its residents shared histories of incarceration, drug addiction, or (most commonly) both.[1] By the time I met Rocky, he had been at La Casita for about three years, and for the foreseeable future, he intended to remain there.

This book follows the lives and labor trajectories of formerly incarcerated men who have been diverted to therapeutic communities as an alternative to prison and who have chosen to stay at these reeducation programs upon completing their mandatory court sentences to assume positions as peer counselors. The book describes the specific arrangements of labor and social life that are crystallizing in therapeutic communities, and it explores how the entrance of self-help into the work of criminal rehabilitation is shaping men's opportunities for social, economic, and political participation. While the events described take place in Puerto Rico—a US colony and former Spanish colony—these arrangements of labor and confinement also speak to many other parts of Latin America. From Argentina to Mexico, overcrowded prison systems are turning to the growing capillary network of self-help organizations, churches, reeducation programs, and gang-prevention initiatives that constitute the region's "soft security" apparatus, providing a rapidly growing, albeit underappreciated, alternative to incarceration.[2]

Puerto Rico's correctional twist on self-help since the late twentieth century has come to rest on a surprisingly simple arrangement. Courts transfer incarcerated individuals from overcrowded prisons to therapeutic communities. These self-help initiatives undertake the work of "reeducating" those entrusted to their care. Eventually, residents who have completed their mandatory custodial sentences are given the option to *stay put*, to live in reeducation facilities *for free*, and are provided with internal positions as therapists, social workers, and counselors. In Puerto Rican therapeutic communities, the men who perform this work are known locally as *re-educados* ("reeducated men"). In exchange for their contribution to the running and functioning of these reeducation programs, re-educados receive free room and board along with various in-house privileges. Some who stay for many years eventually obtain waged positions. For the vast majority though, this is a self-consciously "voluntary" kind of work whose reward is both more and less than a wage.

Whatever one might think of this voluntary work, this key innovation of modern capitalism has so far escaped the radar of past theorizing on incarceration and capitalism. Taking inspiration from Karl Marx's early observation that modern capitalism has a built-in tendency to generate human surplus, scholars who have explored the connections between the rise of mass incarceration and the demise of wage labor since the late twentieth century have come to agree upon a fundamental plotline. Usually, policies pioneered in the United States (the mainland, not the territories) are considered the major milestones of this plotline, which goes something like this.

In response to civil rights protest movements in the 1960s and 1970s, the United States strengthened its carceral state through expanding its policing, surveillance, and incarceration capacity. Then, as changes in economic policy privileged profit making over full employment—what scholars describe as the moment when global neoliberalism brought an end to Fordist-Keynesianism—entire swaths of the population were rendered "superfluous" within the new postindustrial economy. The war on drugs soon emerged as a key mechanism for controlling this expelled postindustrial proletariat. Key legislative innovations during this period included law-and-order policies, broken windows policies, mandatory minimum sentences, and three strikes legislation. Taken together, this punitive legislation differentially targeted US citizens along lines of race, class, and gender, and the overall effect was a gendered and racialized penalization of poverty. Soon, the carceral turn spread to other parts of the globe, especially to Latin America and northern Europe, expelling ever greater swaths of the world population. This growing expelled population is today's version of the "surplus" laboring population that emerged in the brutal beginnings of modern capitalism.[3]

But as Saskia Sassen, herself a theorist of this plotline, points out: "When dynamics of expulsion proliferate . . . the space of the expelled expands and becomes increasingly differentiated." What is left is not just "a dark hole."[4] As useful as theories of expulsion and surplus are for linking prison expansions to twentieth-century labor market contractions, this plotline cannot yet account for the set of developments that are occurring in a host of different sites across the Americas; namely, the carceral state, the nonprofit sector, and self-help are coalescing, and through this odd unification, formerly incarcerated people are carving out new, meaningful, and encompassing social and economic lives for themselves in various alternatives to the prison—alternatives that they themselves are increasingly responsible for running.

This book offers an ethnographic portrait of this development and a reflection on its social significance, with Puerto Rico—a US colony with a drastically different racial history to the mainland—as its focal point. In conversation with scholars of capitalism, colonialism, and race formation and drawing on insights from Northern and Southern carceral studies, it explores how this unexpected amalgamation of confinement, labor, and self-help came into existence historically, and it explores what these perplexing new labor opportunities mean for the people whose livelihoods now nest within them. By exploring how formerly incarcerated people bring new livelihoods and new social memberships into being—using the case study of self-help and therapeutic communities in Puerto Rico—this book will add a fresh chapter to contemporary understanding of capitalism's dynamics of expulsion and confinement. It will lead me to conclude that capitalism's "surplus" masses are not so superfluous after all.

Rocky (a pseudonym) was among a dozen men at La Casita (another pseudonym) who described themselves as "volunteers." These men had typically resided at the center for at least a year and had access to certain privileges (such as a bedroom with fewer roommates or a permit to drive La Casita's in-house vehicle). Volunteers were often responsible for supervisory tasks, such as allocating chores and assignments and acquainting new residents with the center's numerous rules and norms. Like most volunteers, Rocky did not have to pay the $250 monthly residence fee. Instead, he received free room and board along with a sub-minimum-wage stipend. While two staff members at La Casita were paid monthly salaries that enabled them to live off-site in their own private homes, Rocky's situation was by far the more common.

Fifty-three years old and heavily tattooed, Rocky spoke in a smokey whisper that conferred him a raspy, street-elder authority. He had spent over 20 years of his adult life in the Río Piedras State Penitentiary, going in at twenty-seven and coming out in his late forties. Those 22 years, he would hasten to add, were significantly fewer than anticipated. His initial sentence had been for 147 years on thirteen counts of drug trafficking, drug possession, kidnapping, assault, armed robbery, and possession of firearms. But after partially losing his eyesight in a prison riot, having spent years cramped with twenty other men in a small cell designed for six inhabitants, Rocky joined the dozens of inmates who were relocated by Puerto Rican prison authorities in the early 2000s to therapeutic communities of the nonprofit sector to ease overcrowding. In Rocky's case, he was referred to La Casita to fulfill the remaining two years of a much-reduced sentence.

Much like the prison Rocky had just come from, La Casita's explicitly stated aim was to "reeducate" and "rehabilitate" its residents by creating "independent" and "hardworking" men with the requisite skills to become "useful members of society."[5] But when Rocky compared life at La Casita to the 22 years he had spent in prison, a comparison he volunteered sparingly, reserving for pep talks with skeptical residents, the differences were clear. For Rocky, prison had spelled twenty-two years of dirty water, thirst, blunt needles, ulcers, hepatitis, broken ribs, bedbugs, and, most harrowingly, dead cellmates. It was at La Casita, in contrast, that Rocky had found safety and shelter and had finally stopped using heroin, a drug he had injected almost daily and throughout his time in prison. It was at La Casita, Rocky said, that he had learned "how to really relate to people" and acquired new theories for interpreting his past, or what he now referred to as his "disorder of character." "Before," he would say, "my personality wasn't fully formed. I was stuck. But La Casita taught me how to strengthen my character." Beneath the therapeutic scripts of character transformation that circulate in therapeutic communities across the Americas lay something else. As well as internalizing a historically particular way of understanding himself (an understanding whose history I trace in chapter 2), Rocky had also acquired a feeling he'd never had before. You could call it a sense of belonging.

"Why did you choose to stay here?" I said, repeating a question I'd come to ask numerous therapeutic community residents that year. Rocky stared at me for a moment. "I made it through the first year," he said, "and I guess I was noticed as a hard worker. They told me: 'If you keep this up, you will go very far here.'" And so he did. After two years Rocky graduated from La Casita. There had been a boisterous graduation ceremony in a town hall, a day he recalls fondly for the hundreds of families who had attended and the evening of dancing and live music. Once the festivities had died down, Rocky had met with La Casita's director and asked to be kept on as a volunteer. The director said, "Let's see how you manage for a few months." Rocky stuck it out. Two months later he was hired. His preferred title was "therapist." He was paid $325 a fortnight in cash "as an incentive," which works out at about $8,450 a year. He shared La Casita's best bedroom, the one with just two bunk beds in it. He remained on-site full-time, seven days a week, and said, "I'm always working, really, except when I'm asleep." He did not have a car or driver's license, though he said someone could usually give him a ride into town when he needed one. "But I don't really like being out of the *hogar* [home]," Rocky said, with a shrug.

"On Saturdays I'll leave in the morning and get into town around nine a.m." Rocky said this gesturing toward the road that conjoined La Casita to nearest town, a breezy commuter village just shy of a thousand inhabitants. "But in like two hours I'm back here. I prefer it here," he said. When my head cocked to the side, inviting clarification, Rocky leaned in. "Carolina, I have my family here," he said, seeming to eye my expression. "These men are my brothers, and I'd do anything for them. This is my first legal job, and I do it with all my heart." I struggled to meet Rocky's gaze, doubt prickling within me, a doubt that felt ill-matched and even rude in the face of Rocky's earnest positivity. "I love what I do," he said, raising his hands to his chest. "I'm fifty-three years old, and before this, I hadn't done a thing with my life. When I was in prison, I never imagined I could do this, be here, helping others, just as I was helped."

I began working with Rocky in the summer of 2015. At that time, I was traveling around the island interviewing directors of therapeutic communities to understand the factors driving the growth of mutual-aid care systems. Many of the therapeutic community staff members I encountered spoke passionately about the work they were doing. Like Rocky, many of them were formerly incarcerated, and landing an opportunity to become a peer therapist was the lucky break they had been waiting for.

But back in the university hospitals and government bureaucracies of San Juan, public health workers and government employees I interviewed told a dramatically different story. Therapeutic communities and the re-educados that ran them were yet another depressing symptom of the state's failure to respond to the drug problem. At best, they were well-intentioned amateurs who provided basic shelter to drug users but fell woefully short of providing adequate treatment. At worst, they were pseudoprofessional profiteers who were exploiting Puerto Rico's most vulnerable.

These professionals were not alone. For decades, researchers have dissected therapeutic communities' clinical and social outcomes.[6] With only shaky evidence that they protect their graduates from substance-related harm in the long term, some consider the whole therapeutic community enterprise as a sham whose only real achievement lies in poverty management.[7] This interpretation, powerful as it is as a structural analysis, omits a fundamental social scientific question. As incarceration, self-help, and labor coalesce within a quasi-autonomous US colony, what kind of life and what kind of citizenship become possible? And more to the point, what can the terms "self-help" and "volunteer" mean in these quasi-correctional, quasi-therapeutic, quasi-vocational settings?

. . . . .

The last exit before Comunidad-Luz is full of potholes. Screeching cars and trucks grind to a halt in the jammed slip lane. A municipality-wide electrical fault has immobilized the traffic lights, bringing highways and thoroughfares to standstills for miles around. In the city of Guayama, where Héctor and I are now headed, police officers have been instructed to shepherd vehicles through the city's major junctions until the traffic signals regain power. There have been three car accidents and two fatalities in the last twenty-four hours. Héctor snickers at my anxious driving. After half an hour of slow crawling, we finally put the highway behind us and begin the four-mile ascent to the compound. Burned-out cars and peeling billboards soon give way to wild grasses and *flamboyán* trees thick with orange flowers. The front tire of my decrepit Chevrolet goes flat just as we are entering the parking lot. Through the gate, we are greeted by residents eager to help unpack crates of bottled water. A drought has put the whole municipality on rationed water: one hour per "household" per morning, but Comunidad-Luz is a household of thirteen.

Comunidad-Luz is really just a few concrete outbuildings bordering an asphalt basketball court. A sign overhead reads: "Addiction is curable!" Another reads: "God Loves You!" Like many of Puerto Rico's therapeutic communities, Comunidad-Luz is built on abandoned land: in this case, the grounds of a now-defunct primary school that closed down many years ago amid fiscal pressures and sustained depopulation. Héctor, who used to be a security guard but has done time in prison for drug trafficking and armed robbery, is now in his sixties. "If you'd met me back then," he'd say, letting out a mischievous whistle, "well, put it this way, you wouldn't wanna go near me." Like many therapeutic community founders, Héctor has an eye for opportunity. The very land on which Comunidad-Luz is built, as he would often remind me, "used to be just jungle, full of dead animals and wrecked cars." But where others saw ruin, Héctor spied potential.

Having successfully wrangled a couple of modest loans—one from his mother, another from a Pentecostal church—Héctor purchased the old school grounds on which Comunidad-Luz now stands in the late nineties, when local governments were selling off public property cheaply. Once the building work was done, he got Comunidad-Luz incorporated as a community-based organization in 2000. Then, putting his own personal history of therapeutic community treatment to use, he designed his own reeducation program, making a list of "what addicts need" based on his own personal experiences. What addicts needed, according to Héctor, was "moral character," "new norms and values," "an education in hard work," and, last but not least, "a place to call home."

Héctor got Comunidad-Luz licensed as a residential drug treatment program through Puerto Rico's Mental Health and Anti-Addiction Services Administration in 2001. The accreditation process had been relatively pain-less: a government inspector told him to lock the kitchen at night "because of sharp objects," to put the television behind bars, and to pay a license fee. Héctor thought the $125 fee was steep given that, in his words, "they give us nothing in return." Nevertheless, he duly paid the fee. When people asked, "Why work with drug addicts?" Héctor would reply with some talk of "not just standing by and watching the suffering." But there was more to it. Héctor shared something with other therapeutic community founders: an unshakable conviction that he was uniquely positioned by virtue of his own life experiences to help other men like him. Like other therapeutic community founders, he had a fundamental faith that he knew something those doctors and probation officers did not.

Héctor now had twelve residents living at Comunidad-Luz, twelve men for whom he, and he alone, was responsible. He talked like a youth coun-selor, telling men he'd just met, "I used to be just like you," and handing out warnings of "falling into vice" and "going down the wrong path." He would often say: "These men need everything because they got nothing. I got twelve brothers depending on me now." As Héctor liked to put it, he had found his calling.

To understand the experiences of men like Héctor and Rocky, this book develops two concepts: *carceral citizenship* and *carceral livelihoods*. Pared down, the former refers to a profoundly contradictory mode of belonging, and the latter, to a way of making a living that has been crystallizing in devolved outposts of the carceral state since the late twentieth century. As conceptual lenses, they draw attention to how late capitalism, incarceration, and the entrance of self-help into the work of criminal rehabilitation are generating new and highly paradoxical modes of economic, social, and civic participation for formerly incarcerated people. The many paradoxes of these carceral livelihoods and their associated genre of citizenship are elaborated ethnographically through the book's chapters. But before I get to these paradoxes, let me outline my grounding concepts.

First, what do I mean by "carceral"? A distinction is usually made between the carceral state and its "penal" counterpart. Whereas the penal state comprises the criminal justice institutions, policies, and instruments that adjudicate "penal power" (the power to punish) through criminal law, the carceral state encompasses a much more expansive collection of institutions and instruments that exercise this power to impose punitive sanctions.[8] Gang rehabilitation initiatives, probation hostels, and civil courts, for example, may all be considered elements of the carceral state. Like therapeutic communities, these sites of civil and administrative authority are "carceral" in the sense that they actively wield penal power, though they are not prisons, and though their authority does not stem entirely or even solely from criminal law.

These not-entirely-criminal sites of not exclusively punishment are not new and certainly did not originate in Puerto Rico. The ungated, unguarded French Juvenile Reformatory of Mettray opened its doors in France as early as 1839. As Foucault famously argued, Mettray's minors were not straightforwardly locked up.[9] They enjoyed a circumscribed freedom of movement and were committed to a humanistically inflected daily schedule of religious instruction, apprenticeship, education, and work. This was reflected in Mettray's clientele, which in addition to minors serving custodial criminal sentences also included minors who had been acquitted, boarders who had never been charged, and the law-abiding children born of convict parents in France's overseas penal colonies.[10] As much as Mettray was designed to punish then, it was also designed to educate and to cure; in Foucault's deft summary, it was "a prison, but not entirely."[11]

Puerto Rico's therapeutic communities present a similarly strange containment. They lie at the limit of strict penal confinement. With no imposing walls, no barbed-wire fences, and no padlocked gates, their clientele extend beyond the criminally detained to include residents whose court orders have expired and who have chosen to remain there, residents committed via civil rather than criminal courts, and residents who have enrolled voluntarily (without a court order, though these are a small minority). Thus, therapeutic communities are not exclusively designed to confine. Beyond confinement, these ungated facilities also seek to reeducate, to achieve a radical transformation of character, and, most importantly, to instill a sense of self-help and mutual obligation (*auto-ayuda-mutua*) in their members.

But what kind of citizenship is possible within these carceral jurisdictions of a US colony? "Citizens," recall, are conventionally understood as equal members of a nation-state, a liberal conception that immediately encounters problems in a territory like Puerto Rico, which does not amount to a nation-state.[12] In 1901, the legal status of Puerto Rico (along with the Philippines and Guam) became that of an "unincorporated territory" defined paradoxically as "belonging to" but not "part of" the United States.[13] Puerto Rico's ongoing coloniality is a stark reminder of liberalism's chief conceit—namely, that membership within a democratic nation-state necessarily guarantees something called "full" or "equal" citizenship. Instead, as a growing chorus of historians, political philosophers, and scholars of citizenship now concur, modern citizenship turns out to be a fundamentally stratified and differentiated project, one that attributes rights and benefits to some while systematically denying them to others. When I write of citizenship in this book then, I channel this critique of liberal citizenship. I acknowledge that Puerto Ricans, like other colonized and racialized minorities in the United States and its territories, are part of a stratified, racialized, and highly differentiated US citizenry. All exist in a world where colonialism and structural racism are part and parcel of liberal citizenship and always have been.[14]

From its inception in 1790, recall, US citizenship was granted only to "free white" people, which effectively excluded most women and all those who were nonwhite, enslaved, or indentured. Though the debate about whether to extend US citizenship to Puerto Rico took place between 1898 and 1917 (so several decades after African Americans were granted US citizenship in 1868 but before Indigenous Americans were granted US citizenship in 1924), legal arbitrations of US citizenship were shot through with plain and potent white supremacist ideology. In the congressional debates about whether Puerto Ricans were good candidates for US citizenship, those in favor decried the "un-American" injustice of denying citizenship to a people, "in the main, of Caucasian blood . . . [and] desirous of casting their lot with us."[15] Those opposed to extending US citizenship to Puerto Ricans cast doubt on islanders' whiteness. During the final congressional debates over the Jones Act in 1916, Representative Joseph Cannon of Illinois objected that "the people of Porto Rico have not the slightest conception of self-government. . . . Porto Rico is populated by a mixed race. About 30 percent are pure African . . . [and fully] 75 to 80 percent of the population . . . was pure African or had an African strain in their blood."[16] Between 1898 and 1917, US Congress would debate upward of thirty bills containing citizenship provisions for Puerto Rico, with most failing to get through the House. So tightly intertwined was this issue of race and citizenship that it was only through legislating a highly ambiguous and "empire-friendly" conception of citizenship—one that would forever remain open to interpretation—that US Congress eventually managed to grant Puerto Ricans US citizenship in 1917.[17]

But what did this citizenship amount to? The Jones Act of 1917 did not smoothly upgrade or subsume Puerto Ricans into a homogenous US citizenry. All it did was introduce one additional axis—"residency" (island or stateside)—to prevailing legal stratifications of US citizenship. The most egregious discriminations at that time consisted of Jim Crow laws forcing African Americans into slave-like conditions on the plantations, voting restrictions denying women equal suffrage with men in all but four states, and, among many other examples, laws requiring Mexican American and Chinese American children to attend segregated schools.[18] For all *these* US citizens, there was nothing remotely equal about US citizenship. So when, in 1917, approximately 1.2 million Puerto Ricans were "collectively naturalized," these freshly minted US citizens joined the uncertain ranks of a highly stratified and differentiated US populace.

This brings me to my first grounding concept: carceral citizenship. Criminologists and sociologists have rightly noted that formerly incarcerated people in the United States are subject to a range of legal barriers and exclusions—often for the rest of their lives—across foundational institutions of voting, employment, and housing.[19] From the 4.6 million people currently unable to vote because of a felony record to the millions more who are permanently denied vital state services, the alternative legal-regulatory universe awaiting the nation's felons is often decried a "second-class" citizenship—that is, a "purgatory status"[20] said to be "less than average citizens."[21]

But for the 3.2 million Puerto Ricans residing on the island, there has never been anything "average" about US citizenship. Since 1952, Puerto Rico's constitutional status has been that of an Estado Libre Asociado (Free Associated State, commonly translated as Commonwealth).[22] As an Estado Libre Asociado, Puerto Rico is granted partial autonomy in some domestic areas, including elections, taxation, education, and health. But Puerto Rico remains subject to US federal legislation at the discretion of Congress, it does not have voting representation in US Congress, and Puerto Ricans continue to be denied the right to vote in US presidential elections. Federal government remains in control of most state affairs, including citizenship, immigration, customs, defense, currency, foreign trade, and diplomacy. Meanwhile, various US constitutional provisions—such as the requirement of indictment by grand jury, trial by jury in common law cases, and the right to confrontation of witnesses—do not extend to the territory. That "first class" citizenship has never existed in Puerto Rico points to the need for carceral theorists to reckon more directly with the colonial, racialized, and fundamentally stratified nature of citizenship to begin with.

In addition to considering citizenship's many exclusions, Miller and Stuart make an important intervention when they point out that formerly incarcerated people also accrue some unique state provisions and benefits too (such as dedicated health and employment services, however shoddy or inadequate they may be).[23] They theorize carceral citizenship in this strict legal sense: as the legal restrictions, duties, and benefits that are uniquely accorded to people with criminal records. This legal conception has usefully shed light on the alternative legal regime of social welfare and surveillance that is set in motion with the issuing of a criminal record. Like Miller and Stuart, I am also interested in what incarceration can be said to add or bring to the experience of citizenship, beyond exclusions. But my interest in citizenship's social dimensions leads me to a distinct conceptualization of carceral citizenship.

Extending criminological perspectives that conceive carceral citizenship as a legal-juridical status bestowed top-down by nation-states at the moment of a criminal conviction, I conceive carceral citizenship anthropologically: *both* as a formal classification that revokes rights and confers legal rights and duties on formerly incarcerated people *and* as a shared sense of mutual obligation that can be cultivated among formerly incarcerated people. By my anthropological formulation, carceral citizenship is neither the opposite of "full" citizenship nor a purely legal-juridical matter. Instead, carceral citizenship is one among many stratified and unequal forms of citizenship to be found in the Americas today. Like all forms of citizenship, carceral citizenship is brought into being gradually, over time, and through human practice.[24]

For the formerly incarcerated people running Puerto Rico's therapeutic communities, we cannot begin to appreciate their lives, motivations, and their labor trajectories if we confine our attention solely to the legal exclusions imposed on them by virtue of their criminal records. Beyond any legal-juridical restrictions, my work with re-educados has alerted me to the surprising manner in which the shared experience of incarceration is igniting some striking new social affinities. These new affinities are encapsulated by Héctor's and Rocky's decisions to assume positions as volunteers in the name of self-help.

As I show in this book, the historically emergent form of citizenship I am calling carceral citizenship owes its form in no trivial part to Puerto Rico's ongoing coloniality and ambiguous racialization. This is why I do not posit carceral citizenship as the opposite of a homogenous or full citizenship, which has never existed in the United States, neither on the mainland nor in its territories. Instead, my formulation of carceral citizenship draws attention to how the ongoing extension of penal power since the closing decades of the twentieth century, and across ever broader elements of social life, has come to redraw what were *already highly differentiated possibilities* for social belonging in specific and highly circumscribed ways. These new modes of belonging come hand in hand with new economies and new ways of making a living, which brings me to my second grounding concept.

"Livelihood" is one of anthropology's oldest and most enduring categories of analysis for how people live. Since nineteenth-century ethnology, livelihood has comprised two elements: first, "work," in the sense of "making a living," and second, "living," in the sense of a "way of life." What I am calling carceral livelihoods refers to *both* the ways of working *and* the ways of living that are taking shape with carceral jurisdictions. This formulation confers at least two conceptual advantages. First, "livelihood" remains helpfully agnostic regarding mode of production, positioning it to account for ways of working in the contemporary moment that do not conform to wage labor or formal employment. Second, carceral livelihoods highlights the fact that for the re-educados who live and work in therapeutic communities, the work they do is providing more than just a means to survive. It is also providing an encompassing way of life that addresses social and existential needs.

Studies of precarious and oppressive modes of existence are increasingly heedful of the fact that precarity and structural violence do not preclude moral experience. Even the most abject and violent of livelihoods—dispossessed women who smuggle drugs across the US-Mexico border, mothers who pass injection drug use and addiction onto their daughters, the laboring poor who collect and sell recyclable trash on the peripheries of megacities, and teenagers whose coming of age in narco culture is predicated on murdering their friends—are recognized to *mean something* and to *bring something*, beyond suffering, to the people involved.[25] Yet quite strikingly, the idea that labor (broadly defined) performed under the auspices of the carceral state might provide something positive or meaningful to those who perform it is a point that carceral theorists have been loath to consider, and for understandable reasons.[26] Doing so can easily be mistaken for an endorsement of the carceral state and its practices. But this hesitancy, I argue, is restricting our understanding of the vast changes to work, life, and social belonging that are occurring across the Americas.

In Latin America, 1.5 million people are now behind bars, twice as many as twenty years ago, meaning that the region has now overtaken North America in having the fastest growing prison population worldwide.[27] Alongside formal prison expansions, Latin America has also witnessed an enormous expansion and devolution of its carceral apparatus. A highly devolved network of therapeutic communities, addiction ministries, gang-prevention initiatives, and self-help organizations has proliferated.[28] These "prisons of charity" have assumed critical roles in rehabilitation, reeducation, and reentry, both when prison sentences end and as alternatives to incarceration.[29] A central contention of this book then is that carceral states in the Americas have become sufficiently extensive and variable that a closer examination of ways of living and working emerging within these carceral jurisdictions— and of the reclaimed agency of those inhabiting them—is much needed.

Drawing on eight years of research, this book examines the carceral livelihoods being devised by re-educados in Puerto Rican therapeutic communities. My ethnographic inquiry leads to an important, albeit troubling, realization: The war on drugs has done a lot more than unleash a campaign against the poor. It has also spawned some canny camp followers—men like Héctor and Rocky, who have spied and seized the opportunities presented to them and who are now repurposing a colonially conditioned assault on the poor into a fully fledged way of life.

· · · · ·

Carceral livelihoods and the regimes of coerced labor they reinvent have a colonial anatomy that owe their shape, in contemporary Puerto Rico, to two distinct imperial orders and their intertwined racial legacies. The Puerto Rico of the Spanish Empire—an era marked by Indigenous genocide, African slavery, and a multiracial system of indentureship forcing landless peasants into toiling on the plantations on behalf of European landowners—was a gradually whitening Puerto Rico. That is, nineteenth-century racial censuses suggest that Puerto Rico's racial makeup was growing whiter, with *blanqueamiento* (whitening) generally attributed to *mestizaje* (racial mixing) and

Iberian racial caste systems that coded the light-skinned children of interracial unions as white.[30] Unlike the British colonies, where interracial unions were widely prohibited and, by the time the United States came into being in 1776, the infamous "one drop rule" meant that any person with one drop of "black blood" was rendered Black, mestizaje long provided Puerto Ricans with mixed African and European heritage with an escape from slavery and pathway to social mobility.

Mestizaje set Puerto Rico apart from many British colonies in part by producing a large population of *pardos libres* (free people of color), a class that vastly outnumbered Puerto Rico's enslaved population throughout the eighteenth and nineteenth centuries.[31] Though free from slavery, the term *free people of color* is something of a misnomer since a sizable portion of this non-enslaved population was coerced into working on the plantations. In 1815, Spain had introduced the Cédula de Gracia, which aimed to stimulate immigration by granting land to free male heads of household and thereby creating a new class of landowners (*hacendados*). Racially, most of the new landowners would have been white, generally elite Spanish Catholics or French or Dutch slave owners fleeing Haiti and the other Caribbean colonies, though a minority of the new landowners would have been *pardos libres*.[32] With the land grants, the multiracial peasantry who had eked out a living as subsistence farmers for several centuries suddenly found themselves within the confines of the new plantation system. By law, squatter farmers (*agredados*) were now obliged to work side by side with enslaved African workers cultivating sugar, coffee, and tobacco. As Kelvin Santiago-Valles makes very clear, corralling subsistence farmers into toiling all day for the sole purpose of producing exportable sugar and coffee on behalf of the new and mostly European landowners was by no means a peaceful endeavor.[33] Instead, it was achieved chiefly by means of a novel institutional development: a premodern carceral state.

Beginning in the nineteenth century, a complex mesh of new laws and legal practices had sprung up whose overall effect was the extraction of unpaid labor from the landless peasants, including those categorized as white. During the period 1849–1873, all squatter farmers were required to carry on their person and maintain an up-to-date *libreta de jornalero* (a worker's notebook) logging the days and hours they had spent working on the haciendas (plantations). Peasants who failed to present their notebooks in town hall meetings or who failed to rack up sufficient labor time could be punished by eight days' work at half pay, either in agriculture or domestic servitude on behalf of the landowners.[34] Workers with poor reputations (*malos antecedentes*) could be punished by six months' work at half pay.[35] Additional early appendages of the carceral state were the antivagrancy laws (Leyes de Corrección de Vagos) passed in 1832, 1833, and 1844 and the day labor codes (Leyes de Reglamentación de Trabajo) passed in 1839, 1847, and 1878.[36] Together, these laws effectively locked the multiracial landless peasantry into servile labor contracts with the European landowners.

These histories of coercion haunt the way race is conceived in Puerto Rico but in ways that are markedly different from the US mainland. To drive a wedge between themselves and their enslaved ancestors, Puerto Rico's freed slaves came to eschew the racial identification *negro*, which became synonymous with slave, choosing instead *pardo, liberto*, or *mulato*.[37] This eschewal of Black identification was common throughout the Spanish empire. In the Dominican Republic, freedmen and women would often represent themselves as *blancos de la tierra* (whites of the land).[38] Thanks to Spain's infamous Cédula de Gracias a Sacar of 1783, Puerto Ricans of interracial unions had the option of purchasing "legal whiteness" by paying a sum to the Spanish Crown.[39] With legal whiteness came the right to serve in public office and in the military, along with important forms of social mobility. While the purchase of legal whiteness was pervasive throughout the Spanish Americas in the eighteenth and nineteenth centuries, the disappearance of key historical records renders it unclear exactly how common or tightly regulated Gracias a Sacar was in Puerto Rico. Nonetheless, the deeply engrained social expectation that Puerto Ricans of African heritage should seek to marry someone lighter than themselves—encapsulated in the phrase *mejorar la raza* (improve the race)—is well documented historically and surfaces frequently in contemporary studies of *blanqueamiento* too.[40]

When the United States seized Puerto Rico from Spain in 1898, twenty-five years after the abolition of slavery on the island, the United States introduced new rules of race formation to a people who had learned over the course of four centuries to flexibly navigate white supremacy through racial mixing and whitening. This was a Puerto Rico where "color" was based on a gradient, not a binary, with multiple intermediary categories between Black and white. These intermediary categories were highly unstable and tended to change over time according to changes in geography, occupation, status, and class.[41] Ignoring Puerto Rico's flexible color spectrum, the US War Department pressed ahead in 1899 to conduct the first US-led racial census on the island. Administrators were instructed to categorize Puerto Ricans into two racial categories: "White" or "Colored." That year, the majority of Puerto Ricans (62 percent) were categorized as white.[42] Enthused by the finding that "the pure negro blood has lost ground,"[43] many US officials looked to Puerto Rico with optimism. Its inhabitants were said to be "tending towards whiteness,"[44] something that was seen to bode well for their future assimilation into white Anglo-Protestant culture.[45]

As the flexible Spanish-era rules of race formation intermingled with the comparatively more rigid rules of the United States, early attempts to categorize Puerto Ricans by race produced highly volatile results. Official censuses suggested that the island's racial makeup was transforming at breakneck speed: jumping from 62 percent "White" and 38 percent "Colored" in 1899 to 79.8 percent "White" and 20.2 percent "Negro" in 1950.[46] Faced with these results, US officials at the Federal Census Bureau came to treat racial data from Puerto Rico with suspicion. As Jorge Duany tells the story, US officials dropped the race question from the census in 1950 in the face of what they called "considerable evidence . . . that color is misreported [in Puerto Rico]."[47] The 1950 census, the last national census to collect racial data in Puerto Rico for a fifty-year period, noted the following: "The comparison of the 'white' and 'nonwhite' . . . reveals the tendency of the enumerator [nonwhites] to report persons with varying amounts of Negro blood as 'white.'"[48] With Puerto Ricans of African ancestry failing to uphold the one drop rule— itself an antebellum principle dreamed up by white segregationists—US officials lost interest in gathering Puerto Ricans' racial data. So, from 1950 to 2000, no government gathered population-level racial data in Puerto Rico.

Puerto Rico's first democratically elected governor (Luis Muñoz Marín of the Popular Democratic Party), a former independence activist who abandoned the campaign for Puerto Rican independence that had defined his earlier career, oversaw the 1952 plebiscite that formalized Puerto Rico's constitutional status as an Estado Libre Asociado. Rather than pursue political independence, Muñoz Marín instead pursued a compromise. He based his mandate on economic development and sought to counter decades of "Americanization" by fostering a sense of Puerto Rican culture and shared national heritage. A key ideological strand in this project of cultural nationalism was the promotion of a reformulated national origin story that celebrated mestizaje (mixing) and conceived Puerto Ricans as the product of a harmonious encounter between Indigenous Taíno, Spaniards, and Africans.[49] Through centuries of mestizaje, these "three roots" were said to have fused together into one nation and one race: Puerto Ricans. Omitting the violence of plantation slavery, indentureship, and Indigenous genocide and stoking cultural nationalism in place of desires for political sovereignty, this "three roots" origin story was disseminated through cultural institutions and school curricula throughout the 1950s and holds powerful cultural relevance today.

Puerto Rico's intertwined histories of colonialism, slavery, indentureship, mestizaje, and cultural nationalism render "race" a profoundly ambiguous concept that continues to confound researchers today. Consider the ongoing saga of the census. When I began my fieldwork in Puerto Rico in 2015, official statistics proclaimed Puerto Rico to be whiter than the US mainland.[50] Five years later, the census of 2020 sent shockwaves through the research community when, in a striking reversal of a four-century trend toward whitening, the proportion of Puerto Ricans identifying as "White alone" dropped from 80.5 percent to 17.1 percent between 2000 and 2020.[51] The drop in white identification was accompanied by a rise in the proportion of Puerto Ricans identifying as "Two or More Races" (from 3.8 percent in 2000 to 46.8 percent in 2020) or "Some Other Race" (from 6.8 percent in 2000 to 25.5 percent in 2020). Meanwhile, the proportion of Puerto Ricans identifying as "Black or African American alone" held relatively constant, at 8 percent in 2000 and 7 percent in 2020 (albeit with a brief peak in 2010 at 12.4 percent).[52] The ongoing topsy-turvy of Puerto Rico's racial census offers much food for thought, but for now, suffice to say that consistent racial identification with either Black or white was never the rule in Puerto Rico. Instead, most of my interlocuters avoided using explicit racial terms, in particular the term *negro*, more commonly relying on euphemisms such as *colorito* (a little colored) and *de barrio* (from the barrio) or on comparisons like "a little darker than him" and "a little lighter than her."[53] For most *re-educados* I knew, and with striking consistency, "race" was not a straightforward or explicitly vocalized part of their identity.[54] Like my middle-class colleagues at the University of Puerto Rico, the more salient identity was ethnonational. Men were "Puerto Rican," not "American," and often proudly so.

Notwithstanding how ambiguous and volatile racial identification has proven to be in Puerto Rico, census data show that Puerto Ricans who identified as "Black alone" in the 2020 census were 47 percent more likely to be incarcerated than Puerto Ricans who identified as "White alone." If one were to make direct comparisons between Puerto Rico's racial disparities to those on the US mainland—an epistemologically complicated comparison because of the radically different configurations of race in both places—the degree of racial inequality on the island would appear to be of a smaller order of magnitude. On the US mainland, people who identify as "Black alone" are between 300 percent and 400 percent more likely to be incarcerated than those who identify as "White alone."[55] But direct comparisons are complicated by the incongruous conceptions of race operating on the island and mainland.[56] When I began presenting portions of this book, in fact, US audiences would sometimes ask me whether the 49 percent of Puerto Rico's prison population who identified as "White alone" in 2020 were "*really*" white," a question that casts doubt on Puerto Rican's whiteness and speaks volumes about the incommensurability of whiteness between the mainland and colony.[57] I have learned a great deal from Puerto Rican authors who have interrogated white identification in Puerto Rico, including those who have "uncovered" Blackness through attuning to racial scripts.[58] For my own project, I focus less on the unpacking the 'truth' of racial categories and more on how *mestizaje* and Puerto Ricans' ambiguous racialization have mutually paved the way for carceral citizenship's expansion on the island. As a form of social membership that has arisen in the oldest colony in the Americas and among a people who have long had to battle to assert a national identity within the confines of colonialism, the carceral citizenship that has taken shape in Puerto Rico is shot through with the same racial and ethnonational currents that define national identity in Puerto Rico today. As I will show, carceral citizenship draws on long-standing cultural currents of mestizaje and cultural nationalism. Transcending race and color distinctions, carceral citizenship unites partial US citizens who are marked with multiple intersecting stigmas into a unified and proudly Puerto Rican collective whole. Riding waves of deeply entrenched patterns of raceless racialization, carceral citizenship builds upon and extends the paradoxical and ambiguous US citizenship that has endured in Puerto Rico for over a century.

Carceral citizenship is not unique to Puerto Rico and can in fact be found in distinct manifestations in prisons, reeducation programs, gang prevention initiatives, and religious reinsertion programs operated by formerly incarcerated people across Latin America.[59] That said, the specific kind of carceral citizenship that has taken shape in Puerto Rico has a distinctly imperial formation whose architecture owes its shape at least in part to the US mainland and its particular encounter with mass incarceration.[60] Throughout the late twentieth century, Puerto Rico was subject to the same US federal legislation that drove up criminal convictions as the US mainland. Influential was the Federal Comprehensive Drug Abuse Prevention and Control Act of 1970, which criminalized the manufacturing, distribution, and possession of five newly categorized kinds of illicit substances. Then, in 1986, came the Federal Anti-Drug Abuse Act, which introduced mandatory minimum sentences for most drug offenses. In 1995, the US Office of National Drug Control Policy proclaimed Puerto Rico a High Intensity Drug Trafficking Area (HIDTA), which massively increased island surveillance by the US Drug Enforcement Agency (DEA). In 1996, President Bill Clinton passed the "One Strike and You're Out" policy, which meant that Puerto Ricans living in public housing faced the threat of eviction if they or a family member living with them was convicted of a drug crime. All this came to a head in 2000, when incarceration peaked—hitting a whopping 384 per 100,000—and earning Puerto Rico the calamitous title of having the third-highest incarceration rate in Latin America, superseded only by Cuba and the Dominican Republic.[61]

But as Marisol LeBrón, points out, it is a mistake to read Puerto Rico's carceral turn as a straightforward story of the United States foisting punitive policies onto its passive colony.[62] In fact, as she painstakingly demonstrates, Puerto Rican politicians not only supported federal law-and-order policies during the 1980s and 1990s but also pioneered some of the most punitive approaches to law enforcement in the region. One action taken locally was to massively expand the island's police force. By the early 2010s, Puerto Rico had one of the most bloated forces (relative to population) in the United States, with 510 officers per 100,000 inhabitants, compared to 423 in New York City.[63] Another notorious innovation pioneered in Puerto Rico was Mano Dura ("Strong Hand"), launched in 1993 by the pro-statehood party. Under Mano Dura, Governor Pedro Rosselló dispatched the National Guard to occupy and stage mass arrests at public housing complexes in low-income neighborhoods, all under intensive and carefully orchestrated news coverage. As LeBrón tells the story, this highly publicized effort to be tougher on crime than the United States was an attempt on the part of the Rosselló administration to demonstrate Puerto Rico's worth to the mainland at a time when the island's strategic value to the United States was felt to be in decline.

LeBrón's analysis demonstrates the benefits of looking beyond federal policies and prison building initiatives to consider the respective roles of a wider range of differentially empowered local actors. The focus of her analysis was on Puerto Rico's own legislators, but another group of actors to remain conspicuously absent from carceral historiography is a group seldom considered *actors* at all: incarcerated people. Yet formerly incarcerated people in Puerto Rico have played a critical (albeit unsymmetrical) role in crafting the carceral state through establishing a highly variable array of reeducation, rehabilitation, and reentry programs grounded in self-help.

One of the more surprising consequences of this blending of self-help and the carceral state, as I explain in chapter 1, is that considerable penal power now lies in the hands of re-educados, who perform a wide variety of correctional duties on behalf of the Department of Corrections. These include (but are not limited to) delivering therapies, taking urine samples from court-ordered residents, informing police of bad behavior or unauthorized absences, writing case reports, and even (as I explore in chapter 4) making recommendations to court. Anthropologists have observed a similar "informalization of containment" in many parts of Latin America, where scholars have described a tendency for governments to implement US-style criminal justice policies that accelerate criminal convictions without making concomitant investments in prison infrastructures.[64] This shoestring approach to "law and order" is said to have given rise to an array of informal institutional arrangements theorized as ad hoc "prison survival strategies."[65] In Rio de Janeiro, for example, prisons have been found to delegate the work of enforcing order to prisoners themselves, who are sometimes recruited to work as prison guards owing to a lack of resources for employing and protecting professional guards.[66] Similarly, underfunded prison authorities in Ecuador have been shown sometimes to shift responsibilities for providing basic food and medical supplies for inmates onto family members.[67]

The work of re-educados could thus be analyzed as an extension of the same demands animating the informalization of containment in Latin America—demands to enforce security and to crack down on drugs—all cobbled together in haste and on a shoestring budget. More, though, seems to be at stake.

For one thing, there is a striking voluntary element at play here. Many re-educados choose to stay on for years after their compulsory treatment periods have ended, sometimes for decades at a time. For another, these enterprises fulfill various social roles—beyond containment—as evidenced in their hierarchical vocational structure. In theory, one can enter as an apprentice (*aprendiz*), pass through two years of learning and adaptation (*aprendizaje y adaptación*), graduate, and then become a certified reeducated ex-addict (*re-educado ex-adicto certificado*). On graduating, re-educados may then choose to stay on at the organization to assume positions of responsibility as therapists, counselors, or case workers—all commonly used terms to describe a range of labor arrangements that exist in these self-help communities. This is not confinement in its classic form then. Many residents could leave, in theory, if they wanted to. Many choose not to.

These therapeutic, vocational, and voluntary elements push us to ask what more, besides efforts at cheap confinement, underwrites these enterprises?

. . . . .

By the time I met Héctor at Comunidad-Luz in 2016, Puerto Rico's incarceration rate stood at 308 per 100,000, equating to roughly 12,000 people in prison, 96 percent of whom were men, 49 percent of whom were categorized as "White alone," 29 percent as "Black alone," and 22 percent as racially mixed (either "Two or More races" or "Some other Race.")[68] An additional 4,500 people were held in 132 licensed therapeutic communities, which, again, were mostly for men.[69] Keen to understand the growth of self-help organizations, I obtained a copy of the government registry of licensed therapeutic communities, eventually succeeding in visiting 15 out of a total of 132 in the registry. All of the therapeutic community directors I interviewed were formerly incarcerated; all of them had first encountered therapeutic communities as residents undergoing some form of compulsory drug treatment: frequently via drug court (explored in chapter 1) but also via civil commitment (explored in chapter 4). Across the 15 programs I visited, anywhere between two-thirds and three-quarters of residents had initially enrolled under court order, usually either via drug court or involuntary civil commitment. Yet the proportion of residents serving an active court sentence on any given day was significantly lower than this (between one-third and one-half). This was because many residents who had entered via a court order wound up outstaying their compulsory internment. Intrigued by the motivations of these overstayers, I endeavored to get to know them.

Compared to the Narcotics Anonymous and Alcoholics Anonymous collectives I'd encountered in church basements in Santo Domingo and Washington Heights back in New York, Puerto Rico's therapeutic communities immediately struck me as a more somber species of self-help.[70] They exuded at once a punitory and monastic-like feeling, one I found surprisingly hard to categorize or pin down. "Somewhere between penitentiary, monastery, shelter, and sanctuary" is what I wrote in my notebook. While a small minority of facilities had barriers barring their entrances, most of the compounds were ungated and unguarded. But despite their characteristically open facade, residents in these facilities were typically accorded relatively few freedoms.

Residents were generally prohibited from leaving the premises without prior authorization, granted exclusively for doctors' appointments, court appearances, church services, and (occasionally) for family funerals. Institutional prohibitions were copious and often extraordinarily specific. At La Casita, by no means the strictest facility I visited, rules enveloped many basic elements of social interaction: from speaking ("new residents are not permitted to talk to each other without an older resident present"), to eating ("no talking during mealtimes"), to smoking ("never light a cigarette that has already been put out by another person"). The last rule—"Always ask authorization for everything"—was plastered onto the wall outside the men's dormitories. Then there was the daily schedule to contend with. At the programs I visited, days tended to be filled with a busy daily schedule of chores, therapies, and manual labor, all strictly regulated through a system of rules, rewards, and punishments. Depending on the facility, rewards for good behavior might include access to the telephone, extended visiting hours, or an upgrade to a nicer bedroom. Punishments ranged from the benign (unpleasant chores) to the extreme (exhausting physical tasks and humiliating forms of group confrontation).

Despite this austereness, therapeutic communities were remarkably makeshift operations. Many were constructed in structures originally designed for other purposes. Some were housed in defunct schools, donated or sold off cheaply by local governments. Others had set up shop in decommissioned fire stations or abandoned churches. Though retrofits, they cobbled together an unexpected semblance of order. They were uniformly well tended: their floors squeaky clean, their halls bedecked with photographs and certificates.

Officially, one-third of Puerto Rico's 132 residential drug treatment programs is "faith-based," while two-thirds are "community-based."[71] The faith-based programs are generally Evangelical or Pentecostal, while the community-based programs will usually describe themselves as secular. But across all 15 of the programs I visited, Christianity was everywhere. Crucifixion paintings hung in reception rooms. Prayers rang out through the canteens at every meal. Residents greeted each other with "Dios te bendiga!" Signs plastered across the walls announced: "God is with you!" and "Only YOU are the one who can change."

FIGURE 1 · Photograph taken by Jack Delano in 1980, entitled *A Church Building Converted into a Drug Treatment Center*.

Whereas the Pentecostal programs usually required residents to participate in Bible study, fasting, and religious worship, the "secular" programs
invoked a far more vernacular and syncretic Christianity. On Sundays, even
the most outwardly secular centers usually gave their residents the option
of attending Pentecostal and Catholic services in nearby churches. Despite
the oft-repeated platitude that "all religions are welcome here," I never encountered anyone from another faith. Most residents described themselves
as Christian, though few named a specific denomination. The cobbled together Christianity pervading these programs is neither new (see fig. 1) nor
surprising in a place where Spanish Catholicism has long been peppered
with US Protestantism, only to be supplemented (far more recently) with
Evangelicalism and Pentecostalism. Yet all the same, I found it uncannily
congruent with therapeutic communities' makeshift architecture.

In many ways, Christianity's pervasiveness in Puerto Rico's therapeutic
communities and drug ministries mirrors a broader geography of Christian mutual aid, providing a lifeline for the drug-using poor across Latin
America.[72] To immerse myself, I surveyed fifteen different programs before
settling on La Casita to base a portion of my study there. Accustomed
to hosting visitors, mostly therapeutic leaders from other parts of Latin
America, staff were enthused about having a researcher around ("an anthropologist learning about self-help"). From January to August 2017, I
spent four days a week there. I'd get there early with the aim of joining
in time for morning prayer at 7:00 a.m., though not always succeeding.
After the one-hour drive from San Juan, where I lived in a small apartment
near the University of Puerto Rico for most of my fieldwork, I'd observe
group therapies, accompany residents as they completed their assigned
tasks and duties, and chat to residents and staff whenever I could. With
the exception of nighttime hours (when I went home), I was pretty much
permitted to come and go as I pleased.

I became a surrogate taxi driver and often ferried residents to their
medical appointments and family visits. (La Casita's single vehicle, a
fifteen-seater van, was usually in high demand.) Though not an official
"volunteer" (of which there were several, mostly program graduates), I
became a kind of personal assistant to Rocky, who tasked me with managing donations and keeping track of stocks of donated clothes, food, and
supplies. Each evening, I'd drive back to San Juan against miles and miles
of stationary rush-hour traffic, acutely conscious of what the freedom to
come and go felt like.

I chose not to audio record my interviews with residents (though I did
with staff members) since many were under criminal supervision and so the

creation of audio recordings that could easily reference criminalized behaviors seemed like an unnecessary risk. Instead, I talked with residents informally and wherever they were. It was in the shared spaces of the balcony, patio, TV room, or gym (actually just a jumble of weights and punching bags in the corner of a parking lot) that I felt like I actually got to know people. I also returned several times to the residential programs I had surveyed before settling at La Casita. At Comunidad-Luz (discussed above), Comunidad de Elevación del Espíritu Humano, and Mesón de Dios (both discussed in chapter 1), I was able to attend group activities, including labor therapies, on a semiregular basis and conduct follow-up interviews with staff and residents.

When I wasn't hanging out with re-educados and residents, I was getting to know their relatives during visiting hours and interviewing senators, activists, lawyers, and government officials; or I was tagging along with harm-reduction agencies as they delivered clean syringes to homeless encampments and shooting galleries; or I was observing civil commitment proceedings; or I was sifting through narcotics laws and dusty boxes of old newsreel at the Legislative Library and the University of Puerto Rico Archive; or I was doing my part-time graduate research job at the University of Puerto Rico.[73] As time went by, I attended charity fundraisers, graduation ceremonies, and homelessness outreach initiatives. As my fieldwork relationships deepened, I was invited to weddings, birthday parties, and, very sadly, some funerals too.

Of course, a white British woman doing research in therapeutic communities housing Puerto Rican men cannot go very far without justifying, many times over, why she is there. Some professionals I encountered were nonplussed as to why *una joven* (a kid) all the way from England would choose to immerse herself in what was seen to be a bleak and dangerous setting. Nearly everyone I met underestimated my age, something I've grown accustomed to since childhood, so I was often answering questions like: "What's your bachelor in?" and "Are you old enough to be doing this?" Therapeutic community residents had distinct questions for me, though they also usually had their own explanations at hand as to why I might be there. I was there to save the youth from delinquency. I was there to rescue the addicts from their drug problems. As a graduate student, I'd anxiously try to dust off this Christian-missionary identity with some talk of "ethnography" and what I saw as its unique capacity to shed light on social problems not easily captured by epidemiology, surveys, or other methods.[74] But, of course, there was more to it.

For over a century, academics from the US mainland have flocked to Puerto Rico, channeled by the federal institutes, public health initiatives, and private foundations that have funneled researchers to the island.[75] Given the "air bridge" linking San Juan to New York specifically, it is no coincidence that my first ever job in Puerto Rico was on a study funded by the US National Institute of Drug Abuse that had joint PIs (principal investigators) at Columbia's Mailman School of Public Health and the University of Puerto Rico's Medical School.[76] It is even less of a coincidence that during my studies at Columbia University I had gravitated toward Caribbean political economy and the work of Julian Stewart and his team of Columbia anthropology students (including Sidney Mintz, Eric Wolf, Elena Padilla, and Eduardo Seda Bonilla among others), who published *The People of Puerto Rico* in 1956.[77] Eschewing the prevailing psychological paradigms that predominated at the time, these authors adopted a Marxist materialist approach to examine how changes in Puerto Rico's "base structure" had influenced regional "subcultures" in their transition from the agrarian to industrial economy. These Marxist approaches and the critical medical anthropology paradigms they inspired provided an important correction to earlier culture-and-personality paradigms that attempted to characterize "Puerto Rican personality" in its entirety, often leading to flattened-out and unflattering depictions of Puerto Ricans as an *essentially* (and by virtue of a shared "national character") dependent, childlike, and docile people.[78]

True to this political-economy heritage, I analyze carceral citizenship materially as an historically emergent innovation of late capitalism, not as the product of a "Puerto Rican psyche" or "culture of poverty."[79] At the same time, I caution that the stakes of carceral livelihoods risk being missed if we ignore the characterological and essentializing tropes and images that circulate about Puerto Rican re-educados. As I show in this book, a variety of ideas about the "psyche" of Puerto Rican people (in general) and about the "personalities" of "addicts" and "criminals" (in particular) are at play in projects of carceral citizenship formation. These ideas have overlapping historical roots in medicine, psychiatry, Christianity, and social scientific writing about Puerto Rico. However stigmatizing and misleading these tropes are, my approach in this book is to try to unpack them historically and ethnographically rather than to ignore or erase them. In the carceral jurisdictions I write about, highly stigmatizing theories of addiction as a character flaw prevail, as do labels like "addict" and "ex-addict," two widely used terms of identification. So I do not edit my interlocuters' language, for example, by substituting the term "addict" for the more palatable "person with a substance use disorder." Instead, I try to retain the spirit of my interlocuters' words and the underlying concepts of their worldviews. This means facing head on some of the complicated ways that many re-educados understand themselves and each other.

I have chosen not to give a comprehensive, cohesive, or *conclusive* account of carceral livelihoods and their associated genre of citizenship. Instead, each chapter presents a unique, partial image—allowing for dissonance and contradiction—culminating in a provisional fractural portrait of carceral citizenship that moves between four distinct perspectives: that of the seasoned re-educados who operate their own programs, that of the residents ordered by the court into their care, and that of the families who resort to using civil commitment legislation to force their loved ones into institutional care. The composite image that emerges is neither complete nor slickly cohesive, having much more to say about some things (labor and social belonging) than about others (sex and sexuality), a patchiness that reflects both the things that were visible to me as a young female researcher and the things I set out to understand. I did not attempt to understand the experiences of women in Puerto Rico's handful of women-only programs, for example, which are undoubtedly different and which are skillfully documented elsewhere.[80] Nor did I try to assess whether therapeutic communities "work," which would have been a different kind of project entirely. Finally, I deliberately eschew a final, clean conclusion about the absolute blessing or curse of carceral citizenship for the key protagonists.

For some, this partial and fragmented approach to ethnography might seem to fall short as a work of analysis, in part because of a legitimate concern about the applicability of anthropological knowledge. But as I understand ethnography, my goal as a writer is not to posture as an all-seeing witness capable of grasping a complete account of lives in all their human complexity. These are, after all, lives that are still unfolding. Instead, my more modest goal here is to convey the messy work that goes into partially seeing lives that are still unfurling and turning what one has been able to grasp into ethnography. Taking stock of what ethnography is—a way of showing a way of looking—I contend that ethnography should bear visible signs of its situated and partial construction, its fragmentation serving as both a reminder and exploration of what it means to see. Thus, my conclusions about the value of these carceral livelihoods, both for the people inhabiting them and for the communities who surround them, remain unfinished and are explored through a moving, not final, portrait.[81]

The ethnographic material zigzags between La Casita, my primary field site, and several other therapeutic communities where I gathered the bulk of my data, including Comunidad-Luz, Comunidad de Elevación del Espíritu

Humano, and Mesón de Dios (all pseudonyms). To protect my interlocuters and their programs, I have removed, modified, and disguised certain identifying features. The only program I do not confer a pseudonym on is Hogar CREA, a program whose leaders are household names (for reasons I explore) and whose graduation ceremonies are attended by journalists and copiously documented in local newspapers, radio, and television.

Chapter 1, "The Economy of Penance," follows the experiences of re-educados who are responsible for running and directing their own therapeutic communities. These are the men for whom it is probably safe to say carceral citizenship has been most beneficial. Foregrounding re-educados who have made it to the top enables me to convey what this arrangement positively brings, at best, to its most impassioned members, while also unearthing a Christian moral economy that extracts unwaged labor from formerly incarcerated people in part by casting them as penitents who owe a "debt to society."

Chapter 2, "The Voluntary Face of the Carceral State," tells the story of carceral citizenship's historical development in Puerto Rico from the perspective of the island's unique encounter with industrial and postindustrial capitalist development and the subsequent rise of mass incarceration. Specifically, I show how a correctional genre of unwaged self-help work—performed in the name of reeducating "criminals," "drug addicts," and other citizens deemed "characterologically flawed"—has ascended since the late twentieth century to become an increasingly common and publicly recognized mode of social, economic, and civic participation.

Chapter 3, "The Carceral Monastery," offers a phenomenological account of daily life among a cohort of residents undergoing reeducation at a therapeutic community called La Casita and uses this to tell a story about some of the new economies and new livelihoods outside of wage labor that are emerging in capitalist societies. By foregrounding the hopes and disappointments of therapeutic community novices as they are in the throes of adjusting to this alternative way of living, I offer a snapshot of carceral citizenship in formation.

Chapter 4, "Crimeless Confinement," follows the experiences of therapeutic community residents and families undergoing involuntary civil commitment (ICC) procedures. Moving between legal documents, court proceedings, and the viewpoints of civilly committed residents and their families, I explore how a change in civil commitment law has massively widened the valve of justifications for confining people who use drugs and alcohol. Increasingly, civil commitment laws are consigning men without criminal convictions and without clinically diagnosed substance-use disorders to dwell in therapeutic communities for years at a time, signing an expanded recruitment—beyond criminalization—into carceral citizenship.

The concluding chapter, "An Exile's Belonging," considers this study's broader insights. I argue that the emergence of carceral citizenship in the late twentieth century as a contradictory, partial, and forfeitable mode of social membership is not a historical aberration that we can chalk up to neoliberalism nor some curious quirk of Puerto Rico. Instead, the emergence of carceral citizenship in Puerto Rico is just one particularly vivid instantiation of a broader reality of stratified and ambiguous citizenship that has been a defining feature of liberal citizenship in the United States since the Founding Fathers.

· 1 ·

The Economy of Penance

Jorge and I make our way down Muñoz Rivera Street to the municipal sports arena, a relic of an older order of public recreation that can be retrofitted, needs depending, for school tournaments, weddings, and government conventions. On this hot, cloudless Sunday, the parking lot is filling fast. Cars and limousines line up to snake the corner. Puerto Rico's elected officials—the chief justice, the town mayor, and scores of representatives of the Legislative Assembly—have come together with over eighty families to pay tribute to this year's graduating class of Puerto Rico's largest therapeutic community: Hogar CREA (the Home for the Reeducation of Addicts).[1] As the attendees mingle in the entrance hall, Jorge and I join the throng as it moves rapidly through the lobby and trickles its way around the tables that fan out from the stage. Parents, grandparents, partners, and children, all turned out in their best attire, find their tables and take their seats. We find our name cards on a table in the middle. It is decked out with plastic flower table dressings and helium balloons that stream up in ribbons from shiny golden chairs. Jorge looks around, scanning the faces table by table. Through the crowd, his sister Belinda has just spotted him. She hurries her way over, ushering her tuxedoed nine-year-old son into his seat.

A few minutes before Hogar CREA's leader breaks out with the opening speech, Jorge's friend and former therapist finds him. They embrace, and he guides Jorge to a coterie of directors, introducing him as they each shake his hand. They are the district leaders, each responsible for coordinating activities across dozens of Hogar CREA centers. A waiter in black livery and white gloves offers them cups of Coca-Cola from a tray. I recognize him as a former resident from Ponce. A wave of quiet signals that the service is about to begin. Jorge and I rejoin his sister at the table.

When it comes to community recognition, of the scores of public officials up on the stage that day, Héctor Figueroa holds the upper rung. As a household name, only his predecessor, the late Chejuán García Ríos, can claim greater community standing.[2] For Figueroa, the presence of the town mayor and the chief of justice, along with a full house of more than two hundred and fifty citizens, lends proof and authority to the continued eminence of his organization in the Puerto Rican township:

> Honorable ladies and gentlemen. Today is a special afternoon. We are here to award certificates to this year's re-educados, the graduating class of 2017 who have demonstrated, yet again, sí, se puede [yes, it can be done]. Like all of you graduating re-educados here today, I am here too as a product of the CREA program. Like many of you, I am also here as a product of the justice system. And I would like to thank every member of the CREA family, our volunteers who have supported us and without whom we couldn't survive, and our friends here in the Department of Justice who have got us to where we are today. I can tell you all that it's a beautiful privilege to be here.
>
> To our honorable directors, we are also here to thank you for the tireless work and sacrifices you have made on behalf of CREA. Today is a proud day for you too. You have all spent years as internados [inmates], you have all made enormous sacrifices as mentors and guides, and you all know how much effort it takes to make the journey to reeducate oneself. Graduates, now that you have all put in the effort, after all that work and sacrifice, you can now start to enjoy the success. You can return to your community as qualified men and women, as leaders in your communities, and together we can work to recreate and reeducate the Puerto Rican personality.[3]

Today is not a typical rehab festivity, at least not the low-key Narcotics Anonymous kind where members are applauded for achieving thirty days of sobriety before promptly ceding the podium to the next person. No. Today Héctor Figueroa can address a class of soon-to-be graduados exadictos (graduated ex-addicts) under the gaze of Puerto Rico's high and mighty, in an embodied display of recognized leadership and professional achievement. Today, he is able to hail his fellow ex-addicts as graduates and certified professionals, with all the grandeur and fanfare of an academic graduation. None of this is lost on the next speaker, the town mayor, who composes his speech as a commencement address: "Today you can all be proud of your immense achievement," he delivers to uproarious applause. "Now is the time to think about where you want to be in five or ten years. You've already proven you can do anything you set your mind to."

Figueroa reclaims the mike and beckons the audience to rise to sing the US national anthem, a chorus that ends with a trio of flag bearers, tall and proud, making their way slowly down a red carpet that connects the graduates and their families to the high table. As the flags of the United States, Puerto Rico, and Hogar CREA (two horizontal panels, blue over yellow) glide steadily down the red carpet, the crowd rises again, this time to sing the Puerto Rican national anthem, in an equally impassioned performance. Afterward, the guests are invited to take their seats. Today's graduating re-educados stand side by side, fists clenched on hearts, and serenade the audience with Hogar CREA's signature hymn. Then the prerecorded music chimes in, a Spanish string piece warbles out through the speakers.

Finally the graduates, who are nearly all men, are called to walk down the red carpet to the high table where, after shaking hands with Figueroa, the town mayor, and the chief of justice, each is awarded a medal and trophy. Prizes in hand, the re-educados certificados (reeducated certified men) assume their seats one by one in a row of cushioned chairs that face the stage. In time-honored tradition, the next two hours are a whirlwind of tributes and testimonies.

A re-educado from the Bronx gives thanks to CREA for turning his life around. "Thank you to my adoptive family here at CREA, and thank you to God. I am proof the program works. I am proof there is a future out there waiting for you." A wife gives testimony to her husband, clean for fourteen years and now a much beloved director at CREA. Tears streaming down her face, she recounts the story of her husband's transformation from troubled addict to program director and implores this year's graduates to follow in his example. "My husband," she finishes, wiping tears from her eyes, "a symbol of rehabilitation and a pride of Puerto Rico." The audience roars in applause. After the ebbs and crests of speeches, it is Figueroa who closes out the ceremony. He chooses his final homage to pay tribute to Hogar CREA's founder, Chejuán García Ríos, "el padre of the fight against addiction," and to give thanks to the executive table, "for their support in the fight for the well-being of our beautiful island." With the fervor and undulation of a soccer commentator spying a goal in the making, he reaches his final crescendo: "May you never fall back; may you assume your duty to lead in the fight for a future for our island—a future free of drugs—*su honrado certificado re-educado* [your certified and reeducated honoree]!"

As I watched the graduation, a transformation seemed to happen before my eyes. On the stage, criminalized men were applauded by the powerful in recognition of their hard work and in celebration of the opportunities that surely lay ahead. Shirts starched and shoes shined, Puerto Rico's re-educados stood tall and proud as they shook the hand of the town mayor and received their certificates under gaze of family and town. Center of stage for all to see was the idealized embodiment and best-case scenario to which criminal justice can aspire: publicly redeemed drug offenders now remade as upstanding, upwardly mobile professionals and ceremonially promoted to equivalence—for today—with the governing class, the professions, and the whole of working Puerto Rico that stands apart from *la calle*. Aspiration filled the air.

· · · · ·

From a certain perspective, the ambitions that the graduation ceremony tried to promote that day can come off as irresponsibly lofty. For therapeutic community graduates fresh out of drug court and about to brave the storm of Puerto Rico's crumbling economy marked by the stigma of a criminal record, prospects for successful reentry are bleak, at least if the usual measures of recidivism, unemployment, and overdose mortality are anything to go by.[4] But having attended many of these graduation ceremonies over the years, and having traced their cultural imagery in Puerto Rican media, I have come to understand them as something more complicated than simply a drug rehabilitation project whose overblown aspirations have superseded its deliverables. What unites these graduation ceremonies is the rallying cry at their center stage. Recent therapeutic community graduates are called upon to rise to a decidedly Puerto Rican "national" duty: to fight for a drug-free Puerto Rico. Whether congratulated by politicians, local citizens, or by members of the judiciary, the refrain becomes familiar: "You've already proved what you are capable of. Now it's your turn to lead in the fight for a future for Puerto Rico." This explicitly Puerto Rican patriotic duty is a powerful cultural ingredient in the project I am calling carceral citizenship: a troubled social membership project that provides a model and blueprint for criminally stigmatized and partial US citizens to participate *in circumscribed ways* within the larger polity of Puerto Rico. More complicated than a "second-class" citizenship, since Puerto Ricans without criminal records inhabit a stratified form of citizenship relative to US mainlanders, carceral citizenship emerges from the intersecting stratifications of criminalization and penal stigma. More than a purely juridical matter or legal-juridical status bestowed top-down on people with a criminal record, the carceral citizenship that has emerged in Puerto Rico has been brought into being, at least in part, by the human actions of formerly incarcerated people. Today, carceral citizenship constitutes a symbolically rich and publicly recognized mode of social belonging that is cultivated by partial US citizens whose colonization, incarceration, and contact with criminal justice has limited their options for civic, social, and economic participation.

To understand how formerly incarcerated people create and assert their carceral citizenship through everyday human practice, this chapter follows the lives, labor trajectories, and everyday working practices of therapeutic community graduates. Exploring the nature and content of re-educados' labor within therapeutic communities enables me to consider what this social membership project brings, at best, to its members. Conversely, tracing what happens to those graduates who leave therapeutic communities and attempt to make it on the outside reveals the many contradictions of carceral citizenship. The chief shortcoming is that while stoking aspirations for a redeemed citizenship free of criminal stigma and replete with job opportunities and social mobility, carceral citizenship roundly fails to deliver its members to the middle-class positionality or unmarked "equal" citizenship that its own ceremonials imply. Never expunging the penal stigma that durably excludes carceral citizens from the mainstream, therapeutic communities instead position the commitment to reeducation itself as a demonstration of moral worth. Rather than returning their graduates to their communities as unmarked or equal citizens, these initiatives work in practice to channel formerly incarcerated people into a tightly demarcated circuit of unpaid or poorly paid "volunteer" work across the island's therapeutic communities. Unable to leave this carceral circuit easily, and severely punished when they do, the re-educados who embrace self-help and pursue live-in positions in therapeutic communities come to execute their volunteer work gladly, and often very passionately. This is in part because their last realistic option for social, economic, and civic participation depends on it.

The second part of this chapter explores how carceral citizenship comes to feel compelling and appealing, given its many shortcomings. Drawing on media coverage of graduation ceremonies and analyzing their cultural, national, and Christian symbolism allows me to unearth a complicated "economy of penance" undergirding reeducation in Puerto Rico. This moral economy invites re-educados to imagine themselves simultaneously as penitents, duty bound to rescue other "sinners" owing to a moral debt they themselves have incurred through their own past wrongdoings, and also as fledgling "certified professionals," who are objects of Puerto Rican national pride and poised for middle-class success and upward mobility. These two faces of carceral citizenship—the Christian penitent and the certified professional—make carceral citizenship very effective at extracting unremunerated work from a population of partial and ambiguous US citizens living in a colony where wage labor is widely unattainable. Together, these two faces of carceral citizenship give rise to the "certified penitent," the voluntary face of the colonial carceral state. This is the social figure who is happy to perform unwaged work on behalf of the carceral state and in the name of Puerto Rican cultural nationalism, and who thrives in a context where people with criminal records are roundly excluded from most legal avenues for social participation. Before I unpack this economy of penance, let me begin at an important moment in the life trajectories of my interlocuters, one that profoundly and durably alters their experience of citizenship.

. . . . .

Like many re-educados, Salvador describes himself as *un producto del sistema judicial* (a product of the justice system), a reference to the fact that his arrival at a therapeutic community was precipitated by a drug charge, and his first four years there were spent under court order. Bilingual, Salvador had spent much of his childhood in New York but had been sent back to his birthplace of Bayamón in his later adolescence to join his maternal grandparents. According to Salvador, this was one of his parents' many measures to protect him from the gang violence that surrounded their home in the Bronx.

In Puerto Rico, Salvador went on to complete fifth grade in elementary school. At eighteen, he worked as a cashier in a fast-food chain restaurant, later serving as a janitor in an *urbanización* (a middle-class housing development). In his twenties, Salvador began dealing cocaine to supplement his meager janitor income. This side venture led to five drug-related charges between 1975 and 1985, during which time he spent a total of six years in prison, seeing his newborn son only a handful of times over the course of his incarceration and forfeiting his relationship with his then-girlfriend and their child too. Now in his sixties, he was unbitter and candidly philosophical about his relationship's demise. "If she would have been incarcerated," he'd say with a shrug, "I wouldn't have waited around either." Both his parents and grandparents were long dead, and Salvador's only living brother was serving a life sentence in New York. These days, when Salvador speaks of "family" you know he is referring to the other re-educados he came of age with, not the family he was born into.

In 1985, when Salvador was in his late thirties, he was diverted from prison to a therapeutic community in Juncos. After four years, he completed his mandatory treatment and graduated as a certified reeducated ex-addict. Cashing in on his new status, he worked at that program for several years until, in 2009, he succeeded in getting his own sister program incorporated. By 2016, Mesón de Dios was home to some twenty male residents whom Salvador referred to affectionately as his "homeboys." Looking back, Salvador attributes his life trajectory since then directly to the experiences he gained as a therapeutic community resident.

"Before this, I hadn't done a thing with my life. Not a thing," he said, with a sigh of regret. "When I first went to the program in 1985, all I knew was drugs and the street. But soon I was noticed as a good leader." Salvador perked up a bit. "And the program, it helped me to discover talents in me that I never knew I possessed." I wondered if he was performing for me a kind of moral rectitude that he had learned over the course of years of correctional messaging and then felt a pang of shame at my own cynicism. He continued: "And so, after I graduated, I decided to stay. I professionalized myself, as they say. And after a few years, I followed my dreams and started my own program. And thanks to God, I'm still here today, as the founder and director of a program, sixteen years and counting. Me, a director, even though I don't have sixth grade."

Like Salvador, re-educados had labor histories that often spanned low-waged sectors of the legal economy and the drug economy, sometimes traversing Puerto Rico and the US mainland. Prior to enrolling in La Casita, for example, Sánchez had been a deliveryman for Pizza Hut in San Juan, Franco had been a cleaner at Pollo Tropical (a fast-food chain), while Ernesto had held a slightly more lucrative job in the military back in Florida. For all of them, their entrance into a therapeutic community was precipitated by a court ruling, usually via a drug conviction or a civil commitment order.[5]

As one of the older characters on the compound, Salvador had given up on family in the traditional sense. Yet younger residents, in contrast, sometimes had partners and children who were still in the picture. Franco, who was in his midtwenties, had a six-year-old daughter, and whenever his mother visited him, they would scroll through photographs of the child together on her phone. While Franco's ex-girlfriend was now married and living with her new husband, Franco's mother had managed to sustain a friendly relationship with her and was pleased to babysit her grandchild regularly. In hushed tones, she'd quietly fret about Franco missing out on his daughter's life and about the prospect of her and her husband having to support Franco financially when he came out. For his part, Franco was sullen at the prospect of having to live with his parents again. He found his mother's inquiries about his future career plans frustrating and demeaning. As he saw it, his ex-girlfriend had turned his whole family against him when he got the drug charge. "She was always giving me so much shit about being out late, but what she didn't recognize," he'd say, "is that I was working. I was working to put food on the table, but they don't see it like that." When we spoke about the future, Franco would say he planned to move the United States, where he could make better money and start "a new family" with "a wife and kids." He had his whole life ahead of him, and he had no intention of sticking around Mesón de Dios. "I'm gonna do my time and get out of here." Notwithstanding these different horizons, Franco was learning in the meantime to assume very similar kinds of responsibilities as Salvador had done all those years before.

For most re-educados, acquisition of institutional responsibilities begins while they are still under court order. Rubén, for example, was appointed as a "case worker" after eighteen months of compulsory treatment, two and half years prior to completing his court order. Similarly, Sánchez was taken on as a "therapist" after just eleven months of treatment, which was actually seven months prior to completing his court order. A range of professional titles drawn from both professional social care and the third sector ("social worker," "therapist," and "volunteer") were commonly used designations that carried kinds of social status but mapped only loosely onto labor or legal arrangements. For instance, I would often encounter "social workers" who were still under court order, "therapists" who received no income, and "volunteers" who did receive forms of payment. By themselves then, these titles said relatively little about the nature or conditions of the work at hand. Over time, however, I was able to collate a spectrum of labor encompassing a variety of income and legal-custodial arrangements.

At the bottom end of the spectrum were unpaid residents who had acquired positions of responsibility on the compound. Though these men would sometimes describe themselves as "therapists" or "counselors," to my mind (and from the point of view of government audits), they were essentially seasoned residents who had resided at the center long enough to garner some institutional perks.[6] Privileges included such things as sharing a bedroom with fewer roommates, having keys to access the center's various outbuildings, or being responsible for answering the office phone. Men with these positions were often still completing a court order. Because of this, their residence fees were usually covered by either the Department of Corrections and Rehabilitation or some other criminal justice agency, though occasionally fees would be paid by a family member.[7] Residents who had entered *sin presión* (without legal pressure) were required to pay the monthly residence fee, usually in the range of $200–$400.

Next in the spectrum were men who received a sub-minimum-wage stipend along with free room and board. Like the newer recruits, men with stipends tended to live on-site, full-time, and would also refer to themselves as *voluntarios* (volunteers), *terapistas* (therapists), and *trabajadores de caso* (case workers). Stipends varied: some were token "annual bonuses" (typically in the range of $100), while others were more generous and consisted of monthly or biweekly payments (all below minimum wage). Only those residents who had completed their custodial sentences (or entered without one) could qualify for a stipend. These were generally distributed in cash and rarely taxed.[8]

At the top of the spectrum were directors who received a salary paid into a bank account that was equal to or greater than minimum wage (but rarely exceeding $26,000 per year). Usually, center directors were paid a salary and lived off-site in private accommodation, though this was not always the case. I was surprised to learn, for example, that Javier, who had been a director of an Evangelical program for over twenty years when I interviewed him, received only a sub-minimum-wage stipend, courtesy of the church, and did not have his own home. Instead, he lived in nearby private lodgings owned by the Pentecostal church. While some organizations commanded sufficient resources to support several salaried positions, most could support only one or two, and a minority had no salaried positions whatsoever. For the most part, it was the larger organizations and recipients of large corrections contracts who were able to sustain multiple waged positions.

Such breadth of income, living arrangements, and legal-custodial conditions defies a straightforward "informality" reading, a concept widely employed in studies of self-help and precarity to date.[9] Whereas informal work tends to be depicted as marginal, off-the-books work oriented toward survival and undertaken in unregulated and unlicensed zones on the peripheries of global capitalism, in marked contrast the work of re-educados unfurls squarely under the licensing regimes of the Estado Libre Asociado.[10] Indeed, it flourishes in programs that are commonly bolstered financially by corrections contracts. But the more important idiosyncrasy of this work is not its confounding of distinctions between work that is formal or informal, a binary already subject to thoughtful critique elsewhere.[11] Most significant is how this spectrum of work traverses a range of legal-custodial arrangements, raising the question of whether it can usefully be considered carceral.[12]

Unlike prison labor, which includes only that performed by incarcerated people, carceral labor refers to any kind of work performed under the "credible threat" of incarceration.[13] This broader category includes work performed in the "free" market economy by probationers and parolees as part of court requirements. This latter kind of labor is carceral in the sense that for the probationers and parolees performing it, their failing to do so could plausibly result in incarceration. A large portion of the work performed by therapeutic community residents does conform to this definition of carceral labor, in the sense that noncompliance (including failing to perform assigned duties) can and does lead to incarceration. But what about Salvador, who completed his court order decades ago? Or the many residents who had outstayed their court orders for months and sometimes years? Should their labor be classified as carceral? If not, should their work count as "voluntary," as re-educados prefer to call it?

To some, Salvador's self-identification as a volunteer might seem to pervert the concept. The criminalization that precipitated Salvador's entrance to this work and the institutional barriers blocking his exit do seem anathema to "freely given labor" and the spirit of the gift, which, in its purest Maussian form, expects no return.[14] But on inspecting these labor categories more carefully, it transpires that the distinctions among voluntary (gifted), paid (exchanged), and carceral (criminalized or legally coerced) turn out to be far less clear-cut than commonly assumed. Consider, for example, the wageless community service that probationers are sometimes required to perform as a condition of their release from prison or the wageless volunteer work that many countries require their citizens to undertake to access unemployment benefits or the handsomely paid waged work performed by some third-sector employees.[15]

As I collated re-educados' narratives about their work, what their words seemed to suggest was not prisoners masquerading as volunteers but rather the formation of a carceral livelihood replete with its own project of social membership. This project I am calling *carceral citizenship* is centrally concerned with supplying criminally stigmatized men who have little chance of succeeding in the market economy with an encompassing albeit highly circumscribed pathway to social, economic, and civic participation within a context where many ordinarily idealized foundations of citizenship (wage labor, heteronormative households, and successful fatherhood) are not on the menu. The work performed by re-educados cannot be understood purely through a legal analysis of its terms and conditions nor through a political-economic analysis of its relationship to production. Carceral citizenship is better grasped, I think, by exploring its structural, social, and cultural production.

· · · · ·

The drug-conviction-to-volunteer pipeline common to the labor histories of re-educados is a direct adaptation to the social and legal-juridical exclusions that await them as criminally stigmatized citizens. Unlike the US mainland, where decades of "Ban the Box" activism has seen many states adopt policies that remove conviction and arrest history questions from job applications, Puerto Ricans with criminal convictions face the job market without such statutory protection. In fact, it is standard practice for landlords, employers, housing associations, and educational institutions to ask applicants for a criminal record certificate. Issued by the police department, this provides a full list of any past criminal convictions or unresolved cases. Without one, it is extremely difficult to legally obtain employment, public housing, or a private rental.[16] Puerto Rican employment law is equally unforgiving when it comes to dismissal. Any person convicted of a felony in Puerto Rico can be legitimately dismissed by their employer without this being considered an unjust or discriminatory dismissal.[17] This also applies to anyone accused of committing more than one felony, even if the trial has not yet begun. Again, this differs from the US mainland, where it is considered discrimination to fire someone solely for having a felony record and where aggrieved citizens may press charges for wrongful termination (though these legal protections clearly have their limits).[18]

Following release, therapeutic community graduates are also required to comply with a variety of enduring and intrusive court stipulations. These commonly include mandatory attendance at Narcotics Anonymous meetings, mandatory check-ins with parole officers, restrictions regarding where and with whom they may live, and requirements about maintaining a permanent address. For those who lack family support, this last requirement can be particularly challenging. For those who do become homeless, sleeping in a car or even killing time in a town plaza can invite police attention and potentially lead to another court order.

This extension of the carceral state into domains beyond criminality per se becomes clear when we consider the complex mesh of municipal codes, police initiatives, and civil commitment laws regulating homelessness, drug addiction, and poverty in Puerto Rico. Beyond criminal law, many municipalities have devised their own public order codes that prohibit behaviors associated with unemployment and homelessness, such as loitering and vagrancy. Though not criminal laws, these codes effectively criminalize homelessness since failure to comply with any ensuing court orders often results in incarceration.[19] Alongside municipal public order codes, the carceral state also penalizes homelessness in more direct ways. Throughout my fieldwork, a local police initiative called Vuelta a la Vida was in operation, which dispatched specially trained officers to identify unstably housed people and which used public order codes to legally coerce homeless people into enrolling in therapeutic communities.

Complicating matters for anyone with a drug or alcohol problem, Puerto Rico also has some of the most punitive involuntary civil commitment legislation in the country. Since the introduction of Law 67 in 1993, the *sole* requirement for involuntary civil commitment in Puerto Rico is that it be demonstrated in a court of law that an individual is "addicted to drugs or alcohol," and not necessarily by a medical professional (a convincing testimony or confession will often suffice).[20] Under successful petitions, the recipient will find him- or herself legally institutionalized in a therapeutic community or an Evangelical ministry, where failure to comply with institutional rules or unauthorized discharge will place the subject in contempt of court and could lead to incarceration. I explore the history and legality of civil commitment in chapter 4, but for now, suffice to say that civil commitment is one of several noncriminal legal domains—along with employment laws disbarring formerly incarcerated people from the labor market, antivagrancy and antiloitering public order codes that penalize homelessness, and police initiatives that criminalize drug addiction—that constitute the legal-juridical dimensions of carceral citizenship. Together, they sign an expanding entrance to carceral citizenship, beyond criminalization, and together they produce a profile of legal exclusions on the island that overlaps with but is not identical to the alternative regulatory universe awaiting many formerly incarcerated people across mainland US states.[21]

Markedly unlike their US peers, both incarcerated and formerly incarcerated people in Puerto Rico retain the right to vote in local elections. The island does not suffer the same problem therefore of "felony disenfranchisement" as the US mainland, where 4.6 million people are currently denied the vote owing to a felony conviction, including 5.3 percent of the African American population and 1.5 percent of the non–African American population.[22] This absence of racialized disfranchisement *within* Puerto Rico coexists even at the same time that *all* inhabitants of Puerto Rico—criminalized or otherwise—are prohibited from voting in US presidential elections, signing a racially segregated citizenship of a distinct nature.

Ilana Díaz argues that race is "invisibly sutured to citizenship" in Puerto Rico, in the sense that US citizenship invisibly racializes and devalues Puerto Ricans while hiding that devaluation and unequal status "in plain sight" under a liberal mythology of equal citizenship.[23] As I attuned to re-educados narratives about citizenship and national identity, I found there to be much truth in this diagnosis, yet the invisibility of citizenship's racialized stratification had internal dimensions that manifested on local scales too.

The differing degrees to which citizenship's racially stratified nature is acknowledged between the US mainland and its territory, and the contrasting ways citizenship is therefore experienced subjectively, become clear when comparing prevailing racial discourses across the island and the mainland. Studies of formerly incarcerated people's experiences of citizenship on the US mainland will often describe how police persecution, discrimination in labor and housing markets, and felon disenfranchisement all radically transform the subjective experience of US citizenship.[24] Many have noted how formerly incarcerated people, and particularly people of color, gradually come to understand citizenship as a privilege that does not extend to them. The experience of being constantly policed and surveilled is said to expose the whitewashed myth of unmarked national belonging by producing a "distinctive lifeworld" defined by a "deep and totalizing sense of political alienation."[25] In New Jersey, Calvin Smiley's African American interlocuters narrate their experience of racially stratified citizenship very plainly through statements like "being Black in America is a crime" and "I have never been truly free."[26]

Quite strikingly, the intrusive legal restrictions imposed on re-educados, the attention they drew from police, and the massive curtailments of freedom and liberty that re-educados incurred long after completing a criminal sentence did not seem to dampen re-educados sense of "national" belonging in quite the same way. Re-educados would often proudly remind me that they were "Puerto Ricans," not "Americans," with nationality defined not politically or according to the legal provisions afforded by US citizenship but culturally and according to shared language, culture, and territory. Anthropologists have often noted the strong currents of cultural nationalism that circulate in Puerto Rico and, by attuning to those currents, have explored the tendency for cultural nationalism to prevail in the absence of a strong desire for political independence or sovereignty.[27] Duany attributes the popularity of cultural nationalism in Puerto Rico to the island's predicament as a colony and "stateless nation," arguing that Puerto Rican cultural nationalism operates as a kind of compromise, one that sacrifices political sovereignty and opts instead to protect and celebrate a sense of Puerto Rican culture and shared national heritage.[28] In line with Puerto Rico's strong local currents of cultural nationalism, I never heard anyone complain of being a "second-class Puerto Rican," which in itself is quite striking considering that many re-educados believed it was "illegal to be homeless in Puerto Rico." Unlike Puerto Rico's "second-class" positionality in relation to the United States, which was visible and acknowledged, local stratifications of citizenship tended to go unacknowledged and thus to remain hidden in plain sight. Markedly unlike formerly incarcerated African Americans on the US mainland, re-educados communicated their subjective experience of citizenship through discourses that flattened and minimized local hierarchies and ethnoracial distinctions. In line with deeply ingrained and well-documented discourses of cultural nationalism and mestizaje that celebrate racial harmony as a defining feature of Puerto Rican national identity, re-educados often distinguished themselves from their mainland peers through narrative devices that both erased Blackness from Puerto Rican identity and denied the local existence of racism. "We aren't like Americans," they might say. "Here, we don't discriminate based on race." I was initially taken aback when re-educados would say things like: "In Puerto Rico, todo'somo' iguales. It's not like over there, where African Americans have no rights." In hindsight, such statements are perfectly consistent with studies of the silencing of racism and erasure of Blackness from Puerto Rican identity.[29] They reflect a semantic strategy that Godreau and Lloréns have called "fugitive Blackness," whereby Blackness is assumed to lie elsewhere: on the US mainland, in Haiti, or perhaps in the past but never in contemporary Puerto Rico.[30]

Puerto Rico's intertwined histories of colonialism, slavery, indentureship, cultural nationalism, and mestizaje are important dimensions of the local context in which carceral citizenship is able to flourish. As a racelessly racialized form of social membership, carceral citizenship carves out a place in Puerto Rican society for formerly incarcerated people. It does this in part by transcending race and color distinctions and uniting a criminally stigmatized people in danger of expulsion into a unified and nationally proud collective whole. Channeling and extending historically entrenched ideologies of mestizaje and powerful currents of cultural nationalism, carceral citizenship unifies ambiguous and partial US citizens marked by the stigmata of criminalization and asserts a new collective identity grounded in mutual obligation and the power of self-help. In the next section, I unpack how this sense of mutual aid and collective identity is cultivated and brought into being.

· · · · ·

The center was blandly modern. Five graying cement structures bordered a concrete basketball court that had been taken over by parked cars. Red railings barred the windows of the men's dormitories. A graying sign at the entrance read "Comunidad de Elevación del Espíritu Humano" ("Community for the Elevation of the Human Spirit"). Next to it, a mounted billboard advised: "All visitors must register on the way in and out." Inside the reception area, the walls were an innocuous yellow punctuated with the occasional framed photograph. The largest was a portrait of the Comunidad de Elevación del Espíritu Humano's (CEEH's) founder, Rubén, who stood front and center with a medal around his neck, flanked on both sides by rows of smiling residents. "In Recognition for Services to the Free Associated State of Puerto Rico," read the inscription.

Whenever I visited CEEH, I would always encounter Rubén, the seventy-five-year-old founder, and Ernesto, who was in his midthirties and who Rubén would variously refer to as his *estudiante* (pupil) and *hijo adoptado* (adoptive son). Ernesto always came to the CEEH wearing a suit, tie, and leather shoes. He was responsible for counseling residents and for undertaking much of the administrative work of liaising with courts and families and writing case reports. Rubén, as both the founder and director of the organization, undertook the lion's share of pastoral and disciplinary duties. A gold crucifix hung over his white short-sleeve polo shirt, and a large bunch of keys for various outbuildings dangled from his belt. Taken together, Ernesto and Rubén seemed to embody two faces of carceral citizenship, representing qualified professionalism on the one hand and Christian atonement on the other.

Rubén commanded a fatherly kind of respect among residents at the CEEH. He was a talented orator. I first heard his life story in fragments during motivational speeches he delivered to residents, but eventually I ascertained a more detailed chronology over the course of several recorded interviews. The headline events in Rubén's history as a re-educado, as we reconstructed them, are as follows.

Rubén grew up in Cataño, a small town in northern Puerto Rico. He was raised by his mother, who worked in one of the island's many *fábricas*, clothes factories that employed thousands of women in the 1940s and 1950s. Neither Rubén nor any of his three older brothers completed high school. Instead, he left school at fifteen to work construction jobs under the supervision of an uncle. At twenty-one, Rubén was arrested for drug trafficking (along with his uncle) while also working as a handyman for a public housing project. With that case still pending, Rubén was charged with a second drug offense and was ultimately sentenced to seven years at Oso Blanco prison, no parole.

He used heroin throughout his time there. On his release in 1973, Rubén headed to New York but was arrested again in under a year. Rather than do more jail time, he skipped town and spent several precarious years in Yonkers and New Jersey.

In 1985, a year when Rubén recalls being homeless and regularly injecting heroin, he fathered a child with a sex worker who was also a heroin user. Not long after she was incarcerated for soliciting in Central Park, he tired of being on the run and handed himself in to the police. In 1986, when he was offered the option of prison or therapeutic community treatment, he opted for the latter and was sent back to Puerto Rico, where he had family who could visit him, to complete four years of mandatory drug treatment.[31] After twenty-four years of using heroin, Rubén recalls, it was there that he finally managed to stop. He was forty-nine years old when he completed his sentence, and after graduating, he decided to stay there and make a living of it. "And it felt so good," he said, "because I never thought that I was going to succeed. But there I was, doing it and realizing that I could help others. How can I describe it? . . . An immense desire was born in me: a desire to help others. I could see a new path ahead of me, calling me. I finally felt alive."

Ernesto, the *hijo adoptado* of Rubén, had been a military man prior to his incarceration at the Guerrero Correctional Institution in Aguadilla. He had served in Afghanistan and Iraq and, like thousands of US veterans, his addiction to heroin had begun with opioid painkillers, in his case prescribed to treat a shoulder injury acquired during service in Iraq. Prior to his deployment, Ernesto had been living in Florida for several years with his wife and their young daughter. He was one of the few re-educados I met who was married, but by the time we met, he was no longer in regular contact with his wife or daughter. Having struggled to keep up with the cost of opioid pain relievers, he had switched to using illegal heroin. Soon he was selling the drug as well, something that led him to be incarcerated twice and to spend a total of fourteen months behind bars in the late 2000s. In 2010, with his marriage up in flames, Ernesto moved back to Puerto Rico to rejoin his parents in the hope that living with them would help him clean up. Within months, he'd been arrested for drug possession (cocaine and marijuana). Ernesto first encountered Rubén at a prison sermon. Though they only spoke briefly, it was enough to make a mark.

"How can I put it," Ernesto pondered, as I fiddled with the audio recorder. "He had something about him—that kind of mission or zest for life." I stumbled through a question about the credibility of firsthand experience when Ernesto cut in, obviously aware of where I was going. "I'm in prison over here, and in comes Rubén. A Puerto Rican guy like me comes in—only he looks good! Upright, smart, not like the other guys. And he says, 'I'm an ex-addict, and if I can do it, you can do it too.' And it was very clear that, to him, it didn't matter where you came from." I nodded and waited, fearing I might have already steered our conversation too hard. "Since then, he has been a father to me and an angel in my life. Even though at first, I quit the program—I quit a few times even—he always stuck by me. He never turned his back on me. 'Cause we Puerto Ricans, we are oppressed enough. We gotta look out for each other, and so, it's like . . . The way he helped me—that's how I wanna try to help others. I do it for them like he did it for me."

Ernesto and Rubén's relationship was demonstrably loving. Ernesto's palpable affection and admiration for Rubén, and Rubén's concern for Ernesto, reminded me variously of a father-son or favored-pupil-and-teacher relationship. This privileged dynamic did not extend to all residents. Many of them avoided Rubén because of his tendency to dole out punishments for minor rule infractions, most often for smoking, which was not permitted at the CEEH. (This streak of disciplinarianism had also earned Rubén the secret nickname, Darth Vader, which residents used behind his back.) Rather than espousing an earnest pupil role or a brotherly solidarity, there were plenty of residents who kept to themselves, who avoided group activities as much as possible, and who, as far as I could tell, seemed isolated and very unhappy. Newer enrollees seemed to have an especially hard time (some saying, "I fucking hate it here," or "This program is bullshit"). For CEEH's newest recruits, the predominant emotional orientation seemed not to be a profuse passion for self-help. Instead, it was more commonly one of frustration, distrust, and boredom. Thus, Ernesto's strong sense of moral obligation—that it was up to him to and him alone to rescue the others—was not universally shared or automatically adopted. For Ernesto's "students," as he liked to call them, this was something he had to explicitly teach them.

One Tuesday afternoon, I had been invited to observe one of Ernesto's group therapies, something I made a habit of doing weekly over a period of several months. He led them twice a day, one after breakfast, one after lunch. The first time I attended one of his sessions, he passed me a laminated printout of the center's rules so that I could acquaint myself with "the norms and customs of the CEEH family." I jotted them down quickly. To me, they seemed to skew toward a Christian-disciplinary side of family.

1. No smoking, drugs, or alcohol.
2. No pornography or semi-pornography.
3. No shouting or unnecessary noise.
4. No receiving or giving tattoos in the center.

5. No negotiating, selling, or trading chores or favors.
6. No aggressive behaviors including threats of physical violence.
7. All participants must participate in all activities.
8. Do not disrespect anyone.
9. Do not leave without authorization.
10. All possessions can be confiscated at any time at the discretion of the administration.

A few minutes before 2:00 p.m., I followed Ernesto out of the reception to a separate outbuilding where fifteen men were assembled in a circle. After laying down some ground rules, he went on to announce what became his constant drill: "I know you are all smart, capable, intelligent men. But if you're here, it's because you have fallen down the wrong path. You have used your skills in the wrong way. We are here today to begin to learn how to use our talents and skills in the right way. So now is the time to start thinking, 'What kind of man do you want to be?'"

Group therapy followed a broadly set routine. Distilled, it repackaged past experiences of individual suffering into a collective sense of masculine obligation and duty. Rhetorically, this conversion hinged on inviting men to accept moral culpability for their experiences of prison, crime, and addiction, while offering self-help as a pathway to atonement. This acceptance of moral culpability involved recasting past suffering as a misuse or waste of a streetwise kind of expertise or skill set. Possession of this skill set was framed as conferring the bearer a moral obligation "to use the skills you have positively," with "positive use" equated with auto-ayuda-mutua (self-help/mutual aid). This conversion of moral culpability into an ethic of self-help was not straightforward. In fact, as a therapeutic teaching, it was not always explicit, and even when it was, not all residents bought into the new currency. But it was in group therapy that institutional attempts to foster a sense of pride and collective mutual obligation among men was most conspicuous.

Ernesto's pedagogy for cultivating carceral citizenship proceeded through a series of rhetorical moves. The first established a feeling of shared experience grounded in suffering: "Trust me, I know what drug addiction is and what it can do to a person. I know how it can lead a man to do terrible, terrible things. There are so many things I did that I'm ashamed of." Next, there usually came a warning aimed at pressing the point that men's alternative options were limited: "Trust me, brother, when I first got here, I didn't want to be here either. At first, I didn't see the point. So then I left, and what happened? I became homeless; I ended up back on the streets. I fell straight back into vice. I learned the hard way, but the good news is you don't have to." The warning was usually followed by an invitation to recast negative experiences in more positive terms, as a kind of vernacular professional expertise: "People like us, only we know what this life is like. We've lived on the street, brother; we come from the university of the street. If you can survive out there, that means you've already proved you're strong; you've already proved you're smart; you've already proved you're capable. But you need to use the talents that you have in the right way, not the wrong way. We've all done bad things out there, but every one of you is capable of setting things right—if you just start to use the talents that you have for good." Then came a call to embrace self-help as a moral duty. "Every single one of you can repay your debt to society. Every single one of you is capable of doing something important for Puerto Rico. Every single one of you can help get yourselves, each other, and our island back on track. Who else is going to help people like us?" Ernesto would ask, before supplying his own answer: "No one else is going to. We are the only people who can help ourselves and help each other. We owe this to our country, to God, and to one another."

In these sessions, Ernesto promoted carceral citizenship through a register of Puerto Rican patriotism, Christian atonement, and reclaimed opportunity. Becoming a carceral citizen was partly about taking moral responsibility for past wrongdoings, but at the same time, it was also about playing one's part for one's "nation," albeit the stateless nation of Puerto Rico. As Ernesto would constantly repeat, it involved "using the opportunities you've been given to overcome vice and drugs and to find and follow the right path." It was an alchemy of perspective based on asserting patriotic duty and street smarts from a stigmatized masculinity and claiming opportunity and expertise in places where both seemed lacking.

Though Ernesto considered his sessions to be lessons in "self-sufficiency" and "independent thinking" geared toward empowering men to choose their own futures (hence his frequent references to the power of self-belief: "if you truly believe you can be a lawyer, you will be a lawyer"), his lessons invited men to pursue a future that was actually highly specific. After all, he had set up the finale of each session to lead by his own example: "I never imagined when I arrived here that I could become a deputy director. But with hard work, I started to work as a counselor; then I got hired as a social worker," he'd say, before finishing: "I know you can all do it, because if I can do it, you can do it too."

With these words, Ernesto encouraged residents to follow in his direction and to derive confidence from his example in their capacity to do so. His pedagogy for carceral citizenship was made all the more persuasive by the fact that he embodied it. But Ernesto's call for men to interpret their predicament in a whole new light was only the beginning. The next step in the production of carceral citizenship would involve molding this reclaimed expertise into a collective identity as a certified and reeducated ex-addict. This reconstructed masculinity was explicitly and self-consciously educated, qualified, and scientifically literate. The cultivation of this professional identity was mediated by education and certification schemes devised by re-educados themselves, buttressed by state practices and discursive strategies of recognition that produced re-educados as public figures. I examine both of these in turn.

. . . . .

Some therapeutic communities—particularly the larger ones—operate internal training schemes known as *aprendizaje* (apprenticeship) and *la práctica* (practicum) for graduated re-educados, which confer informal forms of accreditation. These programs vary in form and content from place to place and tend not to follow any specified curriculum, at least not one that I could find written down.

At the invitation of staff members, I attended six training sessions for re-educados at two different therapeutic communities. I found myself watching Manuel, a long-standing and evidently much beloved director of a residential program in Guayama. His official title was "district training official," and he was responsible for coordinating and delivering training across several different communities. In a previous life, Manuel had been a shop assistant and then a drug trafficker, but in 1991 he'd been mandated by the court to enroll in a therapeutic community—the same one where we were now all gathered—and he'd stayed and worked there ever since. I watched Manuel teach four classes. He was charismatic and often paced up and down the room as he talked. He always wore a suit and tie and would start each session by inviting the group to give a round of applause and a welcoming cheer to each attendee. Following lively introductions, he'd invite the group to hold hands in prayer: "Being here together, *profesionales entre profesionales*, this is what we strive for. We are happy, we are motivated, we are grateful. Gracias a Dios."

In format, practicums had a hybrid educational-celebratory atmosphere that lay somewhere between university seminar, church service, and office party. Between ten and fifteen re-educados would sit around a table stacked with worksheets and refreshments. The facilitator would introduce the topic, and for the next few hours, the men would listen to a lecture, complete various exercises, and watch online videos. In terms of content, it was a hodgepodge of lessons determined by the presenter's choice. The six sessions

I attended covered a mixture of topics, some based on scientific research ("substance use and DSM-V"[32] and "domestic violence"), others on popular science ("managing stress" and "achieving your potential"), and others on Bible-based thoughts for the day ("the power of prayer") variously inspired by recent news items.

For example, in a session dedicated to "leadership and authority," Manuel talked attendees through the ideas of John Maxwell, an Evangelical American author whose pop-psychology books on leadership have sold millions of copies across the United States.[33] After the presentation, the men were invited to watch online videos and perform role-play exercises. In another session, men discussed how the Christian notion of sacrifice applied to their work, with attendees asked to enumerate specific sacrifices they'd made ("sleeping on the floor when there aren't enough beds," "working hard for little pay," and "working for love, not money"). In another, men watched a TED talk delivered by a clinical researcher about the long-term consequences of childhood trauma and the association between trauma and drug problems.

In format, these sessions borrowed their structure and template from higher education, signing the aspirationally middle-class "professional" vision of untarnished citizenship to which carceral citizenship aspires. In place of a colonized, stigmatized, criminalized status, carceral citizenship proposes an alternative vision of cosmopolitan citizenship by encouraging its members to understand themselves as fledgling, card-carrying, upwardly mobile professionals. This helps to explain, in part, why therapeutic communities go to such great lengths to devise a parallel world of titles, trophies, and certification systems that mimic higher education. It also adds some context to some of their more curious rituals: the elaborate reward ceremonies, the sometimes-grandiose titles (*ex-adicto honrado, re-educado certificado*), and the appropriated professional designations (*terapista, trabajador de caso, trabajador social*).

But the hodgepodge content of these training sessions—pop science, Christianity, and public health research—highlights an intriguing quirk of the kind of self-made professionalism that carceral citizenship promotes. Lacking any stable curriculum and unrestricted by theoretical allegiance, this improvised education system borrows its structure, content, and discourses from its surroundings, mixing and melding medicine, Christianity, and popular culture into a decidedly ad-lib—even *vernacular*—professional identity.[34] In turn, criminalized and stigmatized men with very little in the way of educational capital appropriate cultural images of higher education, customizing and adapting this model according to available resources and local conditions.

Consider a session I attended on "substance use and DSM-V," led not by Manuel but by a visiting graduate student with a BSc in psychology from the University of Puerto Rico. The student began the session by reminding attendees that "addiction" was just a lay term and that "as professionals talking among professionals, we should all be trying to use the correct DSM-V term, 'substance use disorder.'" Before giving his presentation, he asked the class to enumerate some of the characteristics that someone with a substance use disorder might display. "Being manipulative!" shouted one attendee. "A loss of social values!" suggested another. In line with their own exposures to therapeutic community pedagogy (whose intellectual genealogy I explore in the next chapter), "aggressiveness," "irritability," and "conflict with authority" were among the other suggested responses offered by the re-educados in attendance. After noting their responses, the lecturer then turned to his next slide, which listed "eleven reportable or observable symptoms of substance use disorders according to DSM-V."

Unlike the characterological explanations offered up by his pupils, the lecturer's symptoms were mostly behavioral: consuming more substances than originally intended, continued use in spite of harm to personal relationships, spending large amounts of time consuming or obtaining substances.[35] After the presentation, we completed a quiz in groups about observable symptoms of substance use disorders. Once Manuel, the director of training, had thanked the visiting speaker for his presentation, he delivered an off-the-cuff recap: "Today's addicts are complicated. It's not like before, when addicts were just addicts. Now, they have trauma, mental health, dual diagnosis, domestic violence. Addicts have changed," he said, "and we have to change too."

To me, this session stood out as a striking dramatization of how carceral citizenship operates as a kind of "bricolage" for the cultivation of a vernacular, patchworked, and self-consciously *professional* sense of citizenship.[36] At play in this session was an encounter between two seemingly distinct therapeutic epistemologies: a clinical epistemology grounded in the norms of biomedicine and the diagnostic criteria of DSM and a therapeutic community doctrine grounded in characterological theory. Yet the extremely accommodating orientation of re-educados to what (to outsiders) might seem like high-stakes framing tensions reflects the fact that "theory" here (whether of the scientific, popular, or spiritual variety) functions not primarily as a guide for therapeutic practice or as a declaration of tribal allegiance within a contested landscape of addiction treatment. Instead, theory functions as one among various disparate life materials (along with certificates, graduation rituals, and social discourses) that can be drawn upon for the formation of carceral citizenship. Molding and sculpting each other by drawing on whatever is around, carceral citizens blend diffuse kinds of theory and knowledge and then appropriate and meld this into an aspirationally professional, educated, and scientifically literate group identity. By replacing a stigmatized, penalized masculinity into a respected, employed professional one, carceral citizens cobble together *some* of the social benefits and rewards of conventional professional employment, within circumscribed settings, admittedly.

For the day's trainees, attendance was rewarded with tokens of recognition: an embossed certificate for each attendant, a plastic medal for newcomers, and, for the man deemed "most promising leader," a plastic shield. The ceremonial conferral of these prizes was marked by a round of applause, one for each attendee, with absent members calling in to deliver their congratulations on loudspeaker. Afterward, we tucked into the refreshments. There was a large spread with a cake. At the end of each of these joyous sessions, we would pray. Manuel's energy never dropped. "We are so grateful for these opportunities we have been given. Remember to have your certificates in a safe place," he called out to the exiting throng. "That way, if anyone says you aren't qualified, you can show that you are."

For some, the training on offer here might seem like a glorified parody of a higher education, a fanciful counterfeit or flashy kind of group theater whose artificiality is glaringly obvious, and, for those to whom the status value of educational qualifications matter, problematic. Certainly, this was the view of many public health researchers, who often dismissed the title "certified and accredited ex-addict" as illegitimate, fraudulent, and even immoral.

But to dismiss this vernacular certification system as phony is to discount not only the vital social and existential needs it fulfills for re-educados but also the public discursive regimes that have produced the honored and certified reeducated ex-addict as a publicly recognized and celebrated social figure over the course of many decades. So below I revisit the graduation ceremonies that opened this chapter, focusing this time on their local documentation in Puerto Rican press. This will illuminate the public communicative work that has created the honored and certified ex-addict as a recognized and valued kind of citizen over the course of many decades. Through these public proclamations, the economy of penance that channels re-educados into unpaid roles as volunteers on behalf of the carceral state will become clearer. Unpacking this economy, in turn, will help to clarify more precisely the kind of renegotiated social contract that is coming into being.

· · · · ·

"Congratulations—you're rehabilitated," writes a journalist in *Primera Hora*, on observing a graduation ceremony in San Juan in 2000. "Today, eighteen men achieve a new kind of freedom" as "souls free of drugs," now "accredited as rehabilitated."[37]

The moral economy that surrounds and extracts unwaged labor—what I now recognize as an economy of penance—is most clearly expressed in therapeutic community graduation ceremonies. In Puerto Rico, these are time-honored traditions and spectacular works of public theater. A staple event in the mayoral social calendar, they have been hosted annually across dozens of municipalities since the late 1960s and are hotly chronicled by local media. They often draw large crowds and are sometimes attended by Puerto Rico's governing elite—mayors, yes, but also senators, police chiefs, religious leaders, and senior judges. At a CREA graduation ceremony in 1988 in Trujillo Alto, for example, attended by none other than Puerto Rico's standing governor Hernández Colón, a joyful reporter congratulated the cohort of "new men" as they shook the hands of Puerto Rico's government officials.[38] Attendees included José Ronaldo Jarabo (the president of the chamber), Pedro Padilla (the president of association of the mayors), a host of businessmen, a bishop, several senators, an Evangelical leader, and a Catholic priest. Fervently, the journalist described how Governor Hernández Colón "shook hands and hugged many of the hundreds of inmates who had smiles on their faces, reflecting the alleviation of having woken up from the nightmare of drugs." After the ceremony, Governor Colón gave an impassioned testimony: "While other countries are known for exporting drugs, we can be proud that an organization born in Puerto Rico is exporting a message so hopeful and positive."

The public ceremonies that produce the honored and certified ex-addict owe their symbolism to at least two distinct traditions. The first, of course, is that of US higher education. This repertoire, for all its palpable glitz, is decidedly secular. In hailing re-educados as "certified" and "accredited," graduation ceremonies marshal the modern imagery of educational attainment to symbolically recast criminalized and marginalized men as upwardly mobile, card-carrying professionals who are publicly greeted *as such* by the governing elite. Graduation ceremonies may be read therefore as public theaters or staging grounds for the imagination and enactment of an alternative kind of world: one where men who have lost everything can catapult up the social ladder to stand shoulder to shoulder—if only for a brief ceremonial moment—with the governing class.

But graduation ceremonies also owe their symbolism to a second, Christian repertoire. One powerful metaphor that has figured prominently in media coverage of graduation ceremonies since the 1960s is that of the "ex-addict crusader."[39] This is a Christian metaphor that casts drug addicts as lost souls fallen to vice ("lost in an underworld of drugs") and positions re-educados as redeemed soldier-crusaders leading a war against drugs ("may you lead in the fight for a future for our island, a future free of drugs").

Hogar CREA's founder, the deceased José Juan García (Chejuán), is the most renowned embodiment of the ex-addict crusader figure. "The program's success," a fellow re-educado recounts in an interview with the *San Juan Star*, "is owed to the moral conscience of one man who pulled himself from the watery depths of addiction and swam back to save those of us who were drowning."[40] But this crusader image is not unique to therapeutic community leaders. It also abounds in journalists' accounts of program graduates more broadly. Consider one of several similar news items I cataloged that year: "These men deserve our congratulations and recognition," writes a journalist in *El Vocero*, "for their courage [for] leaving a world of indignity engulfed in degrading demands of vice and for taking the decision to return to this world to save others."[41]

Borrowing and blending Christian and patriotic images, the ex-addict crusader metaphor works to redeem criminalized men by recasting them as savior-soldiers and Puerto Rican heroes.[42] But redemption, it turns out, comes at a price. As I delved further into journalists' accounts of graduation ceremonies, and as I juxtaposed them with therapeutic communities' own literature, a more complicated moral economy surrounding the work of re-educados began to emerge, one that threaded together re-educados' desires for recognized achievement and redeemed public standing with Christianity and self-help. As I have come to understand this economy of penance, its logic works something like this.

By virtue of their criminalized status, re-educados are discursively saddled with a moral debt that must be repaid. Within the therapeutic community literature, this takes the form of a blunt call for re-educados to "pay back their debt to society."[43] Journalists, in contrast, usually couch this within the language of personal responsibility. But beneath these conservative overtones is the Catholic sacramental principle of penance: forgiveness of moral wrong requires atonement and restitution.

On these stages of national theater, re-educados are called upon to participate in the economy of penance. Under gaze of family and town, their unfinished pathway to forgiveness is laid out ahead of them: to pay *back* the debt, so the story goes, the re-educado must take up the fight to join the national crusade. Héctor Figueroa, the current director of Hogar CREA, encapsulates this idea in a commencement address he delivered in 2016,

when he implored CREA graduates to "return to their communities as leaders in the fight for the Puerto Rican personality." This Puerto Rican and
expressly characterological emphasis matters. A *fight for the Puerto Rican
personality* is not same thing as a *war on drugs*. Public declarations of a war
on drugs usually operate—at least in the US mainland context—as incites
or justifications for extending the use of police and military power against
people of color. Figueroa's plea for re-educados to fight for the *Puerto Rican
personality*, in contrast, is first and foremost an invitation to Puerto Rican
national service. When re-educados are hailed in *El Vocero* as "beings who
have had the willpower to seize the opportunities society gave them," who
can "return to their homelands as people of means," they are being publicly
called upon to enter into a specific kind of moral contract.[44] Through this
civic inauguration, the carceral citizen is summoned to pay back his debt to
society by undertaking a specific kind of duty that he, as a certified ex-addict,
is both qualified and duty bound to fulfill.

At the center of this economy of penance stands the secular-sacred figure
of the certified penitent. This is the *honrado certificado re-educado* (certified
and reeducated honoree)—part penitent, part professional, part volunteer—
whose penal stigma and lack of educational capital make him an ideal can-
didate for voluntary self-help work. A self-making professional, the certified
penitent is happy to be able to perform this important national service. On
this stage of national theater, logics of debt, penance, and patriotism run
uncomfortably together, but one thing all can agree upon is that everyone
wins when the re-educado joins the fight. "The best thing of all," a reporter
from *El Vocero* notes, is the "double triumph to CREA"—"that it not only
rehabilitates its clients, but also succeeds in creating crusaders."[45] "The legitimate aspiration of every human being is to succeed," echoes Judge Carmen
Dolores Ruiz, who delivered a powerful pep talk at a graduation in 2000,
"but you have to fight for success. . . . The certificate that you receive today is
proof that you have the potential to achieve success. But with that success,"
she warns, "comes the responsibility to be an example [for others]."[46]

Layered onto Christian ideas of debt and redemption is the intoxicating
promise of professional opportunity, publicly recognized achievement, and
national pride. It is this heady cocktail of unpaid debt and promises of redeemed masculinity and civic standing that makes this economy of penance
so very effective at extracting unwaged and underwaged work.

"I feel grateful for what the program has done with me," Rocky said, passing
me a can of Coca-Cola from the vending machine. We stood outside the gymna-
sium, cooling off from the day's festivities. "Grateful?" I asked, masking a prang
of discomfort with a slurp of my drink. "'Cause I've suffered a lot, you know?

I lost my family; I don't see my children. All that I've suffered on the street means I know how to help." I nodded, trying to keep myself neutral but feeling a combination of disbelief, sadness, and a growing sense of shame for prying. Rocky continued. "I went through so much. I know how to help others that are suffering. Seeing these men here today, who are graduating and moving on in their lives, and knowing I've helped them learn from my mistakes—I'm grateful for that feeling," he said, adding, "because these men are my little brothers. And every day I keep learning and keep working. I feel fulfilled, honestly, from not having a roof over my head, to having a job that I like. So, I work eight hours that they pay me and sixteen they don't pay me. They are donated hours. Why do I do it? When I was in treatment, there were people who did it for me, so how am I gonna not do it for others? I owe it to them."

So this middle-aged man stays and works at the same therapeutic community from which he once graduated. He works not just hard but gratefully because, at last, after eight years in prison and having partially lost his eyesight in a prison riot, he has finally landed on the best possible option available to him. "I have a roof over my head, I have my participants, and I can be a useful person. That's my second pay. And I do it with love."

· · · · ·

A vast gulf separates the futures celebrated in these graduation ceremonies and the harsh realities that await re-educados. Perhaps unsurprisingly, graduation ceremonies and the carceral citizenship projects they dramatize do not magically propel men with criminal records into the middle-class professions. What they do is provide fleeting moments of recognized achievement and a transient embrace into the larger polis. But on the outside, the indelible mark of penal stigma remains, and re-educados confront the same exclusions as before. Disqualified from housing, discriminated against in the labor market, their poverty is policed just as heavily, if not more, as before. Thus, the achievement celebrated here turns out to be legal tender within a highly circumscribed carceral market.

My own notes and life histories of dozens of re-educados show that graduation is rarely a one-way ticket. Instead, men routinely oscillate over the course of many years between an *internado* and a re-educado position, with the interim period often being one of extreme vulnerability. On the outside, these endorsements and internal systems of certification turn out to count for very little, often to the great peril of the individual whose viability was dependent on it.

Take Jorge, the graduate who opened this chapter. By the time I attended his graduation in 2017, he had actually already graduated three times before, having spent nearly five years as an *internado* and unwaged *terapista* in several different communities, nearly all while under court order. After his penultimate graduation in 2011, Jorge had enjoyed a period of relative stability. As he recalls, he spent two "good clean years" (without heroin) working as a live-in counselor, during which time he enjoyed free accommodation and a sub-minimum-wage stipend. At the suspicion of a colleague, however, Jorge was issued a mandatory drug test by the center's director, which he duly failed (according to Jorge, he had smoked marijuana). He was promptly dismissed from his post, something that cost him his only means of income, his home, and, worst of all, according to Jorge, his sense of fulfillment and duty: "I couldn't believe I'd let down all my homeboys, all my brothers who were relying on me. It was really hard to understand what was happening." Romantic bridges long burned, and unable to live with his sister who was caring for her own two children, Jorge spent several months sleeping in his car. Eventually he was brought back to his old therapeutic community by way of a police-led outreach initiative. He re-reenrolled at La Casita 2014. As is customary therapeutic community practice, he resumed treatment at the bottom of the pyramid, with none of his previously earned privileges. His "honored and certified" status and years of experience counted for nothing.

Jorge was not alone. By and large, cycles of arrest and rearrest, often compounded by housing insecurity, unemployment, and problematic substance use, are the norm. Consider Luis, who had directed an Evangelical program for eight years when I interviewed him in 2016, and who lived on-site in accommodation provided by the church. While Luis initially narrated his rise to directorship linearly, attributing his personal growth to the therapeutic community system and the re-educados who'd supported him, on further questioning he conceded that it hadn't all happened in one go. Prior to his current stability (he is now in his sixties), Luis had initiated therapeutic communities five times before and successfully graduated on three occasions ("without quitting"), in 1989, 1994, and 1998, respectively. Upon his first graduation, he'd been hired as a live-in social worker, a position he held for twenty months and for which he'd received free room and board. Eventually deciding to try his hand at something else, he obtained a job as a janitor at a mall with the help of a family member. He soon moved into an apartment in a public housing project with a new girlfriend and her child (never officially registering as an occupant, since his felony record would have disqualified him). But that relationship soon fell apart when she came to believe Luis "had eyes" for her teenage daughter (Luis says this isn't true). After the breakup, Luis became homeless and resorted to sleeping on cardboard boxes in the Plaza de Recreo in Río Piedras. After several months of homelessness, during which time he says he "fell back" into smoking crack, he eventually got tired and enrolled "voluntarily" (without legal pressure) in another therapeutic community.

Not that there are no exceptions to this. I did occasionally encounter re-educados who had been able to retain their positions without too many setbacks. Some managed to acquire salaried positions that enabled them to live off-site. Manuel (the former trafficker turned therapeutic community trainer we met earlier) exemplified this kind of therapeutic community success story. By the time we met, he'd held the same job for over twenty years (at the therapeutic community that he himself had been treated in decades earlier), and his salary was relatively high ($24,000) compared to the sub-minimum-wage income of many of his colleagues. He was also married and lived with his wife and child in a lower-middle-class suburb. But Manuel's relative job security, domestic stability, and attentive fatherhood were not the norm. Far more common was Jorge's trajectory: repetitive cycling through a revolving pyramid of unwaged and underwaged labor punctuated by housing instability, unemployment, arrest, and extreme vulnerability.

And here lies one of carceral citizenships most serious shortcomings. While providing its members with vital material security along with socially meaningful forms of self-worth, acknowledged achievement, and male camaraderie—surely important remunerations—it delivers its members into a certified and accredited status that is partial, nontransferable, and constantly at risk of forfeiture. In fact, this reclaimed membership can be revoked at any moment, and it is precisely the trigger events that kick-start this cycle—a criminal charge, a court order, substance use, rough sleeping—that are most likely to exact such a penalty.

But despite carceral citizenship's overblown promises, re-educados continue to volunteer to undertake the work of containment and rehabilitation in exchange for shelter, safety, community, and forms of publicly recognized achievement. They do this in the name of duty and debt and animated by an economy of penance that is extraordinarily effective at uniting a disparate collection of interests, scarcities, and institutional arrangements across the carceral state, self-help, and Christianity. And it is through this economy of penance that carceral citizens come to fill the material and social gaps created by the war on drugs, a war that, in the case of Puerto Rico, is also the war responsible for bringing carceral citizens into being in the first place.

It is vital, however, to see that this economy of penance has complex historical roots; the next chapter delves into the ways that economic, political, and legal forces have intertwined to create the conditions in which carceral citizenship can emerge and thrive.

The Voluntary Face
of the Carceral State

On a sticky afternoon in 2016, an exchange was gathering heat at the conference room of Comunidad de Elevación del Espíritu Humano (CEEH). I was sitting at a table with twelve re-educados who had gathered to receive two hours of training as part of their therapeutic community career development plans. This week's session was led by a government employee and psychologist named Eulalia. She began her session—"Compliance with the New SAMHSA Guidelines"—by reminding attendees that the new federal guidelines, released earlier that year by the US Substance Abuse and Mental Health Services Administration (SAMHSA), called for all drug services to be "grounded in evidence-based medicine." This, Eulalia explained, meant it was critical to understand that "substance use disorder is a chronic recurring clinical condition," she enunciated clearly, "not a sign of moral weakness."

The two re-educados on my left exchanged furtive glances.

For the next ten minutes, Eulalia continued her talk, though an awkward atmosphere had settled into the room. "Participants," she said, "should not and cannot be forced to participate in any therapies that they do not wish to participate in." This especially applied to *terapia laboral* (labor therapy), she emphasized. "If participants don't want to work, they should not and cannot be forced to." Eulalia had barely made it to the bottom of her slide when Alberto, a re-educado in his fifties, jumped up from his seat. "The addict," he interrupted, clasping his hands on his chest, "suffers from a deficiency of moral character, and what you need to understand is that all of us re-educados, every single one of us here, has lived through a personality disorder and gotten over this vice. How did we do it?" he asked rhetorically, looking toward his peers around the table. "By working hard to reeducate our character." Alberto was receiving nods of approval. Emboldened, he returned to face the speaker: "Whenever there's a personality disorder, for example, if you start using at twelve years old, you get stuck at that age. My chronological age might be I'm thirty, but really, emotionally, my personality is stuck at twelve." There were more murmurs of agreement. "The addict is stuck," Alberto said, starting to pace. "His character hasn't grown. We re-educados, we need to work hard in order to rebuild our character and to match our emotional and chronological age. It isn't easy!" he exclaimed, now pontificating rather boldly. "But every single one of us in this room knows how much work, dedication, and discipline it takes to reeducate one's character. Every single one of us knows that you can't reeducate yourself if you just sit around doing whatever you want all day." Alberto continued in this forthright fashion for the next five minutes, during which time Eulalia's mouth opened and closed a few times, without emitting any words. "Eulalia," he said, addressing her. Her flushed cheeks were giving away her discomfort. "I don't see anyone here who helped me reeducate negatively, because they've helped me learn how to put my talents to use. They've helped me to develop my character and to develop a new personality."

Before Eulalia had a chance to respond, another re-educado was chipping in: "They [SAMIISA] tell us a lot of things—that we aren't allowed to make the addict work anymore, that we can't do this and that. They say we should let the participant do whatever he wants to!" This latter comment drew a few cynical chuckles and scoffs. The re-educado to Alberto's right piped up. "The addict likes the easy life. Believe me! He needs to be taught the value of hard work." Now everyone was talking. "You know that *they* [the government] are happy to give us methadone?" one said. "You know that *they* [the government] are happy to decriminalize heroin?" said another. "They want to bring in the doctors, who want to give us heroin *for free* and keep the addict dependent on the government! What kind of treatment is that?"

The day's compliance training had derailed, but it had also ignited a reflex I encountered again and again in my research with therapeutic communities: one where re-educados asserted their allegiance to the paradigm of reeducation and attested to the power of labor therapy—unremunerated labor performed in the name of overcoming drug addiction—as a beneficial therapeutic tool fundamental to their own sense of personal transformation. On encountering a wide variety of external pressures to reform methods of rehabilitation, whether those be calls to medicalize and professionalize drug treatment services or campaigns to decriminalize drug addiction, beyond the specifics the reflex was broadly the same. On campaign trails, in courtrooms, and in documents stored in the archives of Puerto Rico's Legislative Assembly, therapeutic community directors espoused their commitment to the paradigm of reeducation and drew palpable ire in the face of proposed alternatives.

Why should this collective of formerly incarcerated, self-identifying "re-educated ex-addicts" not only endorse the notion that people addicted to drugs suffer "pathological personalities" but also oppose federal and local government efforts to suspend the use of labor therapy as a tool of rehabilitation? Is this just an unusually vivid case of internalized stigma or perhaps a thinly veiled attempt on the part of re-educados to exploit the unremunerated labor of their criminalized peers?[1] What other stakes might be at play here? I began to make sense of this reflex when I juxtaposed the stories re-educados told about the therapeutic communities they were part of with Puerto Rico's intertwined colonial, political-economic, and carceral history. One pragmatic reason that therapeutic community leaders might oppose countervailing paradigms of drug rehabilitation is that a truly "evidence-based" field of medicalized drug services could plausibly spell the end of their careers. But this pragmatic interpretation, I argue, ignores this reflex's conceptual significance: the larger whole of which Puerto Rican re-educados are just a part. What I was witnessing that day was one of the human micropractices of carceral citizenship formation. Through these human encounters, men who were the targets and victims of Puerto Rico's expanding carceral state and its repertoire of punitive interventions were seizing penal authority "from below" and asserting themselves as arbiters and wielders of penal power. Through espousing the punitive paradigm of reeducation, and by rejecting countervailing currents proposing alternative ways to improve the well-being of people who are addicted to drugs, re-educados were claiming ownership over and co-opting a highly devolved domain of state power and authority. The history of this underappreciated "human" side of carceral statecraft is the subject of this chapter, which recounts the history of carceral citizenship and contextualizes this innovation of modern capitalism in relation to Puerto Rico's ongoing coloniality and its unique encounter with capitalist development.

As mentioned in this book's introduction, Puerto Rico has remained largely absent from the historiography of the United States' carceral turn, as have the other colonial territories. So rather than retelling the story of mass incarceration's beginnings on the US mainland—a story that has been skillfully told and retold in many other places[2]—in this chapter I maintain a more circumscribed local focus. Foregrounding the experiences of incarcerated people who are often erased in top-down structural accounts, this

Puerto Rican history of carceral citizenship "from below" positions me to show how a sector of formerly incarcerated Puerto Ricans have creatively responded to the dislocations of capitalism, colonialism, and the rise of mass incarceration in the late twentieth century to coproduce the contours of the carceral state. Highlighting how carceral states and its marginalized targets greatly shape each other's development, albeit asymmetrically, this chapter uses the rise of carceral citizenship to extend a dominant understanding of mass incarceration as a "mass expulsion" that has exiled a "superfluous" proletariat.[3] Specifically, I show how a correctional genre of unwaged self-help work—performed in the name of reeducating criminals, drug users, and other citizens deemed "characterologically flawed"—has ascended in Puerto Rico since the late twentieth century to become an increasingly common and publicly recognized mode of social, economic, and civic participation.

This carceral citizenship project has been carved out from the harsh interstices of a series of macro-level developments that have systematically eroded men's opportunities for social membership. In Puerto Rico, these include a colonial organization of capitalism with complex racial legacies, the mass criminalization and extra-penal supervision of young men, capitalist industrialization and postindustrial decline, and the enduring postimprisonment stigma that excludes the island's felons from housing and labor markets. At the juncture of these multiple intersecting exclusions, these carceral citizenship projects that are taking shape in nonprofit community-based organizations out on the devolved outskirts of the carceral apparatus now offer a durable mode of political, economic, and civic existence for thousands of exiles.

This history of Puerto Rico's therapeutic communities also helps to explain the striking persistence of reeducation, a paradigm that for over six decades has conceived of people who are addicted to drugs in terms of psychopathology (pathological personality). As a therapeutic doctrine, reeducation has been refuted many times over in the history of addiction science, yet it continues to find traction worldwide. In fact, its most ardent champions in the Americas today are men with histories of drug problems and incarceration themselves, precisely those whom this paradigm deems "sociopathic."[4] The widespread endorsement of the paradigm of reeducation among the criminally stigmatized poor stems from the role it has come to play as one of their few remaining avenues for publicly recognized and legal social participation.

This history of carceral citizenship gets going in 1898, the year the United States seized Puerto Rico from Spain. From these events, we can begin to reconstruct how a generation of colonized and criminalized US citizens—men dealing with stigmas and problems of their own—drew upon and reworked North American theories of crime and addiction to develop self-help collectives that would eventually morph into a new genre of carceral citizenship.

· · · · ·

The prison has a colonial anatomy etched in its very structure by the economics of the plantation. After US occupation in 1898, Puerto Rico was declared a US customs territory in 1901 by presidential proclamation. Immediately, the island became privy to the same tariff benefits as those protecting the mainland sugar industry. Assisted by the tariff and other economic policies, US sugar companies poured capital into the island. Within a few short years, US sugar companies had replaced the small-scale Spanish-era haciendas with large-scale and technologically sophisticated sugar plantations. Unable to compete with the US-owned corporate sugar plantations, local coffee production ground to a halt.[5] By 1910, sugarcane monoculture controlled more than 60 percent of the arable land.[6] Between 1909 and 1919, the number of sugar factories belonging to individuals tanked from fifty-one to just twelve, as absentee-owned corporations swept in and monopolized sugar production. According to Sidney Mintz, Puerto Rico's formerly indentured peasants and former slaves had been subjected to one of the most intense processes of proletarianization in Caribbean history.[7]

As agricultural wage laborers, Puerto Rico's rural poor were engulfed by a fresh wave of capitalist exploitation. Unlike the indentured peasants of the Spanish empire, who were forced to work on the plantations by antivagrancy laws and labor codes but who usually held usufruct rights that permitted them to engage in subsistence farming (when not busy producing exports for the plantation owners), Puerto Rico's first generation of wage laborers was denied access to land.[8] With the arrival of wage labor, Puerto Rico's agricultural workers were no longer able to fend for themselves and came to depend entirely on the wages they could earn on the corporate sugar plantations. Beholden to the cane-growing cycle, Puerto Rico's first proletariat was starved of income during the dead months. Plantation owners, in turn, devised new practices of extraction predicated on credit and debt. Many owners required that harvesters live on-site in company-owned accommodation as a condition of their labor contracts, which caused harvesters to rack up housing debt during the dead season. On-site company stores loaned food and other household goods to the harvesters on credit, plunging workers and their families into debt. After housing and food-related wage deductions then, a week's pay for the harvesters could amount to just a few cents.[9] Puerto Rico's multiracial rural poor were no longer required to carry a *libreta*, as they had under Spanish colonialism, but this new imperial order kept them bound to the plantation by debt and hunger.[10] Signing a new "apparatus of capture" and a new form of coloniality rather than a decolonization, Puerto Rico's so-called freedom from Spain had made for a strangled liberation.[11]

As US companies took over the plantations, US lawmakers took steps to enforce law and order in the colony. In 1902, US officials approved Puerto Rico's penal code, itself a direct copy of California's code. Initially, Puerto Ricans who fell afoul of the law were incarcerated in the Spanish-era prison of La Princesa (The Princess) in Old San Juan, which had operated as a penitentiary since 1833, or in one of the handful of antiquated jails or penal labor camps. By the early twentieth century, prisons and new systems of debt and credit had replaced earlier regimes of slavery and indentureship as mechanisms of coerced labor. While labor arrangements on the corporate sugar plantations were changing fast, working conditions for Puerto Rico's prisoners seem to have changed relatively little during the first three decades of US rule.[12] By day, incarcerated people were dispatched to perform broadly analogous kinds of unpaid work ("public works") as they had done under Spanish colonialism. According to historian Fernando Picó, Puerto Rican convicts were made to clean up the mess left by the Spanish-Cuban-American War, and, among other things, they were sent to build roads and bridges on behalf of the new US government, all as an explicit part of their punishment.[13]

In 1920, Puerto Rico's correctional population (including those held in jails, prisons, camps, and reformatories) stood at 2075 people, making for an incarceration rate of 153/100,000.[14] According to census records, Puerto Ricans who identified as Black were disproportionately incarcerated relative to their population share, accounting for 30.8 percent of Puerto Rico's prison population but only 26.8 percent of the general population in 1920. For their part, Puerto Ricans who identified as white in the census were underrepresented in prison, accounting for 69.2 percent of the prison population but 73.2 percent of the island's general population.[15] Compared to the US mainland at that time, however, where Jim Crow laws still prevailed in many southern states, the racialization of incarceration in Puerto Rico was decidedly more mixed, reflected in its much milder profile of racial disparities. On the US mainland in 1920, Blacks were 417 percent more likely to be incarcerated than whites. In Puerto Rico in 1920, Blacks were 22 percent more like to be incarcerated than whites.[16] The relatively milder magnitude of racial inequality in Puerto Rican incarceration in the early twentieth century stems directly from its unique legacy of slavery and its multiracial history of coerced labor.

In Puerto Rico, recall, African slavery was one among several modes of coerced labor forcing the landless classes to work on the plantations. Alongside slavery was the *libreta*, or passbook system, whereby landless subsistence farmers (including those who were Black, mulatto, and white) were forced to register as employees of landowners and planters. Not only was Puerto Rico's history of coerced labor multiracial, but like many Spanish colonies, Puerto Rico was also home to a large population of *pardos libres* (freed slaves). In fact, free people of color accounted for roughly 80 percent of all people of African descent in Puerto Rico throughout the nineteenth century and until abolition in 1873. On the US mainland on the dawn on the Civil War, in contrast, free people of color were a mere 1.5 percent of all people of African descent in 1860.[17] The relatively smaller proportion of slaves in Puerto Rico is sometimes misconstrued as evidence for a more benign slavery there.[18] The more accurate reading is that Puerto Rico's slaves were not alone in their enchainment. Both enslaved Africans and indentured peasants were enchained in one way or another. Accordingly, the system of convict labor that endured after abolition, continuing the extraction of unpaid labor from Puerto Rico's poor, was similarly racially mixed.

In the 1930s came an overhaul of the antiquated Spanish-era prison system. In 1933, US-appointed governor James R. Beverley inaugurated the Puerto Rico Island Penitentiary in Río Piedras, also known as Oso Blanco (White Bear). Set to usher in a new rehabilitative agenda, Oso Blanco's administrators understood their remit in overtly "humane" terms. Gone, or so it was hoped, was the antiquated and brutish Spanish system. The new penitentiary was to be staffed by psychiatrists, social workers, and health care workers from across the human sciences. Through scientific knowledge and modern therapeutic practices, Oso Blanco was to be staffed by health care professionals tasked with inculcating in prisoners the "healthy moral habits" befitting of the "useful citizen."[19] Though most inmates at this time would have been Catholic, the architects of Oso Blanco saw their goal in explicitly scientific and secular terms. Accordingly, they ensured to relegate matters of religion to the periphery and noncompulsory activities of visiting priests and missionaries.[20]

Dovetailing with similar developments on the US mainland, Oso Blanco was a hybrid institution: part prison, part hospital, and part sanatorium, perched on 112 acres of land.[21] Prisoners were expected to work, either in the on-site workshops, where prisoners would build furniture for the government, or in the fields, where 70 acres were dedicated to agricultural production, mostly to sugarcane, fruit trees, and cassava.[22] Historians generally agree that the rehabilitative principles behind Oso Blanco, whatever its ideals, operated primarily at the level of aspiration, not practice. By most accounts, promised medical treatments and therapies were never realized because of a lack of financial investment, and disease and prison overcrowding were persistent problems.[23]

The primary targets for imprisonment between the 1930s and 1950s were agricultural workers (see fig. 2), referred to by prison staff as *jornaleros* (day laborers), *campesinos* (rural people), *agregados* (people attached to someone else's land), and *jíbaros* (peasants).[24]

As historian Alberto Ortiz Díaz makes clear, the racialization of Puerto Rico's incarcerated rural poor was highly ambiguous, in line with broader racial ideologies of mestizaje and blanqueamiento. In prison case files, Puerto Rico's rural population was predominantly racialized as *blanco-trigueño*, an ambiguous category that may be translated as "wheat-white," "racially mixed," or even as "white with sun-toasted skin."[25] As Díaz makes clear, widening social definitions of whiteness in the twentieth century are part of the reason why, by the 1960s, 70 percent of Puerto Rico's prison population was characterized as white.[26] Whatever the meaning of whiteness in this context, it is clear that Puerto Rico's rural proletariat was subjected to intense forms of stigmatization. In fact, the multiracial stakeholders in charge of their care

FIGURE 2 · Photograph taken by Jack Delano in 1941, entitled *Sugarcane Workers, near Arecibo.*

(including psychiatric staff, doctors, and social workers in addition to prison guards) variously categorized rural people as "psychopaths," "maladjusted," "moron types."[27] The circulation of highly stigmatizing carceral tropes at Oso Blanco stemmed directly from the new scientific approaches to managing criminals that were proliferating in the early twentieth century. Signing a scientific stigmatization that approaches a racialization, albeit an ambiguous one, Puerto Rico's "wheat-white" rural convicts were widely characterized by psychiatrists and social workers as "superstitious" and "feeble-minded" alcoholics whose "deficient intellect" was said to have prevented them from exercising the "prudence" of a "normal person."[28]

By the mid-twentieth century then, the bourgeoning human sciences had provided an extensive and stigmatizing vocabulary for the classification and treatment of Puerto Rico's prisoners. Among psychiatrists, social workers, and health professionals, carceral tropes about "maladjusted personalities" and "hot tempers" were part of an international scientific vernacular spanning Puerto Rico, the US mainland, and beyond. As Puerto Rico made its way in the mid-twentieth century from an agricultural to an industrial economy, these carceral tropes would blend with medical and religious scripts, sedimenting a decidedly characterological understanding of drug addiction and positioning the "disturbed personalities" of drug addicts as a target of the modern and postindustrial carceral state.

· · · · ·

With the introduction of Puerto Rico's new Estado Libre Asociado constitution in 1952, the notion that the "moral and social rehabilitation" of prisoners should be the primary goal of incarceration was enshrined in the Puerto Rican constitution.[29] Up until 1959, responsibility for managing drug offenders specifically continued to lie with federal government. Puerto Ricans found guilty of breaking federal narcotics laws (users and dealers) were tried in federal courts in San Juan and, if convicted, were transported to federal prisons or hospitals on the mainland. But in 1959, with the passing of Commonwealth Narcotics Law No. 48, Puerto Rico assumed partial jurisdiction of narcotics control. That is, the island remained subject to the same federal narcotics laws that were driving up drug convictions across the US mainland, but Puerto Rico became financially responsible for locking up those who were convicted.[30] Owing to punitive federal drug policies, Oso Blanco superseded its capacity within a matter of weeks, leading to a crisis of prison overcrowding that would endure for decades to come.

Prompted by this crisis of prison overcrowding, the Center for the Investigation of Addiction (Spanish acronym, CISLA) was established in July

1961. Its formal remit was to conduct research into the nature of addiction and to develop treatments. In 1961, supported by a modest commonwealth grant, the CISLA's first director, Efrén Ramírez—then a psychiatry resident at the University of Puerto Rico—took over an abandoned outbuilding on the grounds of the state psychiatric hospital in Río Piedras. There, equipped with only his education in general medicine and a personal predilection for psychoanalysis, the young Puerto Rican psychiatrist began experimenting with methods to treat addiction.

North American psychiatrists at this time generally considered addiction to be a problem of psychopathology. Indeed, addiction was classified as a "personality disorder" in the first two editions of the *American Diagnostic and Statistical Manual of Mental Disorders* (DSM), published in 1952 and 1968.[31] Particularly influential was the American psychiatrist Lawrence Kolb, who in the 1920s had popularized the idea that addiction resulted from inherent defects of personality. Kolb famously distinguished between "innocent" and "vicious" addicts, innocent being people with "normal personalities" who fell into addiction through accidental means, such as through prescribed painkillers. He reserved the term "vicious" addicts for the illicit drug-using urban poor who, he argued, sought out narcotics and were vulnerable to develop addiction because of their "pathological" personalities.'[32]

Ramírez drew on Kolb's notion of personality defect and on psychoanalytic theories of family origin to argue that addiction was caused by disruptions of childhood development. In a series of publications, lectures, and oral presentations in the 1960s, he advanced a theory of addiction as a personality disorder caused by a failure of "epigenesis."[33] The latter was a concept that the psychoanalyst Erik Erikson borrowed from embryology to describe the staged development of personality over the life course.[34] According to Erikson, personality development progressed through a sequence of predetermined steps, each of which was expressed at a certain time in the life course. The development of specific "human strengths"—fidelity, hope, and care—was contingent upon successful passage through the preceding stages. Applying the epigenetic principle to the problem of addiction, Ramírez argued that the addict's "scant capacity to feel anguish, guilt and sincere remorse" stemmed from a failure of epigenesis during childhood.[35] Specifically, he held that family breakdown had prevented the acquisition of appropriate norms and values of society.[36]

Addicts were not "psychotic," he argued, but part of a "subculture" that had "adopted a system of values and an outlook on life that make their behavior contrary to what most citizens consider normal."[37] They were more accurately classified, he argued, as "sociopathic," in the sense that their "distorted personalities"—products of abnormal childhoods and deviant peer groups—"have oriented them away from the attitudes and activities pursued by the normal productive citizen."[38] According to Ramírez this psychopathic personality development was reversible, however. Through what he called "personality reconstruction," the addict could be rendered "capable of functioning as a productive, nonparasitic member of society."[39]

A remedial project was born. Ramírez set out to rectify psychopathic personality development through a program of intensive resocialization. His vision of a therapeutic community involved a team of professionals and nonprofessional "ex-addicts" who acted as a bridge between clinicians and patients. CISLA's basic program was threefold. Induction described outreach efforts that "utilize[d] ex-addicts to establish contact with active addicts on the streets, to attempt to motivate them so that they will enroll themselves."[40] Next was intensive treatment, a "personality restructuring process" carried out through full-time residency.[41] Finally, during reentry the addict continued the "re-socialization training process" on an outpatient basis. During this phase addicts were expected to recruit other addicts into the program and thereby "pay back their debt to society."[42]

During its first three years, CISLA "resocialized" an estimated 1,083 residents and claimed the implausible relapse rate of just 5.6 percent.[43] CISLA's graduates, who referred to themselves as La Nueva Raza (the new breed), gave impassioned lectures about the method across the island, even initiating their own weekly radio program called *The Voice of the New Breed*.[44] Soon CISLA was making international news, if not always with the hoped-for seriousness of coverage ("Junkie Cure Junkie" was the headline at *The Guardian*, a British newspaper).[45] In 1966, New York City mayor John Lindsay came to visit CISLA to see the results for himself. Impressed, he recruited Ramírez to serve as New York's first commissioner of addiction services and to develop similar therapeutic communities there.

Within months of Ramírez's departure, CISLA was shut down, having found its funding suspended.[46] Bereft of their leader, displaced from their headquarters, and desperately lacking in public funds, CISLA's first generation of therapeutic community graduates found themselves in an institutional vacuum. With drug convictions on the rise, and with no government support for treatment on the horizon, CISLA's graduates assumed a self-consciously antigovernment, antiprofessional stance. Their formerly "professionally supervised" therapeutic community gave way to a new "addict-led" and proudly Puerto Rican formation.

. . . . .

The Home for the Reeducation of Addicts (Hogar CREA) was founded in 1968, by Juan José García Ríos ("Chejuán") with the assistance of three fellow CISLA graduates.[47] An avid reader in Oso Blanco prison and a "star patient" at CISLA, affectionately nicknamed "El Semántico" by fellow residents for both his intellect and argumentativeness, Chejuán had stood out among CISLA staff members as a natural leader and "outstanding member of the group." As one of his therapists recalled: "He was sharp, a fast learner. He had charisma and a following. I noticed that many addicts listened to what he said." Though his adolescence and early twenties had been marked by addiction and incarceration, Chejuán was atypical of CISLA's clientele.[48] He had been raised in a middle-class household, was the son of a successful businessman, and had been educated in business administration.[49]

Politically savvy and well-connected, Chejuán immediately set about generating support from industry, commerce, banks, and associations. His fundraising efforts quickly proved successful. Within a few short months, Chejuán and his associates had acquired not just financial donations but also vehicles, furniture, land, and their first building in Trujillo Alto. Through personal letters to senators, town mayors, and local politicians, Chejuán curated a busy schedule of expenses-paid trips to dozens of municipalities, where he would exhort local residents to help set up programs. His tactics combined political lobbying with street theater: Chejuán once brought a group of teenage drug users, some as young as twelve, to a private meeting with members of the Legislative Assembly, whom they persuaded to donate half a million dollars in funding.[50] Equally impassioned were CREA's graduates, who commonly gave testimony to the press about how the organization had turned their lives around.[51] Figure 3 is taken from a press conference at CREA headquarters in Trujillo Alto about a year after it was founded. The image shows the baby-faced Carlos Pinto, aged twenty-two in 1969, smartly turned out in a shirt and tie with hair neatly combed to one side, speaking of his desire to save others like him: "I've got involved in the program because it is effective. I'm sure I'll never go back, not just because of what this would mean for me, but because I have an interest in saving others from this vice and destruction."[52]

Hogar CREA excelled at community organization. To drum up civic support, it would send representatives into the towns to give talks to interested citizens. Crowds would flock to public gatherings, press conferences, and public speeches where Chejuán would not only exhort citizens to get actively involved in tackling the drug problem but would also offer concrete means of doing so: addict-led therapeutic communities, supported by local citizens and managed through steering committees.[53] For families, as one mother remembers, this meant much-needed relief.

FIGURE 3 · Four graduates of Hogar CREA interviewed in 1969 by
El Mundo, a popular Puerto Rican newspaper, in article entitled
"CREA, Programa Efectivo En Re-Educación de Adictos."

In the late 1960s and early 1970s, ignored by the state and shouldering
a burden few knew how to manage, affected families pressed their mayors
and communities to welcome Hogar CREA with open arms.[54] As one steering committee member recalls: "When CREA started, all these mothers
and fathers who'd been worried about their kids, who were stealing, having
run-ins with police, all of a sudden they had this option." Sentiments of
gratitude were common among parents too: "At least now I could get him
out of the house for a few weeks, a few weeks when I didn't have to worry.
Will he be arrested? Will he die?" Within a few years, CREA achieved broad
civic support: from parents and families, yes, but also from pastors, police,
teachers, social workers, sororities, and a host of civic groups, from the Lions
Club to the Wives Club of the College of Engineers.[55] During its early years,
CREA was widely commended by the press and politicians, who praised
its capacity—not just to treat addition but to produce "conscientious and
responsible citizens . . . capable of getting along with life in accordance with
the established norms of the community."[56]

True to its intellectual heritage in theories of psychopathology and personality development, CREA was envisioned as a home for resocializing
the presumed pathological personalities of its members. Its therapeutic
techniques sought to correct for the childhood "stunting" of character development. Through "reeducation," residents were taught to return to a
childhood state to retroactively cultivate moral character. Programmatically,
this entailed a shock treatment in going cold turkey, during which residents
were often tied to their bedposts (see fig. 4). After this ordeal, residents
would initiate a series of successive therapeutic stages, each corresponding

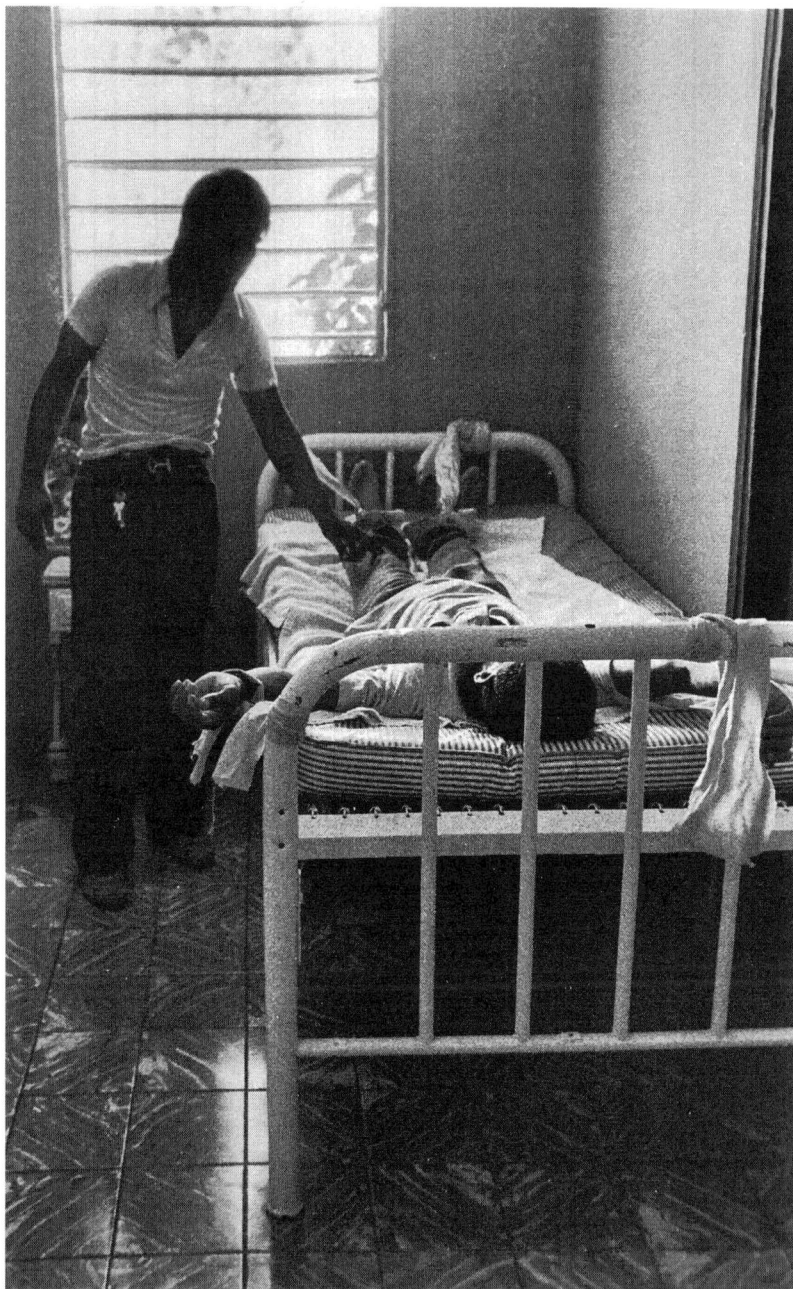

FIGURE 4 · Photograph taken by Jack Delano in 1980, entitled
In a Detoxification Room at the Program Known as CREA in Río Piedras.

to phases of the psychoanalytic life course (e.g., "newborn," "crawling," and "walking"). Male residents were made to shave their heads and wear shorts, symbolizing childhood, with trousers and watches reserved as privileges for residents who had proven their maturity and independence by reaching the final "adult" stage. For their part, "newborn" women were expected to wear dresses and take afternoon baths with fictive mother figures.

The pursuit of successful reeducation would usually take between one and two years, during which time residents would be required to participate in a host of character-building therapies: peer-led confrontation groups where residents challenged each other about their moral failings, group prayer, and a strictly regulated daily schedule of in-house domestic chores. In its characterological framework and emphasis on confrontation therapy, CREA was broadly similar to other therapeutic communities that were proliferating on the mainland during the sixties and seventies.[57] But something that distinguished CREA from its contemporaries, and became its signature enterprise, was its practice of dispatching residents to walk the streets to sell goods—mostly cakes, bread, bottles of water, and garbage bags—to members of the public. This "sales and representation therapy" generated a modest source of revenue for the organization, supplementing the charitable donations upon which CREA depended during its early years. Additional income came from residents' families, who were expected to donate food to the organization on a weekly basis, and in the 1970s CREA enrolled its residents in the Federal Food Stamp Program, pooling welfare checks for collective purchases. Rather than hiring professional cooks or cleaners, CREA maintained low operating costs by having residents perform all institutional upkeep, from domestic chores and gardening to decorating and construction.

Between 1968 and 1972, CREA expanded from three residents living in a single *hogar* to a decentralized federation of twenty-two separately managed centers housing over 1,200 residents.[58] In addition, several new therapeutic communities modeled on CREA were founded, including Hogar Nueva Vida in 1973 and Hogar Nuevo Pacto in 1982. In 1973, the Puerto Rican government hired a team of North American consultants to evaluate existing treatment capacity on the island. The US visitors watched CREA with awe: "The most remarkable thing is the rate at which it has expanded. . . . The ability of CREA to do this is an important indicator of the support which this program has been able to generate within several sectors of the Puerto Rican community. In fact, it is our opinion that CREA's single most significant achievement is the degree to which it has developed a viable and powerful community organization structure in support of its programs."

Having proclaimed CREA "the only program in which the ex-addict and his talents are used well," the consultants went on to prophesize, with surprising accuracy: "Should CREA be successful in its efforts to raise money for staff support, it will have the basis for the most realistic career ladder for ex-addicts in the commonwealth of Puerto Rico."[59]

In hindsight too, CREA's success in kindling civic support is remarkable. Rarely have efforts to engage citizens in caring for drug users proved so successful.[60] Yet, by the midseventies, Chejuán had achieved the kind of household recognition ordinarily reserved for political leaders: the press hailed him "a pride of Puerto Rico," and the government named a plaza after him in Río Piedras (Plaza José Juan "Che Juan" García).[61] In 1974, the Industrialists Association named Chejuán citizen of the year, as did the chamber of commerce in 1976. Even today, over two decades after his death, Chejuán remains an iconic local figure. When he died in 2002, from cancer, at the age of sixty-two, his life and work were widely covered in Puerto Rican media (see fig. 5).

It would be a mistake, however, to ascribe CREA's civic appeal to charismatic leadership alone. Whatever significance journalists may ascribe to

FIGURE 5 · A photograph of Juan José García Ríos (Chejuán) published in 2002 in *Primera Hora*.

Chejuán as "the driving force behind its destiny,"[62] CREA's remarkable marshaling of the citizenry was also the product of a much broader set of social and political transformations that were occurring on the island. During CREA's first ten years, the Puerto Rican township was weathering several storms simultaneously, with real unemployment reaching depression-era levels and a rising tide of criminal convictions further disenfranchising a generation of displaced agricultural workers. Beyond a therapeutic self-help or mutual-aid movement, what CREA was pioneering in the early seventies was a surrogate livelihood for unemployed men who, throughout the second half of the twentieth century, found themselves increasingly locked out of dwindling labor markets and locked up in overcrowded prisons.

To better understand the consolidation and formalization of CREA as it transformed from a self-help therapeutic movement to an alternative carceral livelihood, it is helpful to look at the political and economic transformations that were redefining male opportunity during the postwar period.

· · · · ·

As Hogar CREA grew, extending its reach across the island from a single center in 1968 to sixty-five centers separately managed centers by 1986,[63] Puerto Rico was plunging full speed into a crisis of capitalist development. Having recently and rapidly industrialized its economy, bankrolled by federal government and private US investment, Puerto Rico was starting by the late 1960s to feel the side effects of state-led rapid industrialization.

State-led modernization, or Operation Bootstrap, as it later became known (Manos a la Obra, in Spanish), had been first initiated under the US-appointed governor Rexford Tugwell in the 1940s and later extended under the popularly elected governor Luis Muñoz Marín. Pursuing a development strategy that the economist Benjamin Higgins later dubbed "getting rid of the farmers," Operation Bootstrap transformed Puerto Rico's largely agricultural economy into an industrial one.[64] Agrarian economies of sugar, tobacco, and coffee declined from 44.7 percent to 22.8 percent of the island's total employment between 1940 and 1960. Manufacturing rose from 10 percent of total employment to 19 percent during the same period, a substantial increase without question but not a large enough one to make up for agricultural losses. As Puerto Rico's sugarcane mills and tobacco industries withered, its largely rural population flocked to the towns in search of work in the rapidly expanding factories. By the mid-1960s, consumer products such as garments, textiles, and electrical goods had become Puerto Rico's biggest industries, but many former agricultural laborers were now without work.[65]

For the first time in Puerto Rican history, slums and informal squatter settlements erupted around San Juan.

Operation Bootstrap had rested on a dual strategy: direct state investment in industry, modeled on the US New Deal programs of the 1930s, combined with enticing US investment through tax deductions and other financial incentives. Key was the Industrial Incentives Act of 1947 (amended in 1948), which granted qualifying corporations a ten-year exemption from a host of distinct taxes and trade fees, including federal corporations' tax in addition to nearly all local taxes and license fees. Pharmaceutical and medical manufacturing soared. Owing to the vast tax exemptions awarded to US companies, however, local producers found themselves unable to compete with established US businesses. Local ownership of manufacturing remained minuscule, with around 90 percent of all manufacturing investment during Operation Bootstrap coming instead from mainland US firms.[66]

Growing external ownership and control of Puerto Rican manufacturing combined with the vast tax exemptions awarded US companies meant that the new manufacturing wealth flowed straight back to mainland investors rather than remaining on the island. Puerto Ricans did experience an impressive one-time leap in per capita gross national product (GNP), from $154 per year in 1940 to $716 per year in 1960. But in spite of the enormous growth that had occurred at the level of GNP, real unemployment remained stubbornly high, casting doubt among island economists about industrialization's successes. Between 1951 and 1960, the size of the labor force actually shrank from 603,000 in 1951 to 543,000 in 1960.[67] Between 1950 to 1965, the labor force participation rate (the proportion of the working-age population who are employed or actively seeking employment) for both men and women dropped from 55.5 percent to 45.4 percent.[68] Among men, it fell by 20 percent between 1950 and 1980.[69]

Though the official unemployment rate was low, hitting an all-time minimum of 10 percent in 1969 and hovering around 20 percent from the mid- to late 1970s, this metric was misleading.[70] For one thing, it was artificially lowered by mass emigration. At the encouragement of the Muñoz Marín administration (and as part of the commonwealth state's economic development strategy), thousands were leaving the island each year in search of work on the mainland, something that compressed the unemployment rate only by reducing the total number of island inhabitants.[71] In addition to ignoring tens of thousands of émigrés, the unemployment rate also failed to account for the significant numbers of people who were no longer actively job seeking (since unemployment rates capture only those actively seeking work). Once this group is taken into account, Richard Weisskoff estimates that by the mid-1980s, 67 percent of Puerto Rican adults were unemployed or out of the labor force.[72] The consensus among analysts of Puerto Rico's labor history, then, is that despite Puerto Rico's status as a "showcase" for US capitalism, postwar modernization roundly failed to deliver jobs to the majority of working-age Puerto Ricans.[73]

Young men fared particularly poorly. As women overtook them as the primary work force in several industries (notably apparel and food processing), young able-bodied men found themselves denied work and either ineligible or deprioritized for the various welfare entitlements available to women, the elderly, and the sick.[74] Consequently, young men's access to housing and other social benefits became increasingly mediated by their female partners or parents.[75] It was in this context of colonially induced economic stagnation, widespread unemployment, and declining male opportunity that Hogar CREA assumed a new role locally: supplying a surrogate home to a generation of unemployed men jolted to the margins by capitalist development. What had begun as a low-cost treatment venture had quickly morphed into a safety net whose chief affordance at that time was to supply shelter, sustenance, and community to a cohort of men with vanishing labor opportunities and dwindling household status.[76]

But therapeutic communities were about to undergo another transformation. As the carceral turn swept across the island beginning in the 1970s, the island's prison system found itself wholly unprepared for the hike in convictions that was about to ensue. As Puerto Rico's overwhelmed prison system sank into chaos, re-educados and the therapeutic communities they were part of assumed new roles in criminal rehabilitation.

. . . . .

The seventies marked a well-known turning point in US history. In the face of spiraling oil prices and inflation, postwar economic expansion ground to a halt. Having remained relatively stable in preceding decades, the mainland incarceration rate jumped fourfold from 1970 to 2000, from 161 to 683 per 100,000 of national population.[77] Dovetailing with these developments, if a little later, incarceration in Puerto Rico underwent a similar transformation. The size of Puerto Rico's prison population rose dramatically: from 4,221 in 1981 to 11,239 in 1991, sending the incarceration rate soaring from 130 per 100,000 in 1981 to 315 per 100,000 by 1991.[78]

Both federal and commonwealth policies contributed to this calamity. Key federal policies were the Comprehensive Drug Abuse Prevention and Control Act of 1970 and the Anti-Drug Abuse Act of 1986 (see this book's introduction). A key local policy was the Commonwealth Law of Controlled Substances of 1971, which quickly became the single most common conviction among inmates.[79] During this time, the budget for Puerto Rico's Department of Justice rose from $25 million in 1984 to $62 million in 1992.[80] The budget for the Department of Correction and Rehabilitation rose from $147 million in 1992 to $532 million in 1998.[81] Legal histories provide comprehensive descriptions of the various other war-on-drugs policies that drove Puerto Rico's prison boom in the latter decades of the twentieth century.[82] But alongside top-down policies facilitating prison expansion, Puerto Rico's prisoners, too, were making a mark on carceral state formation.

Lacking the requisite investments in prison infrastructure to keep pace with soaring conviction rates, Puerto Rico's prisons burst past official occupancy rates, leading to riots and mass escapes. Overcrowding reached a boiling point in 1979 when inmates filed a class-action lawsuit against the Puerto Rican Administration of Corrections, alleging unsafe and unsanitary conditions. Harnessing both the Puerto Rican Constitution of 1952 and the US Constitution, prisoners leveled various charges against the Puerto Rican government, including violation of the US constitutional protection against cruel and unusual punishment.[83] Following statements from forty-five witnesses who described astronomical rates of homicide that were said to be a thousand times higher in Puerto Rican prisons than in mainland prisons, and who reported sewage running through kitchens and dormitories, food stocks contaminated by rats and other vermin, and outbreaks of scabies, tuberculosis, and mange, Puerto Rican district court judge Pérez-Giménez ruled in favor of the prisoners.[84] Denouncing the Puerto Rican government for keeping inmates "caged up like animals," without clothes, toilet facilities, or medicines, and for forcing inmates "to eat with their hands," Pérez-Giménez ordered the government to improve prison standards across sanitation, health, and education and fined it $10 per day for each inmate held at an overcrowded prison.[85] When Puerto Rico's government failed twice, neither complying with the mandate nor making good on the initial payments, court fines were hiked to $60 per day and a tidal wave of prisoner-led class action lawsuits ensued. Between 1980 and 1990, the Puerto Rican government hemorrhaged over $68 million in court fines.[86]

Caught between contradictory legal mandates—to crack down on drugs on the one hand (a demand that would only intensify with the introduction of the Federal Anti-Drug Abuse Act of 1986, which instituted mandatory minimum sentences for most drug offenses) and to reduce prison overcrowding on the other—by the late 1980s Puerto Rico's Department of Correction and Rehabilitation was in a bind. So when Hogar CREA representatives proposed an innovative arrangement to prison authorities, offering to take drug offenders off their hands in exchange for a very modest stipend, corrections officials were relieved to have stumbled upon a possible solution. Facing a budget deficit, mounting court fines, chronic overcrowding, and a series of high-profile escapes, the department finally seemed to have found a viable way out in therapeutic communities.[87] Through a combination of rushed verbal agreements (all technically illegal), along with subsequently legalized referral schemes, prison authorities began diverting hundreds of prison inmates each year to Hogar CREA from the late-1970s onward.[88] Other therapeutic communities soon followed suit, with Teen Challenge, Hogar Nuevo Pacto, and Hogar Nueva Vida coming to similar arrangements with the Department of Justice and the Juvenile Institutions Administration.[89] In exchange for each diverted offender, these organizations would typically receive a per diem courtesy of the Department of Correction or the Department of Justice.[90]

By the mid-1980s, diverted drug offenders accounted for over half of Hogar CREA's intake, with similar proportions found at Teen Challenge and Hogar Nuevo Pacto.[91] To accommodate this new clientele, some institutional changes were necessary. Newly minted re-educados became responsible for administering various correctional responsibilities on behalf of the carceral state: taking urine samples from court-ordered residents, informing police of unauthorized leaving or rule breaking, enforcing discipline, and even writing case reports and recommendations for the courts. But this was a decidedly shoestring take on law and order. There were no professional security and no armed guards. As I explore in the next section, to sustain itself financially CREA increasingly turned inward to rely upon the unremunerated income-generating activities of its residents, bringing both a new economy and new way of being a citizen into being.

Though squarely integrated into criminal justice, and though bolstered financially by corrections contracts and referral routes, CREA clung to its "community" identity, touting the fact that it was run by ex-addicts and volunteer citizens—and, pointedly, *not* by government or paid professionals—as a point of institutional pride. Legally speaking, of course, this was correct. Hogar CREA was (and remains) legally incorporated as a "community-based organization."[92] Yet while conjuring an image of a discrete civic domain of practice, apart from both the state and labor market, this community designation obfuscated CREA's most significant innovation: its blending of criminal confinement, unpaid labor, therapy, and community service. Through this amalgamation, it was effectively repurposing a colonially induced crisis of capital and associated criminalization spree into a new carceral livelihood replete with its own signature genre of citizenship.

·　·　·　·　·

Something Hogar CREA caught onto much earlier than its critics was that for many of its members, a life based on wage labor was not about to materialize. Though officially championing residents' return to society, in practice, CREA seems to have committed relatively little time or resources to assisting members with accessing employment and housing or reconnecting with family ("reentry"). Instead, testimonies of former residents suggest it devoted far greater energy to the creation of various unremunerated and poorly remunerated work opportunities. Not only was CREA highly entrepreneurial—its microenterprises including a bakery, a car repair shop, a car wash, and a furniture-moving company—but it was also a master of the art of publicly performed volunteer work. Its signature move was to dispatch its residents into the towns, clad in brightly colored CREA T-shirts, where they could be seen performing an abundance of civic duties: planting trees, cleaning streets, mowing public lawns, and weeding town plazas.[93]

For a very low fee, town mayors, local government officials, and private landlords could hire CREA residents to undertake manual tasks such as these. The residents performing this *terapia laboral* would usually receive a token payment (a few dollars for the day), with the remaining sum channeled back to CREA to support organizational maintenance. In the seventies and eighties, I should note, this was by no means controversial. If anything, CREA's thrift and industriousness appears to have impressed local officials, who appreciated having a cheap pool of "respectful" and "well-behaved addicts" to move their furniture, perform home improvements, and landscape government property. As one long-standing CREA affiliate who helped set up several branches in the 1980s recalled: "They were well behaved, they were courteous, and for a very low fee they could be called upon to [help]."

To historians of Jim Crow, such antics might seem all too familiar. Labor therapy could, in principle, be analyzed as a poorly camouflaged chain gang: a colonial twist on an older US tradition of racialized coerced labor, which has been said to run from chattel slavery through to contemporary prison labor.[94] Certainly, this was the view of many of my Puerto Rican colleagues working in harm reduction, who frequently characterized labor therapy as "modern slavery." But to equate labor therapy with slavery risks overlooking critical differences of racial ideology and political economy. As a form of coerced labor, the differences between contemporary labor therapy and other modes of coerced labor, past and present, are worth unpacking.

The Jim Crow system of criminally regulated extraction that emerged in the southern states after the abolition of chattel slavery was designed, first and foremost, to maintain white supremacy.[95] This was partly (but only partly) about profit. Postbellum convict labor could certainly be highly profitable; indeed, it was thoroughly integrated into the southern industries of coal and steel.[96] Yet convict labor also functioned as a tool of racial terrorism. It was intended not simply to *instrumentalize* but to *intimidate* and *humiliate* African Americans.[97] Exemplifying this project of racial terrorism was the chain gang, perhaps the most visually monstrous of all convict labor. Its harrowing aesthetic served a white supremacist purpose: it stripped African Americans of their humanity by putting them out on show as hardened criminals deserving of public scorn.[98]

By contrast, the *terapia laboral* pioneered by Hogar CREA during the late twentieth century was not driven by racial terror. Nor was labor therapy designed by an established elite or former slave-owning class. Strikingly, power distinctions between those "in charge" (formerly criminalized therapeutic community directors) and those "in custody" (criminalized residents) were remarkably fluid: therapeutic community residents who stuck around long enough were able to progress to the top of the pyramid, and those at the top were constantly at risk of forfeiting their "privileged" position.[99] Posing little threat, if any, to working-class laborers (if its cordial reception among trade unions is anything to go by), labor therapy was a bottom-up and publicly facing redemption effort on the part of formerly incarcerated people to repair a criminalized, stigmatized, and tarnished citizenship. Pithily surmised in one headline in *El Mundo*, the goal was "*CREAndo hombres nuevos*."[100]

The precise nature of the citizenship-formation project at the heart of *terapia laboral* gets clearer when one considers CREA's press coverage in the local media, which, thanks to its leaders' careful orchestration, abounds in the archive. In 1999, under the "serenade of a Methodist choir," CREA directors proudly announced their newest initiative, "planting over a million new trees," to an invited coterie of journalists, one of whom praised CREA's men for their "positive contribution towards Puerto Rico."[101] Or, in the words of one re-educado quoted in a press interview with *Primera Hora*: "It [labor therapy] projects a new image of the ex-addict. . . . It shows that you are putting new good models and manners into practice. . . . In the way that your hair grows [after shaving it], you grow emotionally."[102] In 2000, CREA announced its latest "millennium free of drugs" initiative, earning it the favorable headline: "Good Harvest!"[103] Blending criminal confinement, unremunerated labor, and publicly visible acts of community service, labor therapy placed a civic and voluntary face onto convict labor, proving a powerful tool for the production of carceral citizenship.

In the late eighties and early nineties, CREA took its lead from Evangelical movements and initiated what became the hugely popular Cruzadas de Fe y Esperanza (Crusades of Faith and Hope). On campaign trails that snaked through the island's seventy-eight municipalities, Chejuán led annual demonstrations that drew thousands of people, including interested citizens, politicians, police chiefs, and trade union and religious leaders.[104] At a *cruzada* in San Juan in 1989, broadcast on WAPA-TV and reported in several local newspapers, a CREA caravan "accompanied by thousands of young people, adults, children" made its way from El Condado to the historic center of Old San Juan, "making it clear, once again, that the Puerto Rican *pueblo* can walk united as one single cause."[105]

Under sustained media coverage (see fig. 6), these carceral citizens proclaimed their virtue from the rooftops by continually rehearsing a carefully choreographed performance of Christian rescue and public service. "*Rescatar los adictos!*" announced the banners that hovered above the caravans at a crusade in 1995, leading journalists to gasp as a "swarm of white T-shirts"

FIGURE 6 · A photograph of Hogar CREA members from Trujillo Alto conducting a "crusade of faith and hope" in Río Piedras, published in 1999 by *El Vocero*.

marched on Capitolio in Old San Juan.[106] "We are very happy," exclaimed a jubilant CREA director to a journalist at a crusade in 1990, "because this year, the message has got through. Last year we rescued thirty-six addicts, and this year one hundred and eighty addicts decided to seek help."[107]

Not so much a "spectacle of punishment" as a citizenship pageant, CREA's chief prerogative in these acts of street theater was to redeem criminalized men in the public eye by exhibiting them as exemplars of Puerto Rican and Christian civic duty. But street theater was only one part of a carceral citizenship project that, to be sustainable, had to address the much more difficult problem of what to do after men had completed their own reeducation. In a striking anticipation of the "ethical citizenship" that swept through parts of southern Europe during the neoliberal turn, which, as Andrea Muehlebach has argued, recycled economically unproductive retired and elderly people into unpaid ethical volunteers, the maintenance of carceral citizenship came to depend on the constant replenishing of an internal market of unpaid "volunteer" positions.[108]

During the 1980s, willing volunteers were readily available. With employment opportunities dwindling and criminal convictions soaring, therapeutic community alumni were jumping in droves at the chance to stay on as volunteers after completing their criminal sentences. In exchange for their commitment to reeducating others, recruits were provided with a free place to live, something that was nigh impossible to secure from public housing administrations owing to laws disqualifying people with criminal records. With scant alternatives, the stark reality was that for many re-educados this was by far their best option. "If it wasn't for CREA, I'd be dead by now," a former CREA resident, Papo, told me flatly in an interview. "It was an easy decision. I'd just graduated [in 1982], and my mindset had changed in the extreme. The fact that I could really give myself to something, have a purpose, and it would benefit others too." Re-educados were not the only beneficiaries. "It was a great option for a lot of people," recalled a government official. "At the graduation ceremonies there'd be all these addicts there. The families could see them there in good clothes, looking smart . . . as reeducated ex-addicts. Now they had a job. Now they had a purpose."

In 1982, a government audit reported that 71 percent of CREA's total workforce (of 814) were "volunteer" graduates, a proportion broadly mirrored by Puerto Rico's ninety other residential programs.[109] This carceral twist on volunteer work proved highly successful. By 1986, CREA had 65 facilities in Puerto Rico, with satellite programs in the Dominican Republic, Colombia, Venezuela, Costa Rica, and Pennsylvania.[110] In addition, dozens of new therapeutic communities had sprung up in Puerto Rico, staffed for the most part by unpaid graduates.

This voluntary twist on convict labor not only complicates clear demarcations between free and coerced labor, but intriguingly it conceives its chief market competitor not in the blue-collar sectors, as histories of prison labor might lead us to predict, but in the decidedly white-collar arena of professional health and social services.[111] In the following section, I return to the reflex that opened this chapter: the allegiance of therapeutic community directors to the paradigm of reeducation and their seeming hostility toward alternative paradigms. Tracing therapeutic community leaders lobbying efforts in the archive, I reflect on some of the sad ironies of carceral citizenship, the most potent of which is its tendency to lead therapeutic community leaders to vehemently reject measures that now seem, to many, to hold better prospects for assuring the well-being of people addicted to drugs.

· · · · ·

It was February 2002. Puerto Rico's Office for Drug Control had just announced a radical overhaul of its failed war on drugs to be based on public health (not penal) principles. The new *salubrista* approach—long advocated by island proponents of criminal justice reform—would recognize drug addiction as a "chronic illness" deserving of medical treatment rather than a "moral weakness" requiring criminalization and punishment. One week later, the governor's office received a furious letter from the executive leaders of Hogar CREA. What drew the ire from these therapeutic community leaders was the assumption built into the Office for Drug Control's public health strategy that drug addiction would only respond to *clinical* treatment. This, leaders felt, was a gross dismissal of their forty-year effort to reeducate and resocialize the "pathological personalities of addicts." Worse, it perpetuated the perverse notion that the only hope for the island's drug users was to keep them "legally addicted under narcotics distributed by the government." In other words," the authors typed in bold, "the commonwealth of Puerto Rico is in obvious collusion with the Colombian Cartels."

Setting aside, for now, the unfulfilled nature of the Office for Drug Control's pledge (no, the war on drugs did not end), what matters about these encounters is the human action and moral experience they reveal to be part and parcel of "carceral devolution": the process whereby penal authority is decentralized from government or state-level agencies to private nongovernmental actors.[112] While carceral devolution tends to be understood as a fiscally motivated state practice whereby governments "hand down" authority and responsibility over incarceration and rehabilitation to nongovernmental actors (to, for example, charities and private prisons), the striking thing about Puerto Rico's devolved carceral state is the extent to which formerly incarcerated people have collectively organized to seize this authority "from below," culminating in the cocreation of a circumscribed and highly devolved sphere of penal power. As I waded through the legislative archive, I learned that this was not an isolated incident. On the contrary, therapeutic communities have often sought to amend or forestall legislation that would impinge on their carceral livelihood. In particular, they have frequently opposed government attempts to "professionalize" or "medicalize" Puerto Rico's drug services, especially (and most forcefully) when these efforts have gone hand in hand. Four examples will help illustrate this.

First, in the 1970s therapeutic community leaders lobbied against the establishment of a centralized government-run drug service administration. In the run-up to the law that created Puerto Rico's Department of Services against Addiction in 1973 (Law 60 of 1973), a publicly funded centralized provider of drug treatment services that operated between 1973 and 1993 (before Puerto Rico's public health care system became privatized), therapeutic community leaders lobbied *against* the government provision of drug treatment services. Through written testimonies submitted to the Legislative Assembly and through private letters to Governor Hernández Colón, the CREA leadership proposed instead a US-style subcontracting system in which the government would distribute funds to private providers, ideally those that were peer run and therefore had "special insight" into the "addict personality."[113] When these efforts proved unsuccessful, and the Department of Services against Addiction was established in 1973 and threatened to undermine CREA's intake, Hogar CREA's relationship with the government became highly acrimonious.[114] In June 1978, CREA obstructed the government's efforts to conduct a census by refusing to share its records.[115]

A second and relatively more successful attempt to stall government rollout of drug treatment services came in the 1970s, when therapeutic community leaders launched a vocal campaign against the new department's methadone maintenance program. Along with Evangelical ministers, therapeutic community leaders gave public talks against methadone in the towns, arguing that it kept people addicted indefinitely and failed to address addiction's root cause: pathological personality.[116] Though the Evangelical church and therapeutic community leaders ultimately failed to prevent the Department of Services against Addiction from rolling out methadone maintenance (which expanded throughout the seventies until its federal funding dried up under US president Reagan), this abstinence-only alliance did succeed in making the government's job more difficult. According to state officials responsible for setting up methadone clinics at the time, CREA and Evangelical leaders stirred up vehement community resistance, posing challenges when it came to site selection for clinics. In the end, methadone clinics were consigned to the peripheries of urban centers, where difficulties of access limited patient numbers and hindered the therapy's effectiveness.[117]

A third example of therapeutic communities' opposition to alternative rehabilitation paradigms came in the 1990s, just as Puerto Rico's neoliberal turn was gathering speed. Through a series of policies known as La Reforma, the public health care system that had operated in Puerto Rico since the 1950s was dismantled and a private managed care system installed.[118] The legislative archive reveals that in the run-up to La Reforma, therapeutic community leaders actually lobbied in favor of health care privatization. Through invited policy responses to the legislature, the CREA leadership called on the government to close the "monstrosity that is the health department" and to embrace a "community approach," which would redefine the role of government "from an inefficient provider of services" to a "stimulator and sponsor of community-based services and program."[119] This, they argued, would "reduce bureaucracy" and allow community organizations to provide "more efficient, cheaper, and better services."[120] Although this stance was strikingly compatible with prevailing neoliberal ideology, the aligning interests of therapeutic community leaders and liberal reformers were opportunistic, not philosophical.

The fourth and final example concerns the run-up to the passing of the Mental Health Act of 2000 (hereafter referred to as Law 408), a bill of rights that was supposed to establish minimum standards of care across all mental health facilities, a congress of community organizations including representatives from Hogar CREA, Teen Challenge, and the Assembly of God pressured the legislature to exempt their facilities from new health care regulations, this time successfully. As Helena Hansen tells the story, when legislators drafted one version of the law that would have required all therapeutic communities to employ clinically trained staff and adhere to minimum standards of care (determined by the government), Chejuán, along with several Evangelical drug treatment groups, denounced the proposed law, even threatening to mobilize voters against the governor in the upcoming election.[121] In the end, an additional article that exempted all community-based and faith-based drug treatment providers from the standards set out in the bill was added to the law, as was a special provision that recognized the "monumental labor of rehabilitated and re-educated ex-addicts."[122]

One of the most striking and cruel ironies of carceral citizenship then is the animosity it generates among its members toward other initiatives aimed at promoting the health and well-being of those addicted to drugs. When I interviewed re-educados, I would often ask them what they thought about alternative approaches for managing addiction. Often, they would bring up methadone or buprenorphine, opioid-substitution therapies, only to deride them as "keeping the addict dependent." Older re-educados in particular would often use methadone as a fable against which they could underscore their own moral development. "The problem we have," one seasoned re-educado told me, "is that we addicts like *la vida fácil* [the easy life], and now that we have so many other types of services around—needle exchange, methadone, buprenorphine—the addicts are choosing the easy way out. They don't want to work! Why bother to work if the government will give you drugs?"

Like many of the older re-educados I interviewed, Cartagena considered opioid-substitution therapy a cop-out. He derided it as immoral and lazy. Life as part of a therapeutic community, in contrast, was agreed to be a venerable thing. It was an index of good citizenship in itself and proof, as Cartagena put it, of "strong character." In retrospect, I began to interpret re-educados' criticisms of other approaches as highly informative moments that revealed what was at stake to them as carceral citizens. With their seemingly self-stigmatizing comments, they joined a long-standing debate about what kind of citizen is a worthy member of society. Harking back to a century-old practice of blaming addiction on the "vicious personalities" of the drug-using poor,[123] re-educados sought to define themselves—men who had overcome their character flaws, men who worked tirelessly and independently to reeducate their brethren, as opposed to those who remained characterologically stunted and dependent on the state and on methadone—as the men of stronger character.

Therapeutic communities' lobbying efforts and Cartagena's words both speak to what Elizabeth Povinelli might recognize as the "cunning" of carceral citizenship:[124] re-educados distinguish themselves from the stereotype of the morally stunted "parasitic citizen" by redeploying against each other the same strategies that have been used against themselves. They are continually attempting to counter the century-old stereotypes of psychopathology and criminality that have surrounded drug users, putting forward their "good character" as evidence. But in doing so, the measure of their achievement comes to depend upon the revitalization of the stereotype. As a consequence, the category of "pathological character" and its repertoire of prejudices and derogations is never contested. Instead, reeducation is continuously legitimated, and the same prejudices and stereotypes are re-enacted on a continual basis.

This troubling counterfactual—that if the state decriminalizes drug addiction, men like Cartagena have the most to lose—weighs heavily on the minds of therapeutic community leaders. Cartagena and his peers are acutely aware that their package of reeducation and labor therapy receives a less cordial public reception than it did in the past. Gone are the days of gushing tributes to CREA and its civic contributions. When therapeutic communities do make headlines, it tends these days to be not because of their community service or their crusades of rescue but because of their "unsubstantiated," "abusive," and "exploitative" treatment methods.[125]

"We aren't allowed to make the addict work anymore," Cartagena explained to me moodily in an interview. "We can only encourage him, but it has to be voluntary. So, it's a real struggle," he said. "In the old days, when you'd have two, four, five years to work with a man, you really knew you were making a difference. Now we have residents from drug court who are here for just three months. It's impossible to reeducate a person in three months," he said. "Reeducation takes years. It's not treatment; it's a lifetime's work." As he saw it, increased media scrutiny, increased regulations, increased government interference all signed the end of therapeutic communities. For Cartagena, and for many re-educados like him, this posed more than just a threat to job security. It was a personal torment and threat to their dignity and way of life.

· · · · ·

This history of the rise of carceral citizenship speaks to the unlikely ways that social structures (and attempts to repurpose them) become means through which citizens are made and make each other. Carceral citizenship is a contradictory social membership in several senses. It is an inclusion carved from exclusion, a belonging that never ceases to be an exile. As I have shown, carceral citizenship has been forged over the course of many decades from multiple intersecting exclusions that have eroded men's options for social membership: colonially induced crises of capitalist development, overcrowded prisons, the criminalization of drug use, and the enduring penal stigma that follows citizens long after a criminal sentence. That these exiles have succeed in this herculean task of carving a citizenship out of a sentencing and a livelihood out of waste is remarkable and, *in some ways*, I think, admirable.

But carceral citizenship's unlikely origins also explain its most troubling contradictions. While it succeeds in offering its members a desperately needed and dearly valued alternative to the prison and its crushing inhumanity, this mode of existence depends upon the continued exclusion of many men from the labor market. Mass criminalization and chronic unemployment are, in a very material sense, the structures from which carceral citizenship is wrought and the predicates for its reproduction. Thus, carceral citizenship depends upon the preservation of the carceral turn's most pernicious developments. Once we comprehend the factory defect built into this arrangement, re-educados seemingly self-stigmatizing support for punitive approaches and their ostensibly reactionary tendencies become far less mysterious. We can begin to appreciate why therapeutic communities' advocacy efforts were so uniformly dedicated to killing off government attempts to improve the life chances of the drug-involved poor rather than to advancing social justice causes or to combating the logics of incarceration itself. The reflex that I encountered again and again in my research with therapeutic communities—a reflex geared toward forestalling and rejecting possible developments in the arena of drug rehabilitation services—is best understood not as a straightforward exploitative attempt on the part of therapeutic community directors to profit from the unremunerated labor of their criminalized peers; nor is it as simple as internalized stigma. More fundamentally, this reflex stems from re-educados' understandable concern with protecting their livelihood and hard-earned citizenship. Yet in defending their way of life, re-educados end up opposing the very measures that might improve the life circumstances of the drug-using, criminalized poor.

It is vital, however, to see that this reflex is not automatically or universally internalized by all people who undergo reeducation. In the next chapter, I look more closely at the variable perspectives of therapeutic community novices as they are in the throes of adjusting to (and sometimes rejecting) life in a therapeutic community. Looking more closely at some of the different ways that residents respond to their peers' invitations to carceral citizenship, I offer a moving portrait of a carceral livelihood in formation.

· 3 ·

The Carceral Monastery

Thirty men stood in a circle on a wooden terrace. It was 6:30 a.m. Mountain air pressed moisture onto the windows of the men's dormitories. Each clasping his neighbor's hand in prayer, their voices rang out and filled the valley.

> I give you my hand,
> set my heart in rhythm with yours
> and I pledge us both before God—
> bringing myself and you
> to honor life.[1]

When the prayer was over, each man took his seat. For a few moments there was silence. Rocky, a formerly homeless heroin user and US army veteran, was leading this morning's therapy. Because there had been eight new arrivals this week, he began with a recap of the rules. Confidently, as he had done this many times, he rattled through them. Men were to get up at 6:00 a.m. and have thirty minutes to shower and make their beds. "Why get up at six?" he asked. Then, answering his own question, he said: "To teach independence. The early mornings prepare you for work." Pausing, he eyed the men in the circle. "At six thirty a.m., we pray. After we pray, we eat breakfast." Residents were to wear proper clothes in the canteen, he instructed. "That means no flip-flops, no tank tops, and no talking. Is that clear?" Thirty voices shot back in unison: "*Sí, hermano.*" Straightening his posture, Rocky continued: "At eight a.m., we do labor therapy. That means you clean the toilet, you do the laundry, you prepare lunch, or, for those with experience," he said, nodding toward the jumbled pile of grates and scaffolding that towered beside the terrace, "you can help with construction; there'll be plenty of building work during the next few weeks. Why do we do labor therapy?" he asked, scanning the circle. "By learning how to work, we are learning independence and breaking our dependencies, all of our dependencies."

Rocky continued in this declamatory manner for the next half hour, stopping to take the occasional question. When the short stream of queries dried up, he turned to introduce the other staff members: Rafi, Tito, and Jorge. "All of our counselors are from the streets, just like you. Trust me, we know what you've been through. We know what it is like to lose everything." As the session drew to a close, he turned to face the new recruits, who stood side by side, looking dazed. "Here you are going to work. You will work in construction. You will work in the canteen. You are going to work with your problems and work with yourself. Some of you may need to see a psychologist," he said. "But what most of you need is time. Time is the best psychologist."

I draw this scene from the eight months I spent observing daily life at La Casita, a privately owned nonprofit organization that is licensed by the Puerto Rican government to provide residential treatment for drug addiction. Group therapy took place every morning and was one of several daily practices, along with domestic chores and manual labor, through which La Casita sought to create "independent" and "hardworking" men who would be capable, so the handbook said, of "returning to society." Over the course of a year, which could turn into several, days were filled with a strict and busy schedule of group therapies, prayer, chores, and tasks. Through "keeping busy," treatment leaders said, residents would acquire the necessary work ethic to succeed "on the outside." In time, the center's handbook said, men would gain the requisite skills and dispositions to become "useful members of society."

At first glance, La Casita's regimen of work and its injunction to "keep busy" might seem to confirm what medical anthropologists and scholars of advanced capitalism have been saying for quite some time now: that drug treatment, reentry, psychiatry, and modern medicine are all part of the same neoliberal project of producing tax-paying, independent, economically productive citizens.[2] My time at La Casita has led me to a different conclusion.

The intriguing thing about "keeping busy" is precisely that it is *not* preparing men to live independently or to rejoin the lower tiers of the labor market. For most of these men, a life based on wage labor performed outside of this circumscribed carceral circuit is not about to materialize. Instead,

I interpret La Casita's instruction to keep busy as forming the basis of an alternative carceral livelihood whose "time-discipline"—the rules, social expectations, and meaning given to the organization of time—is anathema to Fordist time.[3] This is an economy where time is overabundant and almost never used productively, and where a spiritually exhausting and frequently tedious effort to "work on yourself" is all that is left to fill the time.

Attuning to the expectations and disillusionments of therapeutic community novices as they are in the throes of adjusting to this alternative carceral livelihood will show that abiding by its constant call to keep busy is both difficult and fraught. Not only are the artificiality and repetitiveness of the tasks available sometimes just too achingly apparent, but also the social engineering of work itself proves unsound. La Casita's residents confront a daily contradiction between an institutional imperative to be "useful" and "productive" and a therapeutic endeavor that fails twice: neither ensuring a steady supply of useful things to do on-site nor preparing men for work outside. Instead, futile assignments are often presented as therapies of last resort, and "work on your yourself" emerges as a secular-spiritual exercise that becomes central to residents' sense of progress. Even in this outpost of men's surrogate employment, boredom, an overabundance of time, and a feeling of futility gnaw away as burning existential pains.

The problems residents encounter on a daily basis at La Casita—an excess of time, a lack of work that feels meaningful, and a frenetic compulsion to "be productive" in a setting where there are fewer and fewer opportunities for productive work—are hardly unique to Puerto Rico or to therapeutic communities. As I argue, this problem of passing time meaningfully in an advanced capitalist economy that valorizes wage labor and simultaneously assures that there is less and less of it to do is a globalizing challenge: it afflicts both marginalized communities in capitalist societies and unemployed educated classes too.[4] Before I begin this inquiry, let me tell you about La Casita.

· · · · ·

La Casita is one outpost within an extensive network of private nonprofit agencies licensed by the Puerto Rican government to provide "residential treatment for drug addiction." Like many of Puerto Rico's residential drug treatment programs, La Casita's bureaucratic trademark is something of a misnomer. I should state from the outset that its clientele was not uniformly (or even largely) defined by addiction. Many of the men I got to know at La Casita had enrolled for other reasons: most commonly, court orders related to drug dealing but also self-referrals prompted by housing insecurity.

Bureaucratically, philosophically, religiously, and architecturally, La Casita exuberated an ad hoc quality that I came to recognize as a defining feature of Puerto Rico's therapeutic community landscape. From the aging bars that lay rusting in the metal arms of three vinyl benches now serving as a gym to the chain-link fence surrounding the creaky office chair serving as a hair salon, La Casita was manifestly makeshift. Much of its supplies— bunk beds, tin cups, hundreds of cans of condensed milk—were donated. Its therapeutic design was a hodgepodge of characterological reeducation, twelve-step techniques, mutual aid, carceral tropes, and highly syncretic Christian teachings. La Casita's objectives now numbered in the dozens and filled a full five pages of the newly written handbook, actually just an office printout fastened together with staples. According to the first few pages of this eclectic manifesto, La Casita's therapeutic objectives were as follows:

1. To help the participant develop a disposition to work.
2. To develop in the participant a sense of belonging.
3. To develop in the participant an understanding of mutual aid.
4. To help the participant to develop the necessary skills to function and live with others in the shelter.
5. To help the participant to identify negative behaviors that need to be modified.
6. To learn how to follow the norms and rules of society.
7. To develop the skills to face society.
8. To develop a sense of identity and to be socialized.
9. To reinsert the participant in the community with the aim of continuing to elevate their behavior and assimilation.
10. To develop an awareness of strengths and weaknesses, in order to confront reality, and to be able to control one's emotions.
11. To develop in the individual responsibility and commitment to positive change, to face up to past errors.
12. To develop, in both the individual and the group, the ability to face situations and conflicts in the correct way.
13. To inculcate positive energy in the participant.
14. To help the participant to identify personal errors or weaknesses.
15. To support participants to commit each day to being a better person, so that they can transcend the obstacles that life presents.
16. To strengthen and support participants' personal faith or beliefs.

The predominant anthropological theorization of therapeutic communities like La Casita—along with other modes of reeducation, rehabilitation, reinsertion, reentry, and drug treatment more broadly—is that these institutions and their widely variable therapies are tools of market discipline. From agricultural work configured as "moral therapy" in early twentieth-century US hospitals,[5] to occupational training mandated by contemporary US drug courts,[6] to labor therapy practiced in Orthodox Christian HIV and drug rehabilitation in Russia,[7] these variable kinds of therapeutic labor have generally been viewed through the lens of capitalist subject formation. The implicit premise is that such therapeutics render their subjects better disposed to submit to "routinized labor exploitation," as Kerwin Kaye puts it, or better able to live "a normal life" under neoliberalism, as Jarrett Zigon surmises.[8]

But capitalist subject formation is less helpful for understanding the work that happens at La Casita, an institution that is strikingly uninterested in promoting market-based employment. Despite its overt commitment to supporting residents' "return to society," La Casita was exceedingly ill-equipped to assist residents with finding paid work. Residents with outstanding court orders were not permitted to leave the premises without special permission (granted for medical appointments, court hearings, and the like). Although voluntary enrollees were permitted *in theory* to work off-site, they were usually unable to do so, not just for a lack of work opportunities but also for a lack of transportation. Very few residents had cars, and La Casita was a seven-mile drive from the nearest town, itself just a small and sleepy commuter village, the descent to which involved traversing two highways, neither of which had sidewalks. The only "occupational therapy" that I witnessed consisted of a single occasion when a visiting student held a workshop on writing résumés. Whatever its stated aspirations then, in practice, La Casita suspended its residents in an enduring state of unproductive economic dependence, fashioning various alternative ways to fill the time for the duration.

If La Casita fails in producing docile wage laborers, what are we to make of its work ethic? Some might read the stubborn injunction to work a residue of the "ghostly presence" of capitalism's affective past.[9] Yet as I showed in the previous chapter, whatever Puerto Rico's ascribed status as a Caribbean "showcase" for US-style industrial capitalism, the consensus among analysts of Puerto Rico's labor history is that a truly Fordist economy never existed in Puerto Rico.[10] For these reasons, the long-valorized ideal of the "male breadwinner" has been decried a "modernization myth."[11]

Rather than treating this injunction to work as a misfitted tool of market discipline for a Fordist economy that never existed in Puerto Rico, a more apposite reading can be found in Helena Hansen's ethnography of Evangelical addiction ministries in Puerto Rico.[12] As Hansen tells the story, addiction ministries are sites where displaced Puerto Ricans create an alternative social order. As is true of gangs, the drug trade, and various other nodes of the informal economy in Latin America and urban centers of the United States,[13] addiction ministries offer surrogate grounds of belonging and operate, in effect, as citizenships "of last resort" for those excluded from wage labor.[14] This explanation provides a powerful and compelling structural diagnosis: carceral livelihoods and their associated genre of citizenship *do* provide an alternative economy and mode of belonging for men excluded from wage labor. But to refine this structural interpretation and to reach a deeper understanding of why residents and staff at La Casita should come to place such strong moral emphasis on "working hard" and "being productive," this chapter repositions the social significance of La Casita's work as an open-ended ethnographic question, allowing me to pursue a series of questions about the nature and meaning of work within our contemporary wage-scarce world.

To understand why a compulsion to labor might persist in a place where opportunities for productive labor are so desperately lacking, and to think about the lessons La Casita might offer for wage-scarce capitalist societies more broadly, this chapter uses early Christian monasticism as a lens to phenomenologically analyze La Casita's time-discipline. By attuning to the points of resonance and departure between La Casita's own work ethic and that of the early Christian monasticism, insights from these older homosocialities enable me to crack open overdetermined accounts of capitalist subject formation and identify a series of paradoxes and affective burdens associated with the passing of time in wage-scarce economies. I will argue that a secular-spiritual throwback to precapitalist monasticism is making a surprising comeback in our contemporary wage-scarce world. At La Casita, men strive to "keep busy" not because capitalist production or reproduction demands it but because embracing a secular-spiritual ascetic practice of continuous work provides an alternative sense of meaning and progress that helps to alleviate, to some extent, the suffering and tedium of being excluded from the market economy. Overall, this chapter illustrates the anthropological value of precapitalist livelihoods for comprehending (and critiquing) new belongings and memberships beyond wage labor.

· · · · ·

Like many of Puerto Rico's "community-based" therapeutic communities, La Casita defined itself as "secular" while exuding a vernacular and highly syncretic Christianity I came to recognize as secular-spiritual.[15] Nearly everyone (residents and staff) identified as Christian, though strikingly few differentiated among denominations. This lack of denominational differentiation reflects Puerto Rico's long history of plural Christianities: with Spanish Catholicism repeatedly cross-pollinated with Afro-diasporic traditions and waves of US Protestant missionaries spanning dozens of denominations.[16] Unlike Puerto Rico's Evangelical programs, which generally require residents to fast, study the Bible, and participate in religious worship in designated *cultos* as part of their therapy, La Casita's vernacular Christianity was borderline lackadaisical by comparison.[17] Its communal spaces were dotted with posters advising: "Anyone interested in spiritual growth should request an appointment with a pastor." Yet La Casita did not have its own pastor. Nor, it turns out, did it have its own church. When I inquired about these opportunities for spiritual growth, I learned that religiously hungry residents were welcome to take the option of attending a religious service off-site each Sunday: either Pentecostal or Catholic, something about a quarter of residents usually chose to do.

Yet even without a pastor or a church, a secular-spiritual worship prevailed. Prayer, though officially "non-obligatory," was an organized daily practice in which most residents participated. It took place several times each day to mark the morning's beginning, the onset of every meal, and the day's end and was usually held in group spaces (canteens and dormitories). Most of La Casita's prayers were concoctions: Christian-inflected snippets from twelve-step programs blended with lyrics picked up from other therapeutic communities. While a small minority of residents chose to remain silent during prayer, most would join the circle to stand hand in hand, with prayers spoken out loud and in unison.

La Casita was founded in 2007 by Jorge Santiago, a former heroin addict and therapeutic community graduate. Jorge had spent ten years living and working as a peer therapist at Hogar CREA, but he split off to establish his own program after inheriting a burned-down property. Initially envisaged as a therapeutic community for the "resocialization of drug addicts," owing to funding necessities, it had recently extended its remit to coserve as an *albergue* (shelter) for men on probation. This bureaucratic makeover procured fresh access to probation contracts, which now provided a valuable stream of support, though none of these arrangements was long-term. For Jorge, the task of maintaining La Casita's ever-changing patchwork of short-term government grants and charitable donations was a constant source of frustration.

By the time I first visited La Casita in late 2016, the formerly incinerated ruin had been converted into a brightly painted two-story home.

Surrounding the main building were several outdoor communal areas: a tiled and spacious terrace where group therapy sessions were held, a stone table and seating area littered with cigarette butts, and an improvised outdoor gym that lay rusting in the corner of a gravel parking lot. Though modest and makeshift, La Casita's design and construction—undertaken for the most part by residents themselves—had been executed with a great deal of care. Flanked on both sides by neatly tended infant palm trees, each encircled by painted rocks, this well-tended terracotta house stood out among the corrugated iron roofs that speckled the mountain. The view of the valley gave the place a healthful, bucolic feeling, undermined periodically by the smell of burning plastic that filled the air whenever the week's trash was put out to burn, leaving patches of scorched earth dotted up the mountain.

· · · · ·

Ángel was one of the people I came to know well. His first day at La Casita had coincided with mine, and as apprehensive newcomers, we had sought each other out. Highly committed to what he saw as his "last chance" to prove himself, Ángel was a former drug trafficker who had spent the last ten years in and out of prison. His heroin addiction had begun about five years earlier, and he'd been cajoled into treatment by his terminally ill mother, who had told him that unless he sorted himself out, he would not inherit a thing, including the house they both lived in. On his first day, he was assigned laundry duty, a role he held onto for several months until being reassigned, to his annoyance, to toilet duty. The laundry room (in fact, a balcony) was usually much quieter than the other communal areas and became a place where we could talk. One afternoon in February, about a month into Ángel's time at La Casita, we sat chatting by the washing machine as he hung up pair after pair of boxer shorts, with a dozen or so laundry baskets lined up waiting their turn.

That day, Ángel seemed to radiate energy. Having just finished hanging a round of laundry, he now stood up on a stool as if it were a ladder. Grasping a pole with a sock wrapped around the end, he stretched upward and began scrubbing the exterior walls of the dormitory as if they were windows. Though the walls were not obviously dirty (in fact, another resident had already cleaned them earlier that same day), Ángel committed himself to the task, his concentration interrupted only by my repetitive questioning. "Why are you doing that?" I asked for the third time. "It's important to keep busy," he eventually answered. "It's important to use my time productively." After several more energetic strokes with the handmade sock-mop, each carefully executed to extend all the way from the top of the wall to the bottom, he stopped. "I didn't used to do any of these things," he said, now turning to me, "getting up early, doing my chores, working up a sweat on my own brow." After several more minutes of intense scouring, he finally got down from the stool and gazed upward to admire his handiwork. The rhythmical tap of a zipper hitting the washing machine filled the quiet that had settled between us.

During the eight months that Ángel came to spend at La Casita, he took the idea of keeping busy seriously. In the eyes of senior leadership, and as explicitly set out in La Casita's handbook, one of the shelter's primary goals was "to help the participant develop a disposition to work." To this end, idleness was frowned upon, and hard work was woven into the choreography of the day. The grounds were kept in a state of perennial improvement: another lick of paint, another coat of varnish, the resuscitation of some donated, now defunct, piece of gym equipment. Time was strictly regulated according to a repetitive series of discrete units of activity. Each unit was therapeutically repurposed so that chore time was "labor therapy," prayer time was "spiritual therapy," and, for one hour a day only, free time was "recreation therapy." Each of these units formed part of a larger temporal ordering of shelter life in which keeping busy *was* therapy.

That tasks of necessity—cooking, cleaning, and other in-house chores— were rarely plentiful enough to occupy the hands of all residents on any given day did not afford license to relax. Instead, when contingencies of group living failed to generate enough tasks to keep all members busy, Sisyphean assignments were concocted: washing a car that had already been cleaned, scouring already pristine floor tiles with a toothbrush, or mopping the kitchen ceiling. Laborious and futile tasks were also prescribed as punishments for lateness or rule breaking: staying up through the night to scrub walls and floors or being sent out, in the midday heat, to cut the grass with scissors.

Residents lived, worked, and prayed to bells. From the 6:00 a.m. handbells that signaled the day's onset to the 10:00 p.m. bells that sent men walking to their dormitories, bells set the time for eating, sleeping, praying, and working. By calling residents to attention and by signaling the onset of a new activity, the bells functioned as summons to labor. In fact, goads to labor were impossible to escape at La Casita. Blending Christian invocations of exertion as spiritual toil with neoliberal notions of personal responsibility, they were posted on the walls: "Work dignifies my person," "Food is not free," and "Responsibility is liberation in action." They sounded in the handbells. They shone out from the paintbrushes and mops that lay drying in the sun. They even seemed to be drawn out, tightly, across the immaculately made bunk beds.

This might feel familiar to students of early capitalism. Writing about England during the eighteenth and nineteenth centuries, E. P. Thompson argued that the advent of industrialism entailed a "re-structuring of man's social nature and working habits," where it ceased to be morally acceptable for workers to merely "pass the time."[18] Through a variety of technologies (e.g., clocks, bells, and fines), a sharp demarcation was enforced between "leisure time" and "work time," with the latter being reconfigured as a valued currency, every last bit of which had to be "consumed, marketed and put to *use*."[19]

In an analogous manner, when residents spoke of their adaptation to La Casita, they described a similar moralization of regular work patterns and vilification of time that is not used. Resocialization at La Casita involved cultivating habits such as getting up early, being punctual, conducting one's assigned tasks and duties properly, and avoiding wasting time. "Before, I didn't do anything with my time," one resident explained to me. "I would sleep until noon, then hang out with *mis panas* [my friends]. But now I get up early. I keep busy. I've learned to use my time productively."

Yet, unlike Thompson's mill owners, for whom the central aim of time-discipline was to maximize industrial output, La Casita derived little in the way of income or value from its residents' labor. Having men do their own chores reduced operating costs, to be sure, but socially necessary tasks were actually in scarce supply, and a lot of the effort that was expended at La Casita appeared—at least to the outsider—to be pointless. Nor was therapeutic labor obviously configured as a stepping stone to formal employment. That considerable time was expended on futile tasks highlights an important characteristic of La Casita's work ethic: the continuity of work is more important than the work's yield. Thus, the careful accounting for time spent, the imperative to keep busy, and the thing that looks like and is often spoken about as "using time productively" has no basis in the production of commodities or marketable services. More encompassing in its reach than the clocks driving capitalist production, La Casita's was the regimen of what Erving Goffman famously called a "total institution," one that was more akin to a convent or monastery than to a factory floor.[20]

The importance placed on continuous work bears a striking resemblance to the Egyptian fathers of the fourth century, as well as that of the Benedictine monasteries of the Middle Ages, who considered idleness "an enemy of the soul," and manual labor was considered itself an act of prayer and "Holy Art."[21] In the monastic literature, "meditation" was the technical term for this hybridization of prayer and manual labor.[22] The Roman monk John Cassian, describing the life of the Egyptian fathers, observed that they were "constantly doing manual labor" in such a way that meditation was "celebrated continuously and spontaneously throughout the course of the whole day."[23] Indeed, the continuity of prayer as extended through manual labor and housekeeping was said to define the monastic condition. "The whole purpose of the monk," wrote Cassian, "and indeed the perfection of his heart amount to this—total and uninterrupted dedication to prayer."[24]

All very noble, but hardly how men like Ángel understood their experiences. When asked about the point of work therapy, they tended to toe the party line: the point was to "learn how to work," "to use time productively," or, as Israel put it, "to get off the street, stop selling drugs, and do something useful with my life." Such worldly narratives seem a far cry from the "otherworldly" aspirations of Puerto Rico's evangelical converts[25] or from the "sublime discipline" of the cenobite.[26]

So what, then, are we to make of this local moral ethic of unending work, of a compulsion to labor that has lost its grounding in the satisfaction of human need or in the execution of divine office? Max Weber might have diagnosed a case of "ascetic compulsion": the affliction that struck modern capitalism's stewards who, on abandoning religion after the Industrial Revolution, found themselves locked in an "iron cage" of disenchanted, hyperrationalized, and bureaucratized labor.[27] But what interested me most was not this correspondence between La Casita and the Protestant work ethic. Rather, what intrigued me was the extent to which residents' accounts of their everyday experiences suggested that what they felt most acutely was not a compulsion to work but its frustration. Instead of feeling busy, residents often complained of having "nothing to do." Instead of feeling that they were advancing toward independence, many worried that they were "stuck," "wasting time," and "falling behind." Less "iron cage," more leaky lifeboat, La Casita's work regime was constantly on the verge of sinking.

Despite the continual injunctions to work hard, it was impossible for residents of La Casita to keep busy. As a disciplinary device for regulating time, the daily schedule was only marginally effective. Assigned tasks and chores—laying cement for a new path, erecting scaffolding to repair a roof, or laying pipework for a new laundry room—were frequently interrupted midway through when some vital material would be found lacking. Continuous work was regularly disrupted by electricity blackouts (of which there were many), water shortages, material scarcities, or, most commonly, by a lack of basic supervision. The latter had to do with La Casita's patchwork of funding sources, which brought with it hefty administrative obligations. Just ensuring that residents made it to their court appointments—which on any day might be held at several different municipal courts—was frequently enough to overtax La Casita's modest workforce. This meant that group therapy sessions, labor therapy, and other repurposed-as-therapy activities were often canceled because no one was around to supervise them.

Residents' everyday talk was often saturated with a bored frustration about *being unable to do anything*. With lengthy sentences to complete, and with so much time to fill, being "stuck" (*estancado*) was a major source of anguish. Take Ángel: By mid-December he was just two months down and had an anticipated sixteen more to go. It was a dreary day. The sky was cloudy, and the rain threw spots on the gravel parking lot. I found him behind La Casita's van, where he was lifting weights. He was visibly irritated. Upon finishing each round of arm curls, he tossed the dumbbells to the ground, allowing them to clang as they knocked into the other equipment. He was sick of it, he said. "It's not easy being stuck up here when you are used to being free." Though he was doing all his assigned chores—"putting in the effort," as he saw it—it was hard to imagine sixteen more months of this. "I'm thirty-eight," he said, his voice beginning to crack. "It can't take me till I'm forty to get over this." Wiping off the raindrops that had settled on his forehead, he resumed another round of arm exercises.

When the 2:00 p.m. bell rang, we trudged up the driveway expecting to attend group therapy, but it had been canceled. Though the chairs had already been set out in a circle, there was no one around to facilitate. Chores completed, we wondered what to do. Taking advantage of a temporary lack of supervision, we sat on the sofa on the terrace and watched *Animal Planet*. I brushed away the flies that kept landing on me. Afterward, we ate pasta and drank iced tea in silence in the windowless kitchen.

Bored frustration. An avowed effort to keep bodies and minds in motion, one that was constantly stymied by a lack of necessary tasks. When work was interrupted, either because tasks were scarce or because planned activities had failed to materialize, questions arose. The acid prickling of doubt could settle in. Rather than feeling improving, soothing, *useful*, the passage of time at La Casita could start to feel unsound, questionable, and even dangerous. "I know I can be a useful person," Ángel said imploringly to me one day. "But it's the boredom. Boredom is bad for us addicts."

Boredom has figured as an illuminating analytic in recent work on unemployment and the experience of time under advanced capitalism.[28] Vivid depictions of daily life among unemployed people have analyzed boredom as a form of social suffering that afflicts a growing surplus stratus that globalization has "cast aside."[29] In places as various as Puerto Rico, Indigenous American reservations on the US mainland, Romania, Ethiopia, and India, anthropologists have described how unemployment inflicts boredom, excess time, and even drug addiction.[30]

Daniel Mains analyzes boredom as an "overaccumulation of time" that instills among Ethiopian youth a heightened and painful awareness of their inability to actualize gendered expectations of progress.[31] Unable to meet culturally valued metrics of manhood, unemployed men have been said to suffer the "temporal hardship"[32] of being stuck in a "permanent male adolescence."[33] Unoccupied, bored, and sullied by the stigma of "doing nothing," this state has been said to afflict millions around the world.[34]

In one sense, Ángel was suffering from this "too much time, not enough progress," kind of boredom. La Casita's haphazard program left many men with a sense that they were "stuck doing nothing" and ultimately failing "to be useful." But as Ángel's words attest, boredom at La Casita was also haunted by the lore of relapse: a temporality of addiction that, in this case, had a discernably Christian meter. It was tinged with the expectation of trouble and moral undoing. In this Christian register, Ángel's experience of boredom was an exposure to temptation, as expressed by the fourth-century theologian Jerome: "Engage in some occupation, so that the Devil may always find you busy."[35] The sense of teetering on the edge of trouble that could creep in during idle moments points to the need for a conception of boredom that can account for these Christian resonances.

Let us therefore return to look more closely at residents' experiences of boredom. As a form of affective hardship, boredom was not actually confined to periods of inactivity. Complaints of boredom were also commonplace during organized activities. Even, that is, when residents succeeded in making themselves "busy," things could still be boring.

· · · · ·

I recall one hot afternoon in April. That afternoon's group therapy was led by an advanced resident, since the entirety of La Casita's staff had been called to a district meeting. That day, the group was restless, and the heat, uncomfortable. Some of the younger members broke into muffled protest as the session began, tutting their way through the prayer halfheartedly. Today's therapy, announced the facilitator, would involve drawing on a piece of paper something that "represents your personality" and then mixing the drawings up in a hat so that they could be redistributed and anonymously discussed in turn. There was a collective moan as the wad of scrap paper made its way around the circle. "There is way too much therapy here," muttered Ángel. "It's just therapy, therapy every day."

Later that evening, I found Ángel in the kitchen, where he was scrubbing the floor. He seemed down, and I asked him if he wanted to watch the

TV show that was blaring out on the terrace for recreation therapy. "I just don't understand how people can live here for years and years," he said. "It's the same thing every day. . . . It's just like, let's do chores and more chores, therapy and more therapy, prayer and more prayer, then chores again until nighttime. How do they just live here for years and years? I just wanna get back to normal life."

Ángel was not alone. Residents' distress as they contemplated the prospect of months or years of the same repetitive daily routine was striking in its resemblance to acedia, a form of spiritual suffering often considered a distinctively monastic affliction. The predecessor to the cardinal sin of sloth, acedia was among the eight types of "demons" or "tempting thoughts" (*logismoi*) that preoccupied Egyptian Christian monks in the third and fourth centuries.[36] While English renditions include apathy, torpor, and lassitude, scholars of Christianity usually understand acedia as a spiritual and sinful species of boredom induced by the rigidities and repetitiveness of ascetic life.[37] Kathleen Norris has described acedia as an "intense and comfortless awareness of time," often likened to a slowing down of time, in which the future looms as an "an appalling, interminable progression of empty days to fill."[38] In *The Praktikos*, the fourth-century Christian monk Evagrius Ponticus marveled at acedia's tendency "[to make] it seem that the sun barely moves, if at all, and that the day is fifty hours long."[39]

For Evagrius Ponticus, acedia was morally threatening because it seemed to mock the monk's good intentions by recalling the worldly life he had left behind by bringing "before the mind's eye the toil of the ascetic struggle."[40] Acedia was said to "instill in the heart of the monk a hatred for the place, a hatred for his very life itself, [and] a hatred for manual labor," and to eventually lead the monk "to drop out of the fight" and abandon ascetic life.[41] To me, this seemed to encapsulate Ángel's anguish as he knelt down there scrubbing the kitchen floor, missing the life he'd left behind, panicking about how much time lay ahead, and wondering whether his efforts might all be pointless.

Left unchecked, acedia could escalate into an outright loss of faith. Something like this happened one weekend in March. It was a Wednesday afternoon, and I was chatting (in English) with Diego, a Bronx-born resident. Diego had come back to Puerto Rico just two years earlier to live at La Casita after being put on probation for drug dealing in New York. Though he had now completed his compulsory eighteen months, he said he was "stuck treading water," with no way of supporting himself and no home to return to.

We chatted as he cleaned the car with a sponge. He gestured over to a group of residents who were pouring cement outside the main building, where there would soon be a new laundry room. "I'm so tired of this bullshit," he said, looking angrily at the bucket of soapy water. He'd spent the whole morning cleaning, and he was exhausted, he said, explaining to me what this had involved: scrubbing all of the floors, moving the fridge, sweeping all of the cockroaches out from underneath, washing all of the walls inside and outside. "I could be working," he said, shaking his head and taking a drag of his cigarette. "I have skills. Back in New York, I was a plumber. I used to make fifty dollars an hour. I could be working now. Instead, I'm stuck here washing walls and floors and not being paid anything." Flicking his cigarette onto the ground, he kicked over the bucket of water, sending slimy liquid gushing around our feet.

Trying to be useful while stuck in a shelter and relying in large measure on a series of draining, repetitive, and not infrequently futile tasks turns out to be a rickety foundation for an alternative way of life. In their efforts to keep busy, men constantly had to reckon with both the tedium and chore of filling up the time. Despite the constant injunctions to labor—the early mornings, the plethora of domestic and manual tasks—idleness was sometimes inevitable. And the boredom that settled in during these idle moments speaks volumes about the design faults of this surrogate labor regime. It is simply unable to ensure a steady supply of things to do.

And yet residents' torment was not reducible to idle suffering. The perhaps more serious problem here was the spiritual acedia that settled in even when men succeeded in using their time "productively." Even as these men took their medicine, so to speak, and duly and piously strove to keep busy as instructed, the repetitiveness and futility of the tasks at hand were often too painfully apparent to ignore. Like the monks of Benedict's abbey, many struggled to maintain their faith in a monotonous way of life that mimicked "eternity in its changelessness."[42] When the effort to keep busy proved too draining, too repetitive, or too meaningless, the thought that these pains might all be futile sunk into La Casita's novitiates as betrayal. Having placed their faith in a rehabilitation program promising recovery and return, after all their efforts they found themselves in exile. "I can't fucking stand it here," said Diego. "I'm wasting my life."

For Diego, the regimen of continuous labor that La Casita devised to try to keep its residents busy was not the kind of work he wanted. It may have "filled the time" (some of it), but ultimately it did not enable him to achieve progressive changes in his life: to get a car, to live independently, and to move back to New York. Diego found work at La Casita to be a "waste of time" because it was not leading him anywhere different or better.

Nor was Diego alone. I encountered many men at La Casita who knew the program could not improve their life circumstances. "This therapy doesn't work," residents told me. "Trust me, all the guys that graduate will be back here in under a year." Still, there were men who *did* value their time at La Casita: men like Ángel and Israel who felt that they were "making progress" and for whom the passage of time at La Casita was personally fulfilling. So below, I dissect those residents' experiences of progress, focusing specifically on their claims to be "working on their personalities." I show that this secular-spiritual genre of self-work made it possible for some men to come to terms with their inability to change their life circumstances, enabling some to commit to this alternative way of life.

· · · · ·

It was my first day back at La Casita following two weeks of nonstop interviewing at other therapeutic communities. I made my way up the driveway and saw Israel, a fifty-five-year-old former truck driver, doubled over and bathed in sunlight. The handlebars of a large wheelbarrow, loaded with cement, were resting on his knees, and he stood panting. As I approached, he gestured up the trail toward the stone table where a group of residents stood smoking amid the construction. Slowly, we made our way up there.

Israel was approaching the end of his third stay at La Casita. Since the 1990s, he had cycled in and out of therapeutic communities, spending years, on and off, as both a resident and live-in re-educado. That day he had just returned from court, where the judge at his hearing had inquired about his "exit strategy." Israel still had none; nor did he seem thrilled by the prospect of leaving: "I try not to think too much about it. I'm very cautious about making plans for getting out. Of course, I want to have a house, a car, a job. I want to be able to call my daughter in Florida that I haven't seen since she was two—now she's twelve. I want to say, 'Come, visit papa.' But I can't. Because when these plans don't work out, that's where the frustration comes, and maybe a relapse." During the various conversations I had with Israel over eight months at La Casita, he would often veer between a peaceful calm at the prospect that he might well be there for a while and a frustrated panic that so much of his life had been spent in therapeutic communities. I recall one occasion, after Rocky floated the idea that he stay on as a *terapista*, when Israel had seemed troubled, even alarmed: "I've already been doing this for many years," he exclaimed. "Next year I'll be fifty-six. . . . That's way too old to be living in programs." He'd visibly shuddered at the prospect.

But today, as he stood finishing his cigarette, his stance toward volunteering for the program as a future life plan seemed more positive. "I'd like to stay on here, if I can," he said. "It's a good option for me. . . . I already have a lot of experience working in addiction." He told me about the two years he'd spent working as a volunteer at a Pentecostal addiction ministry. "It was a mistake to leave that place," he said. "That was how I ended up back on the street." Seeming to collect his thoughts, he continued: "Right now, I'm just focusing on working. And I'm making a lot of progress. I'm working on my personality and working on myself."

This idea of personality reconstruction was an explicit therapeutic teaching at La Casita. Staff often characterized recovery as a process of "reeducation" that involved "rebuilding" or "reorienting" personality. Consider one of several similar statements I cataloged that year, this one made by Rafi, a self-identifying *re-educado ex-adicto*: "When you start consuming [drugs], the whole personality changes. Your temperament gets more aggressive, irritable; you become impulsive; you get violent. A person who is addicted is a person who has lost all their morals . . . and lost the value of life."

During my conversations at La Casita and at therapeutic communities, I encountered many ideas about what addiction was and whether and how it could be treated. Residents and staff members often characterized addiction in characterological terms, though other frameworks were also in circulation. Some residents likened addiction to a chronic disease "like diabetes," for example, while others preferred to call it a "brain disease." It was actually not uncommon for my interlocutors to juggle between these theories, often within a single conversation.

Much can be said about how people in institutional settings take up and internalize scientific theories.[43] As I showed in the previous chapter, for example, the paradigm of reeducation has been widely internalized by re-educados, many of whom now understand themselves as characterologically "restored" from a formerly "flawed" state. But in addition to examining how institutional power can shape subjectivity through scripting, it is also worth considering what scripted ways of speaking can be seen to accomplish for the speakers themselves. Summerson Carr addresses this question in her work on rehabilitation in the United States, where she shows how learning to speak through scripts, such as "Hi, my name is [x], and I am a recovering crack addict," can be a way for people to achieve personal goals. In one example, Carr describes how this script assisted the speaker to stake a claim as a legitimate peer representative.[44]

Similarly, the striking thing about residents' claims to be working on their personalities was not that their speech was scripted—it was—but that it seemed to be meaningfully implicated into their sense of progress. Over time, as I paid more attention to what residents were trying to accomplish when they said they were working on their personalities, I noticed that it often seemed to take the form of a prayer. It was something that residents claimed or even clung to, especially following bouts of boredom or in moments of doubt about the usefulness of time at La Casita.

Consider another conversation I had with Israel, as he contemplated leaving. Shaking his head, he said: "No, it's important to know oneself. I'm not ready. Besides, I'm changing a lot here. I'm developing my maturity, yes, according to my age. I'm developing in terms of being responsible, being tolerant and patient. Here, I'm developing a true personality and way of being." In one sense, Israel's words denote social suffering. Scholars might reach for circulating concepts of "symbolic violence" or "internalized stigma" to grasp how men like Israel, who cannot get jobs, marry, or achieve other liberal markers of male adulthood, come to locate their suffering internally, thus occluding the social conditions that cause their pain.[45]

But in another sense, Israel's words were also prayerful. Prayer, as Marcel Mauss reminds us, is rarely just the outcry of an individual in anguish.[46] More commonly, it is a socialized language that brings people into relationships with one and other and through which people seek to bring about changes in their life circumstances.[47] The contrast matters. Whereas cocirculating theories of addiction ("it's like diabetes") tended to be articulated expositively—as a way of packaging a complicated condition into something recognizable—"working on my personality" denoted *labor* and, more specifically, *continuous* labor. Operating in a manner surprisingly analogous to monastic meditation—the continuous recitation from memory of scripture (albeit a secular therapeutic script rather than a biblical text)—its meaning lay not so much in its lexical connotation (addiction as a problem of pathological personality) but in its total harnessing of time into a form of work.

By sculpting what could look to outsiders like being stuck in a superfluous state of "doing nothing" into the language of internal growth and uninterrupted work, "working on my personality" tore open a window of possibility for existential advancement in a context where opportunities for culturally valued social advancement were lacking, signaling an alternative way of living, based not on wage labor, independent habitation, or family life but rather on a commitment to self-improvement in the shelter unfazed by economic dependency. It thus functioned as a kind of pledge that gave meaning to an investment of time whose purpose or value was not always obviously apparent.

For Evagrius Ponticus, spiritual persistence through praying, reading scripture, and performing manual labor was the remedy for a monk who, battling the demon of acedia, had come to doubt the value of ascetic life:

he instructed, "The time of temptation is not the time to leave, devising plausible pretexts. . . . Rather, stand there firmly and be patient."[48] As residents buckled down to work on their personalities, acutely aware of the pleasures and freedoms they had left behind and facing months or years of the same repetitive routine, persistence was all they had left. I have often wondered, were the Egyptian fathers to have observed these criminalized exiles who for all their many stigmas strive to persist at La Casita—men who let go of modern desires for material advancement and who commit instead to internal growth—might they have seen kindred souls?

Let us consider one final conversation, this one with Ángel. It was a Monday morning in February, and La Casita was in the grip of yet another power cut. I'd joined Ángel on the terrace, where he was drinking coffee and watching the rain. He seemed down. Yesterday, it transpired, had been family visiting day, and his parents had not shown up. *Fue un castigo* (it was a punishment), he said. "I know it. . . . It's because they are trying to test me." Ángel glared into space for a while, seeming to wrestle with himself. I asked him if he'd requested permission to call them, when something like resolve seemed to click in his mind. "No," he said. "I know that wouldn't be the right way. I keep working, I keep working on my personality." Staring into the low clouds that misted around us, he recounted his parents' last visit two weeks earlier. At some point, his father had told Ángel that he loved him. "He's never said that before," he said. "I had to go to the bathroom and cry." In tears, Ángel continued: "I'm thirty-eight years old. That's too old to be learning the difference between right and wrong. At first when I arrived, I was in such a rush, like, I can't be here when I'm forty. But now I'm here and I see there are lots of older men. I know I shouldn't rush because I'm not ready yet. I've been learning who I am here."

Ángel's torment seemed to index several feelings: discomfort with place, regret over a misspent past, a desire for something better, and the early seeds of recognition that his best option might be to stay put. That last feeling might also be read as the initial stages of an acceptance of a life plan based not on advancement to something materially better but instead on a pledge to persist in the knowledge that things might never change. Writing of technological industrial transformation in Europe, Reinhart Koselleck has argued that with the onset of modernity, "progress" became locked into the expectation that the future will be different and qualitatively better than all that has been experienced in the past.[49] For Ángel, in marked contrast, progress hinged precisely on letting go of expectations for a radically different or better future. Progress meant committing instead to harnessing time in the present into internal growth. Largely unconcerned with market discipline, "working on my personality" can be read as a secular-spiritual prayer that involves converting a lack of work into self-work and turning an overabundance of time into a sense of internal spiritual progress.

· · · · ·

Writing of Paul of Thebes, the third-century ascetic, who lived alone in the Porphyrian desert and collected palm fronds each day only to burn every year all the fronds that he had gathered, John Cassian writes: "Although the obligation of earning a livelihood did not demand this course of action, he did it just for the sake of purging his heart, firming his thoughts, persevering in his cell, and conquering and driving out acedia."[50] Here, I have argued that a similar kind of unproductive, socially unnecessary, spiritually exhausting, and isolating self-work is making a comeback in surrogate outposts of male employment like La Casita. Here, the relentless pursuit of constant activity is not merely a requirement imposed by capitalist systems or reproductive demands. Instead, it represents an adherence to a secular-spiritual asceticism, where the continuous engagement in work offers a distinct perspective on both meaning and advancement. Keeping busy helps alleviate, to some extent, the suffering and tedium of being excluded from the market economy, but it doesn't do so reliably.

The problems men encounter at La Casita on a daily basis—a lack of meaningful work, an inability to actualize gendered markers of adulthood, an excess of time, and a monotonous and repetitive daily routine enveloped by a frenetic compulsion to be productive—are not unique to Puerto Rican therapeutic communities. These globalizing afflictions manifest in various permutations among millions of people around the world: from marginalized men with "nothing to do" in postsocialist Europe and postcolonial Africa to the recently laid-off white collar workers in southern Europe desperately trying to be productive while navigating shrinking employment opportunities.[51]

At La Casita, some men responded to advanced capitalism's globalizing challenges by committing to an alternate conception of progress that expresses, in secular-spiritual terms, the asceticism that lay at the heart of the early Christian monastic project. Theirs was a life plan based on a continuous striving for internal improvement in the absence of material advancement, on staying put to work on oneself in the face of eternal boredom. There is, of course, a major difference. Unlike the Egyptian monks of the fourth century or the evangelical converts of Puerto Rico's addiction ministries,[52] residents at La Casita were denied the promise of an afterlife. Some, to be sure, may have privately derived sustenance from this expectation, but La Casita made no promises of eternal salvation. This life, with all its hardship, would have to suffice. But how did it stack up? I have suggested that La Casita offered a "rickety" belonging—"thicker,"[53] perhaps, than other alternatives to wage labor but not necessarily more secure.

I opened this chapter with a prayer:

> I give you my hand,
> set my heart in rhythm with yours
> and I pledge us both before God—
> bringing myself and you
> to honor life.

While La Casita is built on a pledge—of honoring the life you have now, of persisting without expecting material progress, and of continuing to work no matter how unproductive or socially unnecessary that work might be—for many, this pledge proves an unreliable foundation on which to build a life. Boredom, a feeling of futility, and a weariness of soul created by this therapeutic community's inability to ensure meaningful work leave many men questioning their commitment to this alternative way of living. This secular monastery offers a regime of ceaseless work as a surrogate livelihood to jobless men, who embrace it only partially and with great difficulty. What may be most remarkable is the sense of purpose and progress that some of these men, some of the time, could nonetheless derive from this troubled endeavor.

· 4 ·

Crimeless Confinement

Finally, after two hours of waiting, Eric Jr. and his father are summoned to the courtroom. Eric Sr. makes his way in behind his twenty-five-year-old son, panting through labored steps, his hands clutching his hospital cane. The three of us—father, son, and anthropologist—settle into seats opposite the judge's bench.[1] We each confirm our names and relationship to Eric Jr. before a moment of quiet signals things are about to begin.[2] "I have received the results of your urine test," says the judge, looking up from his dossier to gaze inquiringly at Eric Jr. "The test came back positive for both heroin and cocaine, which corroborates your father's statement about your compulsive drug use. Do you have anything you wish to say about this?" Eric Jr. shifts his weight from one leg to another; his hands dig down further into his suit pockets. "The results are correct," he says, lowering his head. "I know I have a problem. I know my father is trying to help me, and that is why I'm here today." Eric Sr. grasps his son's shoulder, squeezing it tight with affection. "Is it still your wish to go ahead with the petition?" the judge asks Eric Sr., who confirms that it is, before adding: "My son is sick, Your Honor. His mother and I have tried to help him in every way we can. We're out of options, so I'm here today asking for your help. Please, make my son accept the treatment he needs."

The judge consults his dossier again. "Your father has come to this court to request that I issue a Law 67. Do you understand what Law 67 is?" the judge asks Eric Jr., who confirms that he does. "Once I grant this petition," the judge continues, "you will have twenty-four hours to enroll in residential drug treatment. If you fail to do this, you will be in contempt of court, and a warrant will be issued for your immediate arrest. Do you understand?" Eric Jr. confirms, once again, that he understands. The next five minutes are a flurry of stipulations. Eric Sr. is formally granted a civil commitment order under Law 67 for his son, Eric Jr., who will be transported that day to an available treatment program. At the recommendation of a family friend, Eric Sr. has chosen to entrust his son to La Casita's care. There, Eric Jr. is to participate in all required therapies and to comply with all of the institution's rules. Should he fail to do so or should he leave without authorization, he will be arrested. After a ten-minute spiel about the importance of compliance, the judge opens the floor to questions. "How long will I be there?" Eric Jr. asks, with commendable calm. "That will depend entirely on your behavior and your progress in battling your addiction," the judge replies flatly. "We all want what is best for you," he continues, "so let us reconvene in two months' time to assess your progress." After five more minutes of stern discussion with Eric Jr., the judge brings the hearing to an end, and the three of us make our way out to the municipal court foyer. "*Gracias a Dios*," Eric Sr. sighs, crossing himself. The knowledge of his son's imminent departure to La Casita has come as a relief.

This chapter charts the journeys of residents like Eric Jr. who are remanded to therapeutic communities via involuntary civil commitment. These are the legal mechanisms that enable concerned citizens to petition local civil courts to forcibly commit individuals who use drugs—and specifically those *not* undergoing criminal proceedings—into some form of treatment. In Puerto Rico, the involuntary treatment of people deemed to have drug problems skews heavily toward inpatient residential care (in either a therapeutic community or Evangelical ministries), owing to island-wide scarcities in clinical drug services. Yet beyond clinical scarcities, this imbrication of therapeutic communities and civil commitment also indexes the critical role that the carceral state has come to play in relieving overwhelmed families of burdens of care.

I came to know many parents, partners, and siblings who had resorted to using civil commitment to forcibly institutionalize their loved ones during the months I spent at La Casita, Comunidad-Luz, Comunidad de Elevación del Espíritu Humano, and Mesón de Dios. The family members I met over the course of numerous visiting hours at these programs were unequivocally adamant that their relatives were *ill* and expressly in need of *treatment*, not punishment. Yet civil commitment's predominant characterization as an expressly noncriminal domain that stands apart from criminal justice is extremely misleading. Though civil and criminal law are adjudicated through distinct court systems, at the level of practice they overlap considerably.[3]

In Puerto Rico, civilly committed citizens are sometimes held in jail prior to their commitment to a therapeutic community, just as those who do not comply are frequently transferred to prisons. Yet unlike criminal justice, civil commitment remains largely immune to public scrutiny, an invisibility that is far from unique to Puerto Rico.[4]

So here lies one of the cruel ironies of civil commitment. Though relatives usually envision civil commitment as an "alternative" measure to punishment, one they hope will ward off a criminal record, imprisonment, or worse, in invoking civil commitment families were in practice doing something that the Department of Correction and Rehabilitation has been doing for decades to people who use drugs. With various degrees of awareness, they were consigning their loved ones to a drastically different legal-juridical world, one where a single step out of line—a dispute with another resident, a failure to abide by institutional rules, or a refusal to participate in therapies—could culminate in imprisonment. Yet markedly unlike the criminal justice mechanisms that revoke citizens' rights and liberties, civil commitment does so invisibly, without being counted and beyond public scrutiny. This murky and expanding entrance into carceral citizenship is the subject of this chapter.

A Bronx-born veteran and father of four, Eric Sr. speaks with a growl and exudes a "no apologies" manner that seems like it might have been useful back in the army. Tall and heavyset with a thick white beard, he wore a single silver hoop earring and his choice of attire for court that day was a bold one: "If you can't get behind our troops," his T-shirt read, "Feel free to stand in front." But even without a suit, it was plain that Eric Sr. meant business. "They call it dual diagnosis," he would explain to insurance companies and detoxification providers over the phone, or even just to other parents in the court waiting room. "It's where the mental illness and the substance abuse exacerbate each other." But in private he was more skeptical. "Some doctors say he's schizophrenic," he told me once. "But it's like me and his mother keep telling him: Look, if you use cocaine so compulsively, you're going to start seeing things." Each of his other three children, as he frequently assured himself, had all turned out just fine.

With these self-assurances Eric Sr. gestured to years of crisis management that had led him to where he was that afternoon in 2017: in the municipal court of Guaynabo invoking an involuntary civil commitment (ICC) order against his addicted and mentally ill child. By then, he and his wife, María, had done the rounds of Puerto Rico's scant psychiatric and substance use services. "Shrinks, antipsychotics, detox—we've tried it all," he'd say, "but it's impossible because of his dual diagnosis." During the last three years, Eric Jr. had been hospitalized on seven different occasions on account of accidental overdose and drug-related psychosis. But just as his drug use had consistently relegated him to low priority among mental health providers, who roundly suggested he "get sober" prior to beginning therapy, so his mental illness had made him hard to place within Puerto Rico's meager network of drug services. Many drug service providers are unwilling to accept individuals with severe mental health disorders.[5] Resultantly, Eric Jr.'s growing repertoire of ever-changing mental health diagnoses (which alternated between depression, anxiety, substance-induced psychotic disorder, and, once, schizophrenia) had left him with only labels, not support. Like many parents and families who resort to civil commitment, Eric Sr. was frustrated by years spent battling waiting lists, navigating complicated service criteria, and paying out of pocket for private detoxification programs that insurance companies somehow managed to refuse to cover. "But no matter what he does, he's still my baby," Eric Sr. would say. But he was getting tired.

"We've had to have him sectioned twice," Eric Sr. explained in a recorded interview, referring to the two occasions in which Eric Jr. had been hospitalized in a state of psychosis, before adding, "but the hospital just let him out again." This was true and, in fact, standard practice for psychiatric civil commitment. One week after his hospitalization, having been diagnosed with substance-induced psychotic disorder, Eric Jr.'s condition stabilized. No longer considered to "represent a risk to the self or others," a legal requirement for psychiatric hospitalization in Puerto Rico,[6] Eric Jr. had been duly discharged from the Río Piedras Medical Center, the island's largest state hospital. But as far as Eric Sr. and María were concerned, it had all happened far too quickly. Within hours of driving him home, Eric Sr. recounted, he had disappeared again, this time for several weeks.

A month of worry later, the police found Eric Jr. in El Condado. Not that they were looking for him, Eric Sr. hastened to add. No, he caught their attention because he was "totally psychotic in the tourist district," making a scene that involved "shouting at cars" and "injecting speedballs" (a combination of heroin and cocaine). Still upset from what they felt to be the hospital's negligent decision to release their son prematurely, Eric Sr. and María decided to send their son to a two-week-long private detoxification program. This would have cost them $400, except Eric Jr. never made it. Instead, he jumped out of his father's moving car while they were en route to the clinic. At that point, Eric Sr. and María decided to take out a Law 67 at the recommendation of a family friend. Unlike psychiatric commitment, this compulsory treatment order was specifically geared toward drug addiction. Importantly, it would allow them to legally force Eric Jr. into long- rather than short-term drug treatment, in a secluded, residential setting.

Petitioning the court had been a relatively simple process. After completing the requisite paperwork and identifying an available program that would accept Eric Jr. (in this case, La Casita), a hearing had been scheduled. At that initial hearing, Eric Sr. and María had testified that their son was a compulsive cocaine and heroin user whose mental health problems, they felt, were "aggravated if not caused entirely" by his substance misuse. Having enumerated their unsuccessful prior attempts to enroll him in treatment, which included nine short-term detoxification programs (just one completed), three voluntary enrollments in therapeutic community care (all aborted within a month), five hospitalizations for accidental overdose, and two psychiatric hospitalizations, they had implored the judge to intervene. "He just won't do it on his own," Eric Sr. had explained. "Each time we get him into a program, he just leaves." As Eric Sr. would later recall, he'd actually gone as far as begging the judge to intervene. Gesticulating in a mock reenactment, he held his hands in prayer: "Look, you are a judge. You are the highest person in the land. If you can't do anything, who can?"

This chapter considers involuntary civil commitment as the place where the carceral state, self-help, and the domestic sphere intertwine. It explores the human consequences of civil confinement, conceived not as an alternative to punishment or as a discrete domain apart from criminal justice but instead as one node in a "carceral archipelago" of institutions and instruments that exercise the power to punish.[7] As a case study of the extension of penal power into ever broader areas of social life, it explores civil commitment's expanding remit, showing that it has long burst the banks of its intended design ("forcing drug users to accept help") and now performs a wide variety of other roles, from poverty management to enforcing domestic order. Unlike criminal imprisonment, civil confinement goes largely uncounted and unmonitored. This lack of accountability, as I show in this chapter, inflicts great pain and suffering on overwhelmed families and their civilly committed relatives alike.

But before exploring civil commitment ethnographically, it is helpful to review the history of civil commitment law in Puerto Rico and to outline some of its particularities with respect to ICC statutes on the US mainland. Clarifying certain idiosyncrasies in Puerto Rican civil commitment law will help to illuminate how otherwise law-abiding citizens can find themselves legally confined for months and even years at a time.

· · · · ·

A few months into my fieldwork with therapeutic community residents, I kept encountering the same weird story over and over again. Men had been ordered by the court into residential drug treatment at the petition of a family member. They had not received legal representation or counsel either before or since their institutionalization. None of the residents I spoke to had been informed of how long they were legally required to remain in a residential facility, and very few were aware of any precise criteria or requirements that must be fulfilled to be released. Instead, residents would often tell me they were "waiting" for a release order, but they were generally uncertain as to precisely when or how they might obtain one.

As it turns out, a fog of ambiguity surrounds civil commitment in Puerto Rico, starting with its legal basis. In Puerto Rico, Law 67 of 1993 is one of two pieces of legislation, along with Law 408 of 2000 (amended 2008) governing civil commitment. Though both laws allow for the civil commitment of people who use psychoactive drugs, they have distinct institutional histories and operate in different ways—so different, in fact, that one law directly contradicts the other.[8] Referred to locally as a "compulsory treatment law," Law 67 is what lawyers call an "organic" law: its primary purpose was the establishment of a new government agency. Part of a series of laws introduced in 1993 under a broader project of health care privatization, Law 67 unified addiction and mental health services into a single new government administration, hence the law's full name: the Law of the Administration of Mental Health and Anti-Addiction Services. Baked into this enabling legislation was a short clause: section 11 (3 L.P.R.A. § 402j), entitled "Juridical Procedure for Addicts."

As an organic (administration-building) law rather than a mental health code, Law 67's procedure for civil commitment was never reviewed by a medical professional society or patient rights group.[9] When I asked government employees who were active during this time about it, many recalled that the clause was the brainchild of a single government employee who had an addicted child (though a lack of relevant archival documentation means it is difficult to verify this now). Whatever the clause's genesis, the result was a throwback to nineteenth-century inebriety laws.[10] Under Law 67, any adult deemed to be a "a drug addict" in a court of law, including those considered "alcoholics," may be legally confined in a residential facility for a statutorily unspecified duration, which can often extend to a year or more.[11] Once committed, the individual's condition will rarely be monitored, let alone reassessed, by a health or social care professional, as this is not strictly legally required. Instead, the individual will be legally obliged to comply with therapies prescribed by their host institution, usually a self-help program. To appreciate Law 67's idiosyncrasies, specifically its unusually lax criteria and long duration, it may be useful to compare it to other ICC laws.

The involuntary civil commitment of people with substance use disorders or alcoholism is currently permitted in at least thirty-eight US states.[12] While ICC laws vary by state, US ICC laws typically stipulate that the following requirements must be fulfilled to justify involuntary civil commitment of drug users. *Either* the individual must have a clinically diagnosed substance use disorder *and* pose an imminent threat of harm to self or others (diagnosis and "imminent danger"), *or* the individual must have a clinically diagnosed substance use disorder *and* be unable to meet their own basic needs (diagnosis and "diminished autonomy," sometimes referred to as "grave disability").[13] According to Supreme Court rulings, simply having a substance use disorder is insufficient justification for involuntary civil commitment: the criteria of "imminent danger" or "diminished autonomy" must also be met.[14] Though ICC legislation varies widely across the United States, with maximum commitment duration ranging from three days in Michigan to two years in West Virginia, most states have adopted some version of diagnosis, imminent danger, and diminished autonomy into their ICC statutes.[15]

Since the enactment of Law 67 in 1993, the only stipulation for civil commitment in Puerto Rico is proving in a court of law that an individual is "addicted to drugs or alcohol," without the need for medical validation.[16] Convincing testimony or a confession may serve as adequate evidence. Upon a successful petition, the individual may be placed under legal institutionalization, often within a therapeutic community or an Evangelical ministry. Noncompliance with institutional regulations or unauthorized discharge can result in contempt of court, possibly leading to incarceration. Throughout this process, legal counsel is rarely provided or offered.

Law 67 is interesting not simply because it is unusually punitive (by the standards of some US states, yes, though not by all of them).[17] More importantly, Law 67 provides an especially vivid example of a broader creep of the carceral state into self-help and into the supposedly private realm of kinship. As the family, the judiciary, and self-help intertwine, configurations of power and authority are being redrawn and families and re-educados become enablers and enforcers of the carceral state. Increasingly, decisions about extending confinement or recommending release fall onto paraprofessional re-educados, who come to wield considerable state power in civil commitment proceedings. The consequences of this dispersal of penal power onto self-help groups and kinship systems seems to have gone largely unnoticed, however, owing to long-standing protections accorded to civil courts.

In my research, families' reasons for using civil commitment varied, but scenarios included the following: a mother whose suicidal nineteen-year-old was stockpiling fentanyl; a couple whose household became enveloped in the fallout of their son's failed foray into drug dealing (leading his discontented associates to open fire on their home); a wife repeatedly beaten by her intoxicated husband; and an ultimatum, issued from neighbors to a father, that either he force his thirty-year-old son to enter treatment for his heroin addiction or they would report him to the police for stealing their car.[18] Such varied circumstances attest to the fact that civil commitment is not necessarily as simple (or benign) as giving a loved one a legally binding motivation to accept help for a drug problem.[19] Quite often, it is a desperate effort to shield the larger family unit from the sequelae of chaos that can come with having an out-of-control (broadly defined) relative.

Complicating matters, local governments and businesses, too, seem to have made use of Law 67. In 2001, to name one particularly troubling example, state officials in the city of Bayamón used Law 67 to rid the streets of homeless people in a *limpieza de deambulantes* (homeless sweep) prior to hosting Miss Universe, an internationally televised modeling contest.[20] Throughout the early 2000s, in a longer series of abuses, a number of municipal governments used Law 67 to relocate homeless drug users from Puerto Rico to Chicago and Philadelphia. Promised "treatment" and provided one-way plane tickets to the mainland, these men were then abandoned to unlicensed flophouses, prompting allegations of human trafficking.[21] These governmental utilities beyond the family serve to highlight the incredible and troubling versatility with which civil confinement is put to use as well as its protean capacity for co-option. But for various reasons, explored below, basic information regarding the number of people civilly confined each year and the clinical-demographic profile of those committed remain a mystery.

· · · · ·

Unlike the forms of confinement that occur under the auspices of the US criminal justice system, which for decades have been scrutinized and quantified by government bodies, researchers, and other critical observers, civil confinement is not statistically monitored. This is partly because there is no centralized surveillance system for civil commitment in the United States and its territories; nor is there for civil court more generally. Researchers decry this as "detention without data," although recent investigations have unearthed some sporadic, if not necessarily satisfying, figures.[22]

One commendable effort came from a study led by researchers at Brown University.[23] The first (and so far only) nationwide attempt to quantitatively assess the prevalence of civil commitment for substance use disorders across the US mainland, its authors solicited ICC estimates from substance abuse departments across the country. Eventually, it succeeded in obtaining certified responses from every US state (itself no small feat), but the findings were disappointing. Of thirty-three US states that had ICC statutes in place in 2015, only seven were able to provide *any* estimate of statewide ICC prevalence. Even there, the details were woefully imprecise. In "recent years" (no further details given), Florida committed "at least 9000 on average," Massachusetts committed "at least 4500," and Colorado estimated an annual average "in recent years" somewhere between 150 and 200. Other states were only able to provide estimates for single sporadic years. Missouri reported committing 166 individuals in 2011; Wisconsin, 260 in 2011; Hawaii, 83 in 2009; and Texas, 22 in 2010. Tellingly, the seven states that reported using civil commitment "regularly or frequently" were unable to provide any estimate whatsoever, while the remaining thirteen states with ICC statutes said they either "never" or "rarely" applied them.[24]

My own attempt to ascertain ICC prevalence in Puerto Rico proved equally unavailing. With no centralized surveillance system for civil court, government figures on civil commitment are limited to those collected by the Administration of Mental Services Administration Health and Addiction (ASSMCA) through its annual provider survey. As part of that survey, which is not publicly available and which focuses primarily on sociodemographic characteristics of participants, all licensed drug treatment providers are supposed to report their annual count of Law 67 cases. Very few programs complete this survey correctly, however, if they do so at all. Owing to widespread underreporting, ASSMCA officials involved in collating the survey declined to share it with me on the basis that it was "not reliable."

Giving up on government figures, I eventually resorted to driving to each of the fifteen municipal courts responsible for processing civil commitment orders on the island, hoping to glean some sort of estimates from the courts themselves. Ten courts kept no records of civil commitment (or at least were not inclined to share them with me). Two courts were inexplicably closed on the days I visited.[25] But three of fifteen municipal courts (San Juan, Bayamón, and Carolina) did share their records with me. According to handwritten logs, these three municipal courts collectively processed 721 ICC cases via Law 67 between 2014 and 2017.[26] As for the other twelve municipalities, their ICC prevalence remains anyone's guess. Thus, after ten days in the car, six separate meetings with senior officials at ASSMCA, five unsuccessful days in the government archive, and multiple phone calls and email exchanges, all I was able to unearth in terms of statistics on civil commitment was its scantiness. Nor had anything been published about Law 67 in either Spanish- or English-language academic journals. With the exception of two brief mentions in reports by treatment activists, in fact, and a short lay summary published online (and pro bono) by a Puerto Rican law school, it was as if the procedure did not exist.[27]

More than a methodological dead end, the statistical invisibility of civil commitment signs one of its distinguishing features: its complete immunity from public scrutiny. Uncounted and therefore invisible, civil confinement's lack of accountability became all the more apparent as I began interviewing professionals involved with civil commitment proceedings. To gain a better understanding of Law 67, I had set about interviewing psychologists and clinicians working in the field of drug addiction, but I immediately encountered vast inconsistencies in their accounts of how the law worked. Some professionals believed that Law 67 could only be applied to someone with a clinically diagnosed substance use disorder, while others maintained that a clinical diagnosis was not strictly necessary: all that was needed was a convincing testimony from a family member. Some thought civil commitment was "very rare these days," used only in "exceptional circumstances," whereas others maintained it was "widely overused" and "prone to abuse." Things became more muddled when homelessness entered the picture. Both the professionals and the re-educados I spoke to usually thought homelessness was *not* a legal ground for civil commitment under Law 67. "That would be totally unconstitutional," one clinician told me. "No, the law is only for addicts to help them get treatment; it's got nothing to do with homeless people," a re-educado explained. And yet many residents told me that they had been civilly committed to residential facilities on *precisely* these grounds. In fact, some had even deduced that it was "illegal to be homeless" in Puerto Rico, owing to their personal experiences of being arrested while homeless (and not necessarily in possession of any substances) and subsequently civilly committed.

Subsequent digging both clarified and further complicated this question. By the letter of the law, homelessness is *not* a legal ground for civil commitment under Law 67. That said, individual municipalities sometimes create their own protocols and agencies for managing Law 67 cases. These protocols differ across the island, but the most striking developments have been in a handful of municipalities that have established designated agencies to commit "homeless drug addicts" to residential drug treatment facilities. In these municipalities, it is a state official rather than a family member who typically acts as the petitioner to the court. That these government agencies exclusively target the homeless population (who then receive no legal advice) probably explains residents' perception that homelessness is "illegal in Puerto Rico."

Murkier still was the question of maximum duration. Across the twenty-four recorded interviews I conducted with therapeutic community staff members, psychologists, and social workers (and, later, lawyers) about Law 67, I never heard a coherent explanation of the precise criteria according to which a civilly committed patient might be released. Some of my interlocuters were adamant that commitment duration was determined by the recommendations of a "health care professional," something that seemed unlikely given the largely unprofessionalized nature of Puerto Rico's self-help treatment landscape. Others maintained that this authority lay ultimately with the petitioning family member; that is, residents would be released at such time as the petitioner chose to "lift" the court order. A third and contrasting account came from therapeutic community staff members themselves, who usually emphasized that it was ultimately "up to the judge," not themselves or the petitioner, to decide when to lift the order.

To clarify what I initially mistook for a straightforward legal misunderstanding, I reached out to several lawyers whom I knew had experience representing people with substance use disorders. It quickly became clear, however, that few had any direct experience dealing with civil commitment. As I subsequently learned, this is because people who are subject to Law 67 proceedings rarely (in my observations, never) receive legal counsel, and neither do their families.[28] These are attorney-free zones. Law 67 recipients usually attend their own hearings accompanied by only their family (including the petitioner) and a representative from their host treatment institution (usually a paraprofessional peer from a self-help therapeutic community). The only lawyer present is the judge.

With respect to the petitioners—mostly parents, partners, and siblings—it is hard to overemphasize the blindness with which they generally initiate this process. The *only* consistent information families receive comes in the form of a one-page information sheet issued by ASSMCA and available in court waiting rooms. This document offers a "practical guide" for initiating Law 67 proceedings, including whom family members will need to contact and what documentation they will need to produce. It says relatively little, however, about the kind of treatment their relative will receive and even less about the legal processes that will follow a petition. Thus, while families tend to be reasonably well versed on how to seek a Law 67 and, for instance, can readily explain how to obtain a *carta de hogar* (a certificate signed by a treatment center confirming availability in the event of a successful petition), in conversations they tended to be much fuzzier on the question of what happens next. By far the most common misconception was that the fate of their loved ones now lay "safely in the hands of professionals."

Not that Puerto Rican families were especially or uniquely ill-informed here. Far from it. On the US mainland, too, families who resort to civil commitment frequently lack a basic grasp of ICC procedures.[29] So too, it seems, do the professionals who administer it. Revealingly, a national survey of practicing psychiatrists in the United States found that nearly half of participants—including psychiatrists who had personally given testimonies at civil commitment proceedings—gave incorrect answers about eligibility criteria for civil commitment for their own states.[30] Given that Puerto Rico has not one but two laws governing involuntary civil commitment (one of which, as I explain below, directly contradicts the other), and given the aforementioned lack of publicly available information, it seems hardly surprising that so few families who resort to civil commitment have a solid grasp of what it entails.

Reminiscent of what Erving Goffman famously termed the "collusive net" uniting kin, state agents, and professionals and resulting in "emergency guardianship,"[31] Law 67 recipients are sometimes misled during the initial phase of their commitment. Gabriel, for example, a twenty-one-year-old resident I met at an Evangelical program who had a history of heroin injection and attempted suicide, was led to believe by his mother that the hearing pertained to her divorce. José, a thirty-year-old heroin user and dealer, was told by his father and girlfriend that the hearing pertained to an accusation of domestic violence. In the cases I followed, this initial surprise element often set the tone for what would later morph into a more protracted state of bewilderment that intensified throughout proceedings.

Thus far, I have eschewed explicit discussion of how Law 67 "really" works, at least in the sense of how a lawyer might approach this question. I have done so to convey how statistical and procedural invisibilities leave petitioning kin to embark on this journey blindly and to show how this effectively abandons committed citizens to a state of acute disorientation. Below, I delve more deeply into civil commitment by the letter of the law, not so much to clarify procedures but rather to show how official legal ambiguities further exacerbate this confusion. Legally ambiguous release procedures in particular set in motion a painful mode of waiting, where release is continually anticipated but constantly deferred.

· · · · ·

Given that the involuntary detention of otherwise law-abiding citizens is at stake, one might expect the institutional procedures of Law 67 to be definitively laid out, "on the books," if not in action.[32] But in fact, the formal specification of procedures that Law 67 recipients are subject to is surprisingly difficult to pin down. The law itself, which none of the people I met affected by it had ever read, lays out various "judicial procedures for the involuntary treatment of addicts."[33] Anyone over twenty-one who is deemed to be "addicted to drugs or alcohol" may be subjected to the law, and anyone over eighteen may act as the petitioner (usually a family member but potentially a neighbor, employer, state official, or any other adult). But even here, details are woefully sparse. While the entire section is just one and a half pages long (1,040 words), Law 67 has several idiosyncrasies that sign a slackening valve of justifications for confining citizens. These are best illuminated through comparison with Puerto Rico's Law 408 of 2000 (amended 2008 and 2012).

Most striking, perhaps, is Law 67's nonspecificity. Whereas Puerto Rico's Law 408 employs the nosological framework of the American Psychiatric Association's DSM-IV-TR manual for diagnosis, explicitly using the terms "substance abuse" and "substance dependence," Law 67 uses the lay term "drug addict" and—remarkably—provides no further elaboration or definition.[34] Divorced from the technical specificity provided by psychiatric nosology, this lay formulation operates as a legal mark and stigma that displaces medical authority as a warrant for indefinitely suspending citizens' liberty.[35] The conditions under which this basic right may be suspended are then outlined in two short paragraphs. Law 67 states that an "evaluation" must be conducted to assess whether there is "evidence" to support the petitioner's claim that the individual is "addicted to drugs or alcohol."[36] Like the term "addicted," the process of evaluation is also underspecified. Whereas Law 408 requires that a relevant "clinical diagnosis" must be conducted "by a psychiatrist in consultation with a multidisciplinary team,"[37] thereby entrusting clinicians with the power to protect or revoke this right, Law 67 diffuses this authority onto a potentially much wider set of actors. Officially, it states that "any person/entity that the Administration of Mental Health and Anti-Addiction Services delegates to" may perform the evaluation, thereby allowing a range of variably qualified (some would say unqualified) parties to perform this assessment.

In the twenty-one hearings I attended, the statutorily unspecified agents who presented their "evaluations" to the court varied widely and included paraprofessional therapeutic community staff members (re-educados), Evangelical pastors, police, social workers, and probation officers. On two occasions, there was no evaluation at all. Instead, the subject of the proceedings simply "confessed" to "being an addict." What counted as an "evaluation" legally marking one as a "drug addict" also varied considerably. Permissible evidence of addiction included a clinical diagnosis (once), a positive urine test of recent cocaine use administered by a probation officer, an accusation from a sibling of reckless drunk driving (confirmed via admission), physical signs of injection-related scarring on the arms, familial testimony (usually more than one and provided they were broadly concordant), and personal confessions.

Just as permissible evidence instantiating "need" for treatment is under-specified under Law 67, so is appropriate level of care. When ICC statutes are crafted as part of mental health laws, they will usually include guidelines for calibrating a patient's clinical condition with a recommended level of care, according to codified standards grounded in a tradition of patient rights.[38] Puerto Rico's Law 408, for example, stipulates that the individual must be placed in the "least restrictive" and "least invasive" level of care according to the "severity" of their symptoms.[39] Moreover, it states that any person ordered to enter restrictive (residential) care must be clinically evaluated regularly by a psychiatrist and relocated to less restrictive (outpatient) care once their condition improves.

In contrast, Law 67 contains no guidelines for establishing the appropriate level of care nor any stipulations regarding monitoring illness severity or adjustments to level of care. Because Law 67 is so thin on details, the question of "appropriate treatment" usually comes down pragmatically (and, in my experience, sometimes exclusively) to availability. By and large, judges will remand "the addict" to the institution that the petitioner requests, provided it is licensed and can demonstrate (by way of a certificate) that it has space available. This helps to explain why therapeutic communities and Evangelical ministries are used so widely in civil commitment: not because they are "appropriate" or "recommended" according to any clinical guidelines or other codified criteria but because in a context of professional service scarcity these self-help programs are the most widely available.

Law 67 is equally ham-handed when it comes to commitment duration. Unlike Law 408 (section 3.06), which stipulates that if a patient no longer reaches the hospitalization criteria ("imminent danger"), he or she must be "released immediately or transferred to another level of care," the criteria according to which a patient ought to be released from involuntary treatment under Law 67 are exceedingly poorly articulated.[40] As a friend of mine (and Puerto Rican academic) acidly put it: "Orwell might have drafted them."

Officially, Law 67 stipulates that patients should remain committed until such time as they have received "the maximum treatment that the institution can offer." (In a later section of the law, this is expressed as "all the treatment the institution can offer.") Unsurprisingly, demonstrating to a court that someone has achieved this principle of "maximum treatment" is difficult. What, after all, does "all the treatment" consist of, in the context of self-help? Might a caregiver need to attest that his or her institution was overwhelmed and had simply run out of some vital resource? Or might he or she have to state, for the record, that there was literally nothing else they could do for a patient and effectively denounce them a lost cause? A clue, if not exactly a guideline, comes in a later section of the law, which states that a "report" providing "recommendations" as to whether a person "should continue with involuntary treatment" must be presented at hearings throughout the resident's institutionalization. But again, basic stipulations regarding the frequency of hearings, the credentials of the reporter, the principles that ought to guide any "recommendations," and, most worryingly, a maximum duration of confinement are all left unspecified. In fact, only at the one-year mark does the onus of explaining why a patient has *not* been discharged fall onto the host treatment center. Effectively, it is only after one full year that the court assumes that the criterion of "maximum treatment" has been fulfilled (and even here, the host institution could theoretically recommend otherwise).

But how is "maximum treatment" adjudicated, in practice? To shed some light on this, I now turn to the story of one family: Camila, Juan, and their son Carlos. Though not a representative or average case, this family's particular story nonetheless conveys the cruel horizon of expectation that characterizes civil commitment proceedings. Here, progress is often presented as residents' ticket to freedom, while the principle of "maximum treatment" works silently against residents' release, culminating in continual disappointment and delay.

· · · · ·

Camila bashed on the vending machine with her fist. Indifferent to the dollar bill it had just swallowed, it belched back a mechanical groan. Giving up, we made our way to the mall cafeteria and found seats at a quiet table, avoiding the worn-out shoppers. "I just need him to be the Carlos he used to be," she breathed, before I'd pulled out my notebook or had a chance to frame a question. A petite woman in her midfifties, Camila was the mother of Carlos, a thirty-seven-year-old recovering heroin user and resident with whom I'd crossed paths at La Casita. At the suggestion of her husband, Juan, the two of them had taken out a Law 67 against Carlos after two trying years. Carlos's drug problem had begun with opioid pain relievers prescribed to treat his back pain. He had soon become dependent on pain relievers, later switching to heroin. For a time, Carlos had tried Suboxone, an opioid-substitution therapy paid for by their private insurance plan, though Juan had never really approved of the medication, suspecting, rightly or wrongly, that Carlos was continuing to use other substances.

Camila explained all this to me quickly and perfunctorily, as though she had told this story many times before. Then, after gazing into space for several minutes, she seemed to return from her thoughts. "Then he started bringing *malos tipos* [sketchy people] to the house. We would find needles in his bedroom. We even found a gun once. Did he tell you that? . . . Of course, when we confronted him, he said it wasn't his. Obviously." Taking a quick sip of water, she continued. "The whole thing is a mess," she said. "My husband has blood pressure problems; he doesn't need this. Now I have emotional problems and need to see a psychiatrist, which is costing even more money. It's not fair that I have to be on medication because my son is an addict. I know he says he's ready to come out," she said, suddenly stern. "But it's not up to us anymore. Let's see what the professionals say."

For his part, Carlos recalls coming home one day to find a police officer who duly issued him a citation summoning him to attend a hearing. At that hearing, he was ordered to undertake a urine test and detained in jail for four days. The urine test, delivered and presented to the court by a police officer, indicated that Carlos had recently consumed cocaine. At that hearing, Camila and Juan recounted that they continued to find needles in their home and confided their concerns about Carlos's new acquaintances. On hearing these testimonies, the judge ordered that Carlos enter a residential drug treatment program. I first met Carlos at La Casita in January 2017 on the day he enrolled.

Day 1: *Carlos is sat outside the office awaiting an entrance assessment. I ask him where he has come from. "El tribunal, Law 67," he replies. "My Dad has really fucked me over with this." There's another guy in the waiting room who says he's a Law 67 too. He says he's recently got out of prison and was incarcerated for two months for quitting another program. "It's much better to be here than there," he says. "I'm telling you; prison is much worse."*

Day 30: *Today is Carlos's first hearing since enrolling. Accompanying him to court is Héctor, another resident who is acting as a peer representative. The three of us find Carlos's parents in the waiting room. We exchange ten minutes of polite conversation. When Carlos's case number is called, the five of us file into the courtroom. The judge asks everyone to swear to tell the truth. We do so in unison. Héctor-the-peer is asked to comment on Carlos's integration into the* *program. He gives a ringing endorsement: "He's participating well," "getting used to the routines," and "working really hard." The judge inquires as to how Carlos is getting on with the other residents. Héctor looks at Carlos, who has his hands folded behind his back and is staring calmly up at the judge's bench. Héctor says, "He never has any problems with anyone, Your Honor; he's showing through his behavior that he is a responsible person."*

Satisfied, the judge takes out an envelope. Inside it is a case report signed by the director of La Casita. The report is one page long and the judge reads it out loud. It is a good report. "Carlos complies satisfactorily with the norms and processes of the center." "Overall, Carlos has shown positive adjustment." The report concludes with a recommendation that Carlos "continue to commit himself to achieving positive change." Placing the report back into the envelope, the judge says she is thrilled the treatment "is working." Then, turning to Carlos, "That is exactly what we and your family want from you." She looks at Camila and Juan, who nod; then she says, "What we all want is for this to be over as quickly as possible. The best way to get out is to keep doing what you are doing. Keep up the good behavior." The judge asks Camila and Juan if they have anything to add. They chat for five minutes about how his physical appearance has improved. Camila is visibly joyful as she explains that he has gained weight and describes the 37th birthday party they'd been able to throw for him the week before at La Casita. At the end of the brief conversation, the judge is smiling. She wishes Carlos a happy birthday and indicates that we will reconvene in two months.

Day 94: Carlos, Héctor-the-peer, and I sit in the waiting room drinking coffee from a vending machine. Today is Carlos's second hearing, marking the start of his third month as a resident. Carlos is cheerfully optimistic. "Today, I'll be out of here," he keeps saying. "My behavior is always good, my report will be great, the judge is going to hear it, and I'll be gone." Héctor-the-peer shakes his head. "You need to not focus on the date," he says. "Who knows what might happen." Carlos lets out a laugh in protest. "No, amigo. You'll see." Soon we are joined by Carlos's parents and caseworker J from La Casita.

At 11:30 a.m. on the dot the five of us enter the courtroom. Today it is a different judge. He asks Carlos if he could please comment on his experience in treatment so far. Carlos says, "I'm doing well, gracias a Dios." Standing straight and confident, he methodically elucidates all the activities, therapies, and responsibilities that he has undertaken in the last five months. Twice he mentions that La Casita have now entrusted him with being a peer-mentor for the new recruits, a responsibility which involves shepherding new residents through the program. "Gracias a Dios," he says again. "It's a big job, ensuring they don't get lost." Next up is caseworker R, who says he's "behaving well" and "settled in nicely." The judge now asks caseworker R, "Do you think he's received the maximum benefit of your program?" Caseworker R replies, "Generally, we recommend that residents complete the entire program, which is eighteen months. But with Law 67 cases, we respect what the court decides."

The judge ponders silently for about a minute, then asks Carlos: "Have you seen a psychologist?" Carlos indicates that he has not. Caseworker R confirms that he has not seen a psychologist. The judge deliberates with himself for a few seconds, then says, "Without the services of a psychologist, he won't be psychologically strengthened and could relapse." Caseworker R explains that this service is available for residents "who request it" and promises she can see this arranged. Looking at Camila and Juan, the judge says he wants to be sure that Carlos gets the "total benefit" of the program. "It would be a mistake to let him out too early," he says. Turning to Carlos. "Without that inner strength, you could relapse." He indicates that we will convene in two months.

After court, I chat with Camila and Juan. "Of course, I'd like him to come home," says Camila. "But it's not up to me. After all, it's the judge's decision." I glance at Carlos, expecting anger, but he doesn't speak. He kisses his mother on the cheek, then leaves us to go and smoke outside. Camila says, "He got it into his head he'd be allowed out. Now he's not, he's traumatized."

By October 2017, ten months after his initial admission, Carlos was still confined under Law 67. By that time, I'd attended two more hearings and had a third recounted to me by phone. Like the preceding hearings, each was presided over by a different judge, each of whom concluded that Carlos should complete an additional two months, after which his "progress" would be reassessed. The specific rationales for continuing his involuntary commitment varied. After the third judge, mentioned above, requested that he see a psychologist, an appointment was duly arranged. This was no easy feat. In fact, it took several weeks of phone calls and tireless advocating on the part of Camila, because at the time the waiting list in Puerto Rico for psychological appointments among publicly insured (mostly Medicaid) patients stood at six months.[41] At the next hearing, however, Camila's valiant advocacy efforts proved irrelevant. The judge in attendance, on hearing Camila's concerns about Carlos's insomnia (including his "dependency" on sleeping pills, which Camila worried was "just another drug"), concluded he was "not confident" that Carlos had "got the most" out of treatment. After advising Carlos to "keep up the good behavior," it was agreed that we would reconvene two months later. Carlos kept up the good behavior, so much so that at his next hearing the judge (again, a different one) was so impressed by Carlos's positive case report—which praised his "hard work" and "commitment to his treatment"—that he concluded it would be "a mistake to remove him prematurely from an environment in which he was so clearly thriving," adding: "We don't want you going back to old friends, bad places, old habits." Afterward, Carlos and I stood in the smoking area. "What shit luck I've had," he said. "Every time a different judge. Every time, two months more. I'm going to explode [*Soy de mecha corta*]," he said.

Carlos's feeling that he was a "short fuse" (*mecha corta*), run down to a dangerous point and on the verge, he said, of doing something he might later regret, came out of (what was then) ten months of frustrated effort. Where initially he had been confident—indeed, led to believe—that compliance with the program's rules and routines was his best ticket to freedom, and though he had duly participated in group activities with zealous dedication, for the last ten months he'd been stuck in a juridical labyrinth where the pathway to release was elusive. Bereft of legal counsel, Carlos was in the unfortunate position of attempting to regain his freedom within a juridical regime where the criteria for doing so were ambiguous and seemingly constantly changing.

Carlos was not alone in his predicament. One judge extended a resident's commitment on the basis that he "had a history of relapse." Another judge told a resident that they would have to remain in treatment "because last time I let you out you went straight back to using drugs." Since residents were roundly unaware of the "maximum benefit" criterion, this repeating adjournment often felt unfair and exceptionally arbitrary. Instead of being informed that, in all likelihood, they would probably complete the recommended program duration (which, for most therapeutic communities, was either one year or eighteen months), residents were repeatedly led to believe by judges, caseworkers, and their families that their release date would depend, first and foremost, on their "progress in battling their addiction." This was what made the whole thing feel so sinister. What was effectively a done deal was presented to residents as an outcome over which they could exercise control. "We all want you to be out of here as soon as possible," a smiling young judge assured Carlos at one of his early hearings. Given what eventually happened to Carlos, this seems in hindsight a cruel condolence.

Stakeholders who I have consulted over the course of writing this book have often wrung their hands in frustration that "clinically expected recurrence" can be used as a justification for extending commitment. Many have assumed (and with striking consistency) that self-help groups must be "exploiting the system" or "profiteering" by holding residents for as long as possible. This issue of who stands to gain from civil confinement is an important one. When framed economically, the answer (again) is not straightforward. In some cases, petitioning families pay a monthly residence fee on behalf of their relative (usually between $200 and $400). In these cases, the hosting programs could conceivably stand to gain from extending residents' commitment.[42] But many programs waive the fee for families who lack the means to pay it, and most faith-based programs choose not to charge fees at all. So this characterization of self-help groups as somehow conniving in a profit-generating ruse is misplaced.

But nor is this some simple and benign misunderstanding. As I delved further into re-educados' understandings of the release process, and as I juxtaposed this against court reports, judges' rulings, and the law itself, a more complicated web of complicity began to emerge. This "collusive net" threaded together re-educados' sense of due diligence as carceral citizens with secular theories of reeducation into a decidedly painful horizon of expectation.[43]

One caseworker, Wilfred, who graduated from Teen Challenge five years ago having been referred there by drug court (and who, incidentally, had undergone civil commitment himself back in the late nineties), oversees all Law 67 cases at La Casita. When I interviewed him, he explained that when writing a court report, it was crucial to "be objective." As he saw it, being objective meant limiting oneself to describing only what one has personally observed "with your own eyes." It meant avoiding interpretation or theorizing about a resident's current circumstances and, most importantly, avoiding making promises about a resident's future. "It's not for us to say when a person is ready," he explained. "We cannot predict what will happen. That would be a fallacy." As Wilfred saw it, to give a recommendation of release was both professionally and morally dubious. This was echoed by other staff members. "We are not supposed to give hard recommendations. We only say if the resident is progressing, adapting well or badly, following or breaking the rules. Practically, we cannot give a total recommendation—*that* person is ready [for release]."

Rather than providing concrete recommendations, caseworkers instead acquired a vocabulary for being objective (describing what they saw) and tended not to bother with diagnostics or prognostics (analyzing what they saw). So, for example, case reports would often note when male residents showed "positive adjustment" or "commitment to improving his personality" or "positive attitude toward change." Conversely, reports would also catalog negative behaviors. These usually consisted of instances where residents "failed to show positive change in interpersonal relationships," "showed a negative attitude," or "demonstrated disrespect toward authority." (Excruciatingly, reports sometimes criticized residents for "making derogatory comments about the program.") As judges ponder their decisions about release then, the information they have to work with pertains to observable modifications in residents' moods, behaviors, and dispositions (in line with the reeducation paradigm) while saying relatively little about residents' capacity to live independently or survive autonomously (in line with patients' rights paradigms).

In response to a question I had posed to a director, Rubén, about whether a resident (a cocaine user) "needed" to be held involuntarily at his institution, he exclaimed: "Look, many of these guys, their families can't deal with them. They've taken out the order because they can't cope. So the best thing we can do to help these men is to give them a new family. If we take them in for just a couple of weeks, only to toss them back out again, *we all know what will happen*." When I stayed silent, leaving the point I thought he might be making to hang in the air, he continued, though now he seemed irritated. "Look, when I first got out of Teen Challenge in the late 1990s, I thought I was ready. I didn't want to be there anymore, and besides, I thought my character was strong." Again, that word, *character*, a word that seemed to creep into the crevices of so many of my conversations with re-educados. Rubén seemed to perk up a bit. "But what happened? *Me deambulé y caí en vicio* [I became homeless and fell into vice]. Why? What I learned at Teen Challenge is that to overcome addiction takes a long time. Rebuilding your character is a life's work. You can't do it in a couple of months."

On rereading this snippet of conversation four years after it took place, I am struck by how clearly it conveys the ethic of carceral citizenship. As Rubén saw it, his professional and moral obligations as a re-educado were clear. As a carceral citizen, it was his duty to rescue other men like him from all the suffering he had endured, by putting his own suffering to work as a prophylactic kind of experiential expertise. As an ex-addict and embodied example of his method, his role was to guide men like him down a path of reeducation that would enable them to overcome their pathological personalities. Rubén's sense of duty also helps us to understand the cruel temporality of waiting that civil commitment's subjects are left to endure. Civil commitment is predicated upon an underlying idea that at a certain point in the future, the confined citizen will overcome their problems. Thus, it does not anticipate its subjects will relapse, in line with prevailing clinical understanding of the chronicity of addiction. We can see this expectation of overcoming at work in the legal principle of maximum benefit, which, in its specification that the confined individual will be released at the point when they have reached the maximum benefit in their treatment, implies a transformational end. Time here appears as a linear horizon with a beginning and an end. At some point, it is implied, the sequalae of suffering will stop. As opposed to the chronicity model of addiction, which, in its purest form, anticipates relapse in a never-ending cycle of recurrence,[44] the picture here is a lot closer to Koselleck's discussion of the early Christians and their long wait for the Second Coming. Way up until the sixteenth century, as Koselleck tells the story, time in Christian Europe was characterized by a constant expectation of an imminent transformation. There was a "constant anticipation of the End of the World on the one hand and the continual deferment of the End on the other."[45] Similarly, the difficult thing about the temporality of waiting that characterizes civil commitment in Puerto Rico is that instead of just being endless, it is the end itself that keeps moving. This is a game of linear time: of constantly anticipating an end point that is always on the horizon but that retreats as one gets closer to it.

· · · · ·

Around the thirteen-month mark, things started to change for Carlos. Camila first got whiff of this when her weekend visit to La Casita was canceled. According to Jorge, Carlos had forfeited his visiting privileges for rule infractions, though he was vague on specifics. I later learned that Carlos had given a cigarette to another resident whose own supply had been confiscated. Since there was a rule against sharing cigarettes at La Casita ("it causes too much conflict"), Carlos lost his visiting privileges and his preferred post (in the kitchen), and his own cigarette supply was confiscated too. When I spoke with him later that week, he'd seemed wrung out and defeated. "*Estoy loco por irme de aquí* [I can't wait to get out of here]," he said.

Camila, too, seemed to be growing inpatient. Perturbed at not being able to visit her son and inundated with increasingly miserable WhatsApp messages from Carlos (all sent from a clandestinely acquired cell phone, a procurement privately of great comfort to Camila), both parents seemed to be coming around to their son's point of view. By January 2018, thirteen months after committing their son to La Casita, they, too, wanted him home. Emboldened by this fresh surge of parental support, when Carlos attended his seventh hearing, his composure was serene. When questioned by the judge, he spoke with the somberness of a minister. "God has put me here," he said, crossing himself solemnly. "And God is showing me the way." When Camila and Juan's turn came around, they recounted the significant improvement they'd seen in Carlos. They were happy with his progress, they said, and ready for him to return home. "We've seen an immense change in him," Juan confirmed. "We are proud of the hard work he's made to overcome his addiction."

Things were looking good, but then came the case report. Handed to the judge by caseworker R, it was the first negative report Carlos had received so far. Three snippets I got down in my notebook were: "disruptive in therapy," "disregard for rules," and (redundantly) "conflict with authority." His fate was sealed. "It saddens me to see your behavior deteriorate so considerably," the judge said. "I cannot release you at this point, when you are so clearly unstable." After enduring a full eight minutes of stern admonishment, Carlos's hearing was brought to an end. It had lasted thirteen minutes. Back in the foyer, caseworker R swiftly disappeared, probably sensing the bad atmosphere. Camila fought back hot tears. "He's getting worse in there, and we can't even bring him home. This is all our fault," she said, before proceeding to round on Juan. Outside, Carlos was chain-smoking his way through bronchitis. His whole composure seemed to be cracking at the seams.

Later that week, Carlos self-discharged from La Casita without authorization, placing himself in contempt of court. One week later, he returned to his parents' home only for his older brother to alert the police and for Carlos to be arrested. Following fifteen days in police custody, Carlos finally came before a civil court. Presented with the ultimatum of more jail time or returning to La Casita, he reenrolled there in February 2018. His release date, he was assured, would depend on his "progress in battling his addiction."

. . . . .

This chapter has followed the experiences of families undergoing involuntary civil commitment procedures. Moving between legal documents, court proceedings, and the viewpoints of civilly committed residents and their families, it has considered the variety of legal mechanisms that enable family members to petition courts to forcibly remand their relatives—specifically those who have not been convicted of crimes—into therapeutic communities. I have shown how a change in civil commitment law in 1993 served to massively widen the valve of justifications for confining people with drug problems, consigning families and their civilly committed relatives to navigate a legal labyrinth they are ill prepared to comprehend. There is some sign of light at the end of this tunnel, however.

As of October 2023, dogged campaigning efforts on the part of my Puerto Rican colleagues at the University of Puerto Rico have finally shed public light on the issue of civil commitment and drawn desperately needed attention from legislators. Through their tireless efforts and those of others working to protect the rights of people who use drugs, section 11 of Law 67 (Law 67's civil commitment clause) has just been overturned in Puerto Rico's House of Representatives and is pending a vote at the Senate.[46] It remains to be seen whether and how this will alter civil commitment at the level of law and practice or how due process will be guarantees for those who find themselves civilly committed under Puerto Rico's other civil commitment law (at time of writing, Law 408, which contains both psychiatric and substance-related civil commitment clauses). What is clear is that the increasing use of civil commitment across the United States and many parts of Latin America points to a broader change in the production of carceral citizenship. Increasingly, simply using drugs serves as legal justification for stripping poor and marginalized citizens of key rights and liberties. In the coming years, it remains to be seen how civil and criminal legislation will reshape the legal dimensions of citizenship across liberal democracies, or how the expanding reach of carceral states into diverse aspects of social life will alter the lived experience of citizenship. Those under court orders and their associated stigmas will undoubtedly devise new ways of living, working, and being citizens. The exact forms of these emerging social memberships and their moral economies are yet to be determined. The account provided is thus one chapter in an ongoing and unfinished story, with the next chapters yet to be written.

An Exile's Belonging

In June 2018, I was back at La Casita after a year back in New York. Like many of my friends and colleagues, I'd spent much of the past year transfixed by the news of Hurricane María and Puerto Rico's unfolding humanitarian crisis. When the category 4 hurricane hit on September 16, 2017, engulfing the island in 155 mph winds, Puerto Rico's infrastructure had collapsed. Thousands endured months without electricity or safe drinking water. In the year that followed, some two hundred thousand Puerto Ricans left the island, many heading to Florida, New York, Massachusetts, and Pennsylvania, with over half of those relocating permanently.[1] Many of the re-educados I knew either went quiet or disappeared entirely from WhatsApp. From New York, I scrolled anxiously through social media looking for clues as to their whereabouts as images of failing federal aid initiatives spread like wildfire.

So it was with some surprise, on my return to La Casita ten months after the hurricane, that I encountered the same well-tended terracotta house along with three familiar faces: Jorge, the director, sporting a new beard; and two former residents, Rocky and Israel. The damage inflicted to the roof by the hurricane had been extreme, but Jorge and the residents had repaired it within just a few weeks, he explained proudly. Since the hurricane, they'd had to learn "to adapt fast," he said, "to become more self-sustainable." "But this comes naturally to us. After all, we are professionals in self-help." Half an acre of land was now devoted to growing crops, mostly casava and pumpkin, and residents had installed a new chicken coop, home to six young hens. Aside from these new fixtures and the unfamiliar faces of the new clientele,

La Casita seemed to have changed surprisingly little. Its grounds of loose soil and crawling vines bled out indistinctly into acres of open grassland. Nestled in the valley, this therapeutic community for the "resocialization of drug addicts" still made for a cloistered, if not exactly monastic, sanctuary.

Later that afternoon, I was able to interview Rocky, who (as I was surprised to learn from Jorge), had only recently returned to La Casita. When I asked Rocky about his time away from the program, he brought all my questions back to the here and now, back to La Casita. I remember finding him hard to read that day; he seemed fervid, a little phrenetic even. Beard freshly shaved and shoulders draped in a black apron while a fellow resident shaved his head, he leaned toward me when making his grandest claims about personal transformation, his efforts to reeducate, and the power of hard work to restore character and morality to himself and to all of Puerto Rico.

I revisited a question I'd posed to re-educados many times before: "What made you come back?" Rocky gazed for a moment at himself in a shard of handheld mirror. He was reinitiating La Casita's eighteen-month reeducation program for the third time in six years, he explained, for the very same reason he was getting up at 6:00 a.m. each morning, praying, and committing himself to a physically taxing regime of hard work. He did all this, he explained, to reeducate himself, to rebuild his character, and eventually—he hoped—to reassume his former position as a certified reeducated ex-addict. As a re-educado, he said, sitting tall in his chair, he could dedicate his life to saving other men just like him. "We addicts," he said, gesturing toward a huddle of residents who were laying out chairs for group therapy, "it is better for us that we stay here and work in reeducation. This way, we can pay back our debt to society by helping others like us. Our place is here. This is where we can be most useful."

· · · · ·

For the men in this book, entrance into a therapeutic community frequently turns out to be more than a temporary stopover or way station on the way toward or back to something different or better. For many of them, life after a court order is profoundly circumscribed by penal stigma. Whether incurred through a criminal conviction, a civil commitment order, or any of the public order codes or policing initiatives that penalize the behaviors associated with unemployment, homelessness, poverty, and drug addiction, the events that trigger this penal stigma turn out to matter surprisingly little in the long term. When it comes to the kind of life that is possible in the aftermath of this carceral embrace, men with widely different prior life circumstances encounter a strikingly similar profile of legal and institutional exclusions. They struggle to find jobs or housing legally, they invite police attention and incur court orders for participating in behaviors that are ordinary (and perfectly legal) for many other citizens, they lose key state entitlements and access to social welfare protections, and they are denied key opportunities for achieving liberal markers of male adulthood.

Yet it is no longer tenable to comprehend the changes that citizenship has undergone since the advent of the carceral turn since the late twentieth century solely through its exclusionary dimensions. As it turns out, there are many ways to make a living and many ways to find belonging along the extensive channels of the devolving carceral apparatus: the therapeutic communities, addiction ministries, gang-prevention initiatives, and Christian mutual-aid groups that absorb large swaths of Latin America's criminalized and marginalized populations. Along this devolving carceral apparatus that reorganizes confinement, labor, and self-help, new livelihoods, new moral economies, and new modes of citizenship are being brought into being.

As I have tried to show, carceral citizenship has arisen in response to a scheme of mid- to late twentieth-century exclusionary developments. In Puerto Rico's case, these include recurring crises of colonially administered capitalist development, the mass criminalization of young men, overflowing prisons, the criminalization of drug use, and the enduring stigma that clings to individuals long after their time served. On the heels of postindustrial decline and Puerto Rico's subsequent prison boom, these are the material structures from which carceral citizenship is wrought: a project that is both one of "self-making" and "being-made."[2] Far richer and more socially encompassing than a just a legal status bestowed whenever a court issues a criminal record, carceral citizenship is also a social and economic membership woven by criminalized and marginalized people themselves from the intersecting threads of their exclusion. Through self-help, formerly incarcerated Puerto Ricans who are in one sense the targets and victims of the carceral turn have carved from their exile a publicly recognized and legally formalized carceral livelihood. By seizing upon the opportunities that these structural dislocations present, people who are colonized, racialized, criminalized, and stigmatized have reworked an expulsion into a sense of belonging.

In the therapeutic communities I have described, these carceral citizenship projects and their associated livelihoods are providing their members with undeniable and desperately needed benefits. This arrangement offers shelter, sustenance, various degrees of agency, and protection from more oppressive forms of confinement (the most terrible and isolating of which is imprisonment). It also holds a system of internally recognized qualifications, the possibility for a career path, of sorts, and, in some cases, publicity and media recognition. Then there is the brotherly sense of community, companionship, and even family that therapeutic communities can nurture. For penally stigmatized men gazing down the barrel of Puerto Rico's bankrupt economy, armed with little in the way of educational capital and about to encounter some of the harshest colonial austerity policies seen in generations, these are hardly trivial benefits. So, as I have argued, carceral citizenship should not be dismissed out of hand as just more exploitation of a powerless, docile people.

Yet what the re-educados who embrace this carceral livelihood will probably never obtain is the kind of life that is routinely idealized—indeed *promised*—by its contemporary reeducation, rehabilitation, and reentry projects—namely, a "return to society" as an unmarked "full" citizen unencumbered by penal stigma with a fair and equal shot at obtaining employment, housing, and recognition outside of this circumscribed carceral circuit.

Instead, as Rocky had learned over the course of two very difficult months prior to our last interview, his previously earned status as a *re-educado ex-adicto* counted for very little on the outside. Though "reeducated," he remained unappealing to employers by virtue of his felony record, which also rendered him ineligible for public housing. Jobless, homeless, and hungry, Rocky's last attempt at reentry had been a flop. Eventually, he had resorted to sleeping in parking lots and was found begging at traffic lights and rearrested. Rocky estimates that this was his thirteenth arrest. This time, he was detained in jail not for breaking any criminal law but for violating a public order code prohibiting vagrancy. Unable to provide proof of stable address, as required by the municipal court, Rocky was ordered to readmit himself to La Casita just two months after his failed departure. At the point of his reenrollment, Rocky did not resume his former position as a reeducated ex-addict and peer counselor, with all the perks, status, and responsibilities he had so laboriously accrued over the last five years. Instead, he rejoined La Casita's reeducation scheme at the bottom of the pyramid. His formerly reeducated status—so painstakingly achieved—was disregarded entirely.

Herein lies one of carceral citizenship's fundamental flaws. Though it can offer material security along with socially meaningful self-worth, recognized achievements, and a sense of belonging—undeniably valuable affordances—it confers a membership that is partial, nontransferable, and perpetually vulnerable to loss. This hard-won citizenship can be stripped away at any time, often due to the very incidents that initiate this cycle: a criminal charge, a court order, substance use, or rough sleeping.

What are we to make of carceral citizenship's signature shortcoming? When seen through the lens of nearly three centuries of US citizenship, the invention of a partial and forfeitable membership is not exactly a historical aberration. For most of the nation's history, US citizenship has systematically denied options for social and political participation to whole swaths of the population based explicitly on race, ethnicity, or gender. Through racial slavery, Jim Crow laws coercing African Americans to work on the plantations, voting restrictions denying women equal suffrage with men, laws requiring Mexican American and Chinese American children to attend segregated schools, or national quota systems preventing Asians and southern Europeans from applying for US citizenship explicitly because of their race or ethnicity, US citizenship has always apportioned rights and benefits to some while systematically denying them to others.[3] Nor has linear progress been the pattern. Many hard-earned rights won at one moment in history have turned out to be losable and temporary. As early as the 1820s, and in states as far south as North Carolina, many African Americans were acknowledged to be US citizens and exercised the right to vote for several decades, only to forfeit their citizenship and franchise in 1857, when the Supreme Court ruled that African Americans were not legally US citizens after all.[4] Later, in the 1870s, hundreds of thousands of African Americans regained citizenship and franchise, only to be divested of the vote again in 1905, not regaining it until the Voting Rights Act of 1965. And as we now know, 4.6 million US citizens have now forfeited this right again, this time in the face of laws barring felons from voting. Such forfeitures repeat themselves again and again in the history of US citizenship.

Even now, six decades after the civil rights movement in the United States, 2 million people are incarcerated in prisons, local jails, immigration detention facilities, civil commitment centers, and psychiatric hospitals across the United States.[5] Of this 2 million currently incarcerated, a disproportionate 38 percent are Black, who represent just 12 percent of the US population. An additional 4.7 million US residents are living under some form of correctional supervision in their communities where they are subject to wide-ranging court-imposed restrictions and conditions on how, where, and with whom they may live. Seventy-nine million US residents— nearly one-quarter of the country's population—live in the community with a criminal record, including 19 million living with a felony conviction, and thus navigate the continued stigma of criminality.[6] Then, of course, there are the 3.5 million US citizens living in colonial territories denied various rights and liberties accorded to mainlanders. For these colonial US citizens, progressions and regressions are part of citizenship's history too. Having gained circumscribed forms of autonomy in the 1950s, Puerto Ricans forfeited many of these in 2016, during the island's debt crisis, when the US president appointed a Fiscal Control Board to override all local government decisions that conflicted with its fiscal aims.[7]

To different degrees then, huge swaths of the US population currently experience a diminished form of citizenship. This fundamentally stratified picture of US citizenship points to the need to reassess how we think about (and critique) contemporary rehabilitation efforts. If citizenship is fundamentally stratified to begin with, to what kind of membership can rehabilitation projects realistically aspire? If not to a full or uncompromised citizenship, then to what?

I have posited carceral citizenship—a contradictory mode of belonging grounded in a reconfiguration of labor, confinement, and self-help—as one variety of stratified citizenship that is thriving in Puerto Rico today in a context of mass criminalization, postimprisonment surveillance, and wage labor scarcities. For Puerto Rico's carceral citizens, reeducation is functioning not as rehabilitation, as is commonly imagined in liberal societies: as a reparative journey from a broken criminalized status that blossoms into an unmarked, employed, tax-paying citizenship. Whether uttered as a therapeutic script, a quiet prayer, or a rallying cry to join a fight against drugs, reeducation now functions as a means through which the penalized appropriate their shared penal stigma and redeploy it—through metaphors of redemption and unpaid debt—as the basis for an alternative social membership.

Like many citizens who volunteer in neoliberal societies today, carceral citizens share a willingness to work for free. But unlike their more privileged counterparts who, animated by the spirit of the gift, demonstrate their worth as citizens by working for free in the public sphere unmarked by the stigma of criminality, carceral citizens work for free under the moral bondage of penance and in circumstances of expulsion. Unable to prepare its members to return as equal-footed or full members of a polis, as terms like *rehabilitation* and *reentry* imply, carceral citizenship offers instead a cunning compromise. In exchange for shelter, community, and protection from incarceration, carceral citizenship invites penalized and stigmatized men to perform unpaid work in devolved outposts of the carceral state. The men who seize this option come to execute their work gladly and often very passionately, in part because it seems their last realistic option for social, economic, and civic participation. Carceral citizenship remains, in the last instance, an exile's membership: a belonging, yes, but an exile all the same.

· ACKNOWLEDGMENTS ·

A book that explores the invention of carceral livelihoods must begin by acknowledging the formerly incarcerated people who opened up their lives to me. My heartfelt gratitude extends to them for patiently helping me to try to understand their work. For the gift of time, I am especially grateful to the organizations I have given the pseudonyms La Casita, Comunidad-Luz, Comunidad de Elevación del Espíritu Humano, and Mesón de Dios and to those whom I have called Rocky, Héctor, Salvador, Rubén, Ernesto, Eric Jr., Eric Sr., Carlos, and Camila.

Staff members of several organizations active in the harm reduction, drug treatment, and outreach spaces allowed me to observe their work and ask innumerable questions. These include the Administration of Mental Health and Anti-Addiction Services, Intercambios Puerto Rico, Iniciativa Comunitaria, and Solo Por Hoy. I also thank staff at La Colección Puertorriqueña and El Centro Médico at the University of Puerto Rico for countless acts of assistance over the years. For their indispensable input both before and during my fieldwork, I extend my gratitude to Luis Ramón, Héctor Colón, Rafael Torruella, and Salvador Santiago. Special thanks are reserved for Carmen Albizu-García and Oscar Miranda Miller, for working tirelessly with me over the years and for galvanizing the House to overturn Law 67. Let us hope its annulment finally passes through the Senate. Special thanks also to Efrén Ramírez, who opened his personal archive to me and who sadly passed away before this project was completed. Thanks to Pablo Delano, for seeing value in the project and for sharing the wonderful images of Jack

Delano included in the book; thanks too to *El Mundo*, *El Vocero*, and *Primera Hora* for their images, also included. And Puerto Rico friends: thank you to José Colón, Edith López, Melissa Marzán, Miguel Marzán, Gabriela Llorens, Eileen Llorens, Claire Kleinman, Ana Negrón, Belinda Negrón, Joaquín Cotler, and Jalen Carreras, whose company has grounded me and sustained me over the years.

Several institutions threw their weight behind this project, which took shape during my years at Columbia University's Department of Sociomedical Sciences. I am immensely grateful to Jennifer Hirsch, who has been a guru, friend, and icon in my life. My only criticism is that you set the advisor bar unrealistically high, so I am doomed to disappoint myself and others. I further extend my gratitude to Kim Hopper for tearing apart my prose, for changing my whole brain, and for sharing many memorable plates of pasta. Through New York's Inter-University Doctoral Consortium, I was fortunate to learn from Richard Parker, Lesley Sharp, Catherine Fennel, Zoe Wool, and Rayna Rapp. I will never forget your teaching. Many thanks to Helena Hansen: you have funneled countless opportunities my way and your ideas and suggestions are all over this book. Lisa Rosen-Metsch, Mark Padilla, Jim Baumohl, Robert Fairbanks, and David Deitch all went above and beyond any call of duty to help me navigate this project's logistical and intellectual hurdles. Amaya Perez-Brumer and Heather Wurtz, you talked me through some of the earliest iterations of my dissertation, edited the grant proposals that facilitated my doctoral research, and welcomed me back after years of research. Philippe Bourgois, I would never have considered a career in anthropology if I had not encountered *Selling Crack in El Barrio* at a young and impressionable age; thank you for unknowingly steering me towards a PhD.

I also want to express my gratitude to everyone who participated in the Latin American Studies Association roundtable Carceral Citizenship in 2021 and to everyone who contributed to the special issue on Carceral Citizenship, especially to my co-organizer Julienne Weegles. Our collaborative writing endeavors with Sacha Darke, Chris Garcés, Hollis Moore, David Skarbek, Kristen Drybread, Chloé Constant, Olga Espinoza, Jean Daudelin, Ramiro Gual, Máximo Sozzo, and José Luiz Ratton have greatly shaped my thinking. To Kevin O'Neill in particular, I am deeply grateful that you supported this project from the beginning. Your encouragement over the years has meant the world to me. Thank you to Anthony Fontes, for reading nearly every piece of writing I've been working on for the last four years and for spending many entertaining hours with me on Zoom. One day we will meet in real life! Thank you to Alberto Ortiz Díaz, whose groundbreaking history of Oso

Blanco prison has greatly shaped this book and who has shown nothing but generosity and warmth over the course of many phone calls and emails.

Finishing a piece of writing, needless to say, is a hustle. I am grateful to the institutions that took a gamble on funding this research, including the US National Science Foundation, the US Social Science Research Council, the Biosocial Society, and the Institute of Latin American Studies at Columbia University.

Dear New York friends, Shimrit, Eva, Hannah, Cami, Anna, Chris, Nader, Saphe, Gabriel, Isaac, Janis, Meril, and Jason, you gave me a sense of belonging and you will forever be my New York. Eva Schreiner, you've held my hand through multiple personal crises and, along with Anna Reumert, you've given me incisive criticism on my work with the perfect amount of warmth. Hannah Scott Deuchar, you've accompanied me through every chapter of my adult life so far and grounded me since I was nineteen years old. I hope there are many more chapters to come.

I moved back to England and found it familiar and strange. I am lucky to have a large, loving, high-octane family supplying me with constant care, coffee, carbs, strong opinions, and periodic free accommodation. Thank you to my parents, siblings, nephews, aunts, uncles, cousins, old friends, and new ones too for carrying me through an eventful readjustment. Thank you to Kevin for poring over census data with me. Thank you to Chris and Magda for coming to my rescue in Manchester during the COVID-19 pandemic and for cooking for me and running with me when I was writing this book. Thank you to Nyasha for befriending me fifteen years ago and doing all the work of making new friends for me ever since. Thank you Fowz for always being in my corner. I'll always be in yours.

I feel tremendously lucky to have undertaken a Presidential Fellowship in medical anthropology at the University of Manchester: I could not have asked for a more supportive and nurturing department for completing this book project. I am indebted to Penny Harvey, Soumhya Venkatesan, Başak Saraç-Lesavre, Gillian Evans, Jolynna Sinanan, Connie Smith, Pete Wade, Karen Sykes, Chika Watanabe, Sebastien Bachelet, and Andrew Irving, all of whom read chapter drafts and offered collegial support throughout my time at Manchester. Tony Simpson's provocative inquiries at Manchester's Departmental Seminar spurred crucial reflections that led me to carceral citizenship. Thank you to Kerry Pimblott and to everyone at the Race, Roots & Resistance Collective for offering profound insights. Thank you to every student in my Racial Capitalism class for thinking with me. I benefited from the terrific research assistance of undergraduates, including Jen Viken, Charlotte Antilogus, Samatha Murphy, and Skyla Baily. The four years I spent at Manchester also involved many months of strike action over working conditions and pay, to which the University of Manchester's administration responded by imposing cruel and unusual deductions of 50 percent on its staff members for many months at a time. I worry for my students' futures, but I thank them and the University and College Union for showing me what solidarity looks like. Thank you Soumhya Venkatesan in particular for balancing unionizing and departmental leadership so gracefully and for sticking your neck out for me on several occasions.

I feel tremendously grateful to have joined the Department of Anthropology at University College London as I brought this project to a close. I could not ask for a better place to reimagine the possibilities of anthropological work, and I am grateful for colleagues who take risks with their anthropological practice.

Portions of chapter 3 appeared in earlier form in Caroline Mary Parker, "Keeping Busy When There's Nothing to Do: Labor, Therapy, and Boredom in a Puerto Rican Addiction Shelter," *American Ethnologist* 48, no. 3 (2021): 301–13.

· NOTES ·

INTRODUCTION

1. In Puerto Rican Spanish, there is one term, *auto-ayuda-mutua*, encompassing both self-help and mutual aid, a distinction sometimes made but inconsistently enforced in the English-language addiction literature. While both terms refer to the phenomena where nonspecialists who share a health or social problem come together to define or address that problem together, mutual aid is sometimes distinguished from self-help because it implies reciprocity, whereas self-help could involve people who themselves have recovered and thus participate primarily as helpers rather than sufferers. Therapeutic communities in Puerto Rico do not to make such a distinction, so in this book I use both terms interchangeably.

2. Writing of Guatemala, Kevin O'Neill uses the term "soft security" to describe the dispersed network of churches, overseas development initiatives, and drug rehabilitation clinics that provide an alternative to "hard security" (prisons and police) for managing the lives of youth susceptible to gang membership. Kevin Lewis O'Neill, *Secure the Soul* (University of California Press, 2015).

3. Many sociologists, criminologists, and carceral geographers have been critical to my thinking, in particular Ruth Wilson Gilmore, *Golden Gulag: Prisons, Surplus, Crisis, and Opposition in Globalizing California* (University of California Press, 2007); Saskia Sassen, *Expulsion* (Harvard University Press, 2014); Loïc Wacquant, *Punishing the Poor: The Neoliberal Government of Social Insecurity* (Duke University Press, 2009); Zygmunt Bauman, *Wasted Lives: Modernity and Its Outcasts* (John Wiley & Sons, 2013).

4. Sassen, *Expulsions*, 222.

5. As the La Casita handbook bluntly put it.

6. Most evaluations of therapeutic communities for drug addiction have been conducted on the US mainland. A systematic review noted the inconsistent results and poor quality of most studies, leading the authors to exclude most of their sample and to conclude that there is "little evidence" that therapeutic communities "offer significant benefits" for the treatment of substance use disorder relative to other modes of residential treatment. See Lesley A. Smith, Simon Gates, and David Foxcroft, "Therapeutic Communities for Substance Related Disorder," *Cochrane Database of Systematic Reviews* (2006).

7. In this spirit, Kerwin Kaye conceives therapeutic communities as racialized sorting mechanisms of poverty management that intensify the racist logic of the United States' war on drugs. See Kerwin Kaye, *Enforcing Freedom: Drug Courts, Therapeutic Communities, and the Intimacies of the State* (Columbia University Press, 2019). This North American framing, useful as it is for capturing the racial dynamics of social control on the mainland, works less well for Puerto Rico or for the rest of Latin America, where race is conceived in incredibly diverse ways. Thus, this book offers a distinctly Puerto Rican reading of therapeutic communities. By considering the racial dynamics of incarceration in Puerto Rico within the context of the island's movement from one imperial regime to another (as detailed in chapter 2), it joins ongoing efforts to provincialize and decolonize carceral studies. See Marisol LeBrón, "Puerto Rico and the Colonial Circuits of Policing: How Reconsidering the History of Policing in Puerto Rico Complicates Our Understandings of the Island's Colonial Relationship with the United States," *NACLA Report on the Americas* 49, no. 3 (2017): 328–34.

8. Katherine Beckett and Naomi Murakawa, "Mapping the Shadow Carceral State: Toward an Institutionally Capacious Approach to Punishment," *Theoretical Criminology* 16, no. 2 (2012): 221–44.

9. Michel Foucault, *Discipline and Punish: The Birth of the Prison* (Vintage, 1977).

10. Clare Anderson, *A Global History of Convicts and Penal Colonies* (Bloomsbury, 2018).

11. Foucault, *Discipline and Punish*, 296.

12. The issue of whether Puerto Rico amounts to a nation has been approached in various ways. Channeling Benedict Anderson, Lorrin Thomas considers Puerto Rico to be a nation in the sense of an "imagined political community." Similarly, Jorge Duany considers Puerto Rico to be a "stateless nation," a concept he uses to capture Puerto Rico's strong sense of collective ethnonational identity but limited political sovereignty. Other constructs aimed at capturing Puerto Rico's ambiguous hybrid of cultural nationalism and ongoing coloniality include Ramón Grosfoguel's "modern colony" and Efren Rivera Ramos's "partial democracy." See Benedict Anderson, *Imagined Communities* (Verso 1991); Lorrin Thomas, *Puerto Rican Citizen* (University of Chicago Press, 2010); Jorge Duany, *The Puerto Rican Nation on the Move: Identities on the Island and in the United States* (University of North Carolina Press, 2003); Ramón Grosfoguel, *Colonial Subjects: Puerto Ricans in a Global Perspective* (University of California Press, 2003); Efren Rivera Ramos, *The Legal Construction of Identity: The Judicial and Social Legacy of American Colonialism in Puerto Rico* (Washington, DC: American Psychological Association, 2001).

13. Jacqueline Font-Guzmán, *Experiencing Puerto Rican Citizenship and Cultural Nationalism* (Springer, 2016).

14. Contemporary studies of stratifications of citizenship in places as varied as the US mainland, Puerto Rico, Brazil, and China have teased apart how various social stratifications that are expressly *not* the basis of national membership—for example, differences of race, ethnicity, religion, language, literacy, education, property ownership, occupation, gender, and sexuality—operate to distribute differential treatment to different categories of citizens in various countries. See Eduardo Bonilla-Silva and Sarah Mayorga, "On (Not) Belonging: Why Citizenship Does Not Remedy Racial Inequality," in *State of White Supremacy* (Stanford University Press, 2020), 77–90; James Holston, *Insurgent Citizenship: Disjunctions of Democracy and Modernity in Brazil* (Princeton University Press, 2021); Thomas, *Puerto Rican Citizen*; Ulla Dalum Berg and Robyn Magalit Rodriguez, "Transnational Citizenship across the Americas," *Identities* 20, no. 6 (2013): 649–64; Nicholas De Genova and Ana Yolanda Ramos-Zayas, *Latino Crossings: Mexicans, Puerto Ricans, and the Politics of Race and Citizenship* (Routledge, 2004); Aihwa Ong, "Mutations in Citizenship," *Theory, Culture, and Society* 23, no. 2–3 (2006): 499–505.

15. These were the remarks of Representative Thomas Spight of Mississippi, cited in José A. Cabranes, *Citizenship and the American Empire: Notes on the Legislative History of the United States Citizenship of Puerto Ricans* (Yale University Press, 1979), 424.

16. Cabranes, "Citizenship," 424–81.

17. Sam Erman, *Almost Citizens: Puerto Rico, the U.S. Constitution, and Empire* (Cambridge: Cambridge University Press, 2018).

18. Erman, *Almost Citizens*.

19. The US mainland literature describes the wide-ranging and often intrusive court restrictions placed on formerly incarcerated people. These restrictions include laws that prevent formerly incarcerated people from accessing state services and state subsidies, along with court-mandated and strict legal limitations on where, with whom, and how formerly incarcerated people may live: from mandatory attendance at drug and alcohol services to regular check-ins with parole officers. See Amy E. Lerman and Vesla M. Weaver, *Arresting Citizenship: The Democratic Consequences of American Crime Control* (University of Chicago Press, 2014); Jeff Manza and Christopher Uggen, *Locked Out: Felon Disenfranchisement and American Democracy* (Oxford University Press, 2008); Reuben Jonathan Miller and Forrest Stuart, "Carceral Citizenship: Race, Rights, and Responsibility in the Age of Mass Supervision," *Theoretical Criminology* 21, no. 4 (2017): 532–48; Calvin John Smiley, *Purgatory Citizenship: Reentry, Race, and Abolition* (University of California Press, 2023).

20. Smiley, *Purgatory Citizenship*.

21. Christopher Uggen, Jeff Manza, and Angela Behrens, "'Less Than the Average Citizen': Stigma, Role Transition and the Civic Reintegration of Convicted Felons," in *After Crime and Punishment*, ed. Shadd Maruna and Russ Immarigeon (Willan, 2013), 279–311.

22. The translation of *Estado Libre Asociado* as "Commonwealth" was highly misleading. Globally, a "commonwealth" typically refers to a former colony turned

independent and sovereign state that has retained some kind of political association with the former colonial power. In Puerto Rico's case, the island remained an incorporated territory and colony of the United States, subject to the broad powers of Congress to govern territories under the US Constitution's Territory Clause.

23. Miller and Stuart, "Carceral Citizenship."

24. As Aihwa Ong famously said, citizenship is a "process of self-making and being-made." Aiwha Ong, "Cultural Citizenship as Subject-Making: Immigrants Negotiate Racial and Cultural Boundaries in the United States," *Current Anthropology* 37, no. 5 (1996): 737.

25. Shaylih Muehlmann, *When I Wear My Alligator Boots: Narco-Culture in the US Mexico Borderlands* (University of California Press, 2013); Kathleen M. Millar, *Reclaiming the Discarded: Life and Labor on Rio's Garbage Dump* (Duke University Press, 2018); Anthony W. Fontes, *Mortal Doubt: Transnational Gangs and Social Order in Guatemala City* (University of California Press, 2018); Angela Garcia, *The Pastoral Clinic: Addiction and Dispossession along the Rio Grande* (University of California Press, 2010).

26. In fact, when it comes to documenting work performed under the auspices of the carceral state today—whether unpaid kitchen or gardening work performed by prisoners or waged work performed in the "free" market economy by probationers and parolees as part of court requirements—scholars have roundly tended to ignore, minimize, or dismiss the potential of these activities to bring anything positive to those performing it. See Erin Hatton, *Coerced: Work under Threat of Punishment* (University of California Press, 2020); Noah D. Zatz, "Get to Work or Go to Jail: State Violence and the Racialized Production of Precarious Work," *Law and Social Inquiry* 45, no. 2 (2020): 304–38.

27. In the first two decades of the twenty-first century, a time when aggregate incarceration rates in Europe and the United States fell by 21 percent and 18 percent, respectively, incarceration rates in South American and Central American countries grew on average by 145 percent and 80 percent. See Roy Walmsley, "World Prison Population, 11th Edition," Institute for Criminal Policy Research, 2016, https://www.prisonstudies.org/sites/default/files/resources/downloads/world_prison_population_list_11th_edition_0.pdf.

28. Fernando Avila, "'El Preso-Emprendedor': Responsabilización y Co-Gobierno En La Prisión de Punta de Rieles En Uruguay," *Delito y Sociedad: Revista de Ciencias Sociales*, no. 53 (2022): 98–122; Sacha Darke et al., *Carceral Communities in Latin America: Troubling Prison Worlds in the 21st Century* (Palgrave Macmillan, 2021); Daniel M. Goldstein, "Flexible Justice: Neoliberal Violence and 'Self-Help' Security in Bolivia," *Critique of Anthropology* 25, no. 4 (2005): 389–411; Helena Hansen, *Addicted to Christ: Remaking Men in Puerto Rican Pentecostal Drug Ministries* (University of California Press, 2018).

29. Chris Garces, "Prisons of Charity: Christian Exceptionality and Decarceration in Ecuador's Penal State," in *Governing Gifts: Faith, Charity, and the Security State*, ed. Erica Caple James (University of New Mexico, 2019), 79–97).

30. Spanish-era censuses show that Puerto Rico was 48 percent white and 52 percent nonwhite in 1802. By 1897, it was 64.3 percent white and 35.7 percent nonwhite.

See Jorge Duany, "Neither White nor Black: The Representation of Racial Identity among Puerto Ricans on the Island and in the U.S. Mainland," in *Neither Enemies nor Friends: Latinos, Blacks, Afro-Latinos*, ed. Anani Dzidzienyo and Suzanne Oboler (Palgrave Macmillan, 2005), 173–88.

31. According to recent estimates by Slave Voyages, Puerto Rico received approximately 43,000 enslaved Africans during the Spanish colonial period (1493–1873). But at any given time, Puerto Rico's enslaved population was much smaller than its non-enslaved Black population. Between 1779 and 1830, enslaved Africans accounted for 10–15 percent of Puerto Rico's total population. Between 1773 and 1840, free people of color accounted for between 47.7 percent and 54.1 percent of Puerto Rico's total population. In Barbados during the same era, in contrast, free people of color accounted for just 2.8 percent to 25.5 percent, and in Cuba between 25.5 percent and 27.3 percent of national population. See Jay Kinsbruner, *Not of Pure Blood: The Free People of Color and Racial Prejudice in Nineteenth-Century Puerto Rico* (Duke University Press, 1996). Slave Voyages Database, accessed October 12, 2023, https://www.slavevoyages.org/.

32. Kinsbruner, *Not of Pure Blood*, 42.

33. Kelvin A. Santiago-Valles, "Forcing Them to Work and Punishing Whoever Resisted: Servile Labor and Penal Servitude under Colonialism in Nineteenth-Century Puerto Rico" *Birth of the Penitentiary in Latin America* (University of Texas Press, 1996): 123–68.

34. With successfully longer penalties for peasants who repeatedly failed to present their *libreta*. See Labor Gómez Acevedo, *Organización y reglamentación del trabajo en el Puerto Rico del siglo 19 (proprietarios y jornaleros)* (Instituto de Cultura Puertorriqueña, 1970).

35. Gómez Acevedo, *Organización y reglamentación*.

36. Santiago-Valles, "Forcing Them to Work."

37. Isar P. Godreau, *Scripts of Blackness: Race, Cultural Nationalism, and US Colonialism in Puerto Rico* (University of Illinois Press, 2015).

38. Frank Moya Pons, "Dominican National Identity: A Historical Perspective," *Punto 7 Review: A Journal of Marginal Discourse* 3, no. 1 (1996): 14–25; Ginetta E. B. Candelario, *Black behind the Ears: Dominican Racial Identity from Museums to Beauty Shops* (Duke University Press, 2007).

39. Provided, that is, that the individual could prove at least four generations of "free and legitimate descent." See Kinsbruner, *Not of Pure Blood*, 22.

40. It is clear that in nineteenth-century Puerto Rico, parents of mulatto children sometimes went as far as petitioning the courts to prevent their offspring from marrying someone of a darker complexion. It is also clear that parents in mixed unions (one white, one *pardo*) generally opted to list their children as white in their birth certificates. See Kinsbruner, 90–101; Duany, *Nation on the Move*.

41. Sidney Mintz's observation in the 1950s that "an individual's 'color' may 'vary' in accord with changes in his socioeconomic status" finds fresh support in contemporary studies of racial geography. Studies show that many Puerto Ricans who identify as white in Puerto Rico come to be culturally coded as Black upon emigrating to the US

mainland. On the island itself, anthropologists have explored how certain spaces—low-income neighborhoods and heavily policed public housing projects—become culturally coded as Black and how this cultural coding, in turn, becomes intertwined with biopolitical valuations of human life, including understandings of who is worthy of police protection and who is deserving of police punishment. See Sidney Wilfred Mintz, "Cañamelar: The Contemporary Culture of a Rural Puerto Rican Proletariat," in *The People of Puerto Rico*, ed. Julian H. Steward et al. (University of Illinois Press, 1956); Zaire Zenit Dinzey-Flores, *Locked In, Locked Out: Gated Communities in a Puerto Rican City* (University of Pennsylvania Press, 2013); Marisol LeBrón, *Policing Life and Death: Race, Violence, and Resistance in Puerto Rico* (Berkeley: University of California Press, 2019); Petra R. Rivera-Rideau, "From Carolina to Loíza: Race, Place and Puerto Rican Racial Democracy" *Identities* 20, no. 5 (2013): 616–32; Mark Q. Sawyer and Tianna S. Paschel, "We Didn't Cross the Color Line, the Color Line Crossed Us": Blackness and Immigration in the Dominican Republic, Puerto Rico, and the United States," *Du Bois Review: Social Science Research on Race* 4, no. 2 (2007): 303–15.

42. Duany, "Neither White nor Black."

43. Lanny Thompson, *Imperial Archipelago: Representation and Rule in the Insular Territories under US Dominion after 1898* (University of Hawaii Press, 2010), 99.

44. Thompson, *Imperial Archipelago*, 99–100.

45. Careful to distinguish between "law-abiding" and "industrious" Puerto Ricans on the one hand, who were said to be "of Spanish origin" and, non-incidentally, "of high intelligence and culture," with the "barbarous" and "uncivilized" Pacific Islanders on the other, even the anti-imperialists in favor of bestowing US citizenship on Puerto Ricans were adamant that this privilege was not to be extended to "the alien races." The "alien races" included Filipinos, for example, who were derided by US congressmen as "head hunters" and "weaklings." Cabranes, "Citizenship," 431–436.

46. Duany, "Neither White nor Black."

47. Duany, 179.

48. Duany, 179.

49. Godreau, *Scripts of Blackness*.

50. The "race question" had been reintroduced to the national census in 2000, this time by the pro-statehood party as part of an effort to achieve "statistical equivalence" with the US mainland. See Isar P. Godreau, Hilda Lloréns, and Carlos Vargas-Ramos, "Colonial Incongruence at Work: Employing US Census Racial Categories in Puerto Rico," *Anthropology News* 51, no. 5 (2010): 11–12.

51. Damayra Figueroa-Lazu and Yarimar Bonilla, "Puerto Rico's 2020 Race/Ethnicity Decennial Analysis," CentroPR, October 13, 2021, https://centropr .hunter.cuny.edu/reports/puerto-ricos-2020-decennial-analysis-datasheet-series/.

52. Between 2000 and 2020, Puerto Rico's national census found that the proportion of the population identifying as "Two or More" races rose from 4.2 percent to 10.2 percent and the proportion identifying as "Some Other Race" rose from 6.8 percent to 8.4 percent. See US Census Bureau, "Puerto Rico Population Declined 11.8 Percent from 2010 to 2020" Census.Gov, accessed July 19, 2024, https://www.census .gov/library/stories/state-by-state/puerto-rico-population-change-between-census -decade.html. The reasons for the rise in Black identification in 2010 (from 8 percent in 2000 to 12.4 percent in 2010) are unclear, but studies of *concientización*

(awareness raising) suggest that Afro–Puerto Rican affirmation strategies are kindling Black pride and providing a significant counter current to century-long ideologies of *blanqueamiento*. It remains to be seen how and whether Afro–Puerto Rican affirmation strategies could also be behind the uptick in 2020 in Puerto Ricans identifying as "Two or more races" or "some other race." Hilda Lloréns, "Beyond Blanqueamiento: Black Affirmation in Contemporary Puerto Rico," *Latin American and Caribbean Ethnic Studies* 13, no. 2 (2018): 157–78.

53. Re-educados' avoidance of explicit racial terminology echoes with studies of race talk in Puerto Rico. See Isar P. Godreau "Slippery Semantics: Race Talk and Everyday Uses of Racial Terminology in Puerto Rico," *Centro Journal* 20, no. 2 (2008): 5–33.

54. My own impressions of the relative silence surrounding race in Puerto Rico find multiple precedents in the ethnographic record. In 1990, to take one example, the Puerto Rican anthropologist Jorge Duany and his team of fieldworkers were tasked with investigating why so few people in a poor neighborhood in Santurce had completed the national census that year. On posing what they presumed to be an innocuous, ice-breaker question—What race do you consider yourself to belong to?—Duany's researchers stumbled head on into a powerful cultural injunction against talking explicitly about race. With informants' responses ranging from "embarrassment and amazement" to "ambivalence and silence," Duany's fieldworkers were taken aback that so many informants simply "shrugged their shoulders and pointed to their arms as if skin color were so obvious that it did not need to be verbalized," and as if they, the researchers, were somehow Martians (and morally dubious Martians, at that) for asking the question. See Duany, "Neither White nor Black, 2."

55. These data come from the American and Puerto Rican Community Survey for 2020, which is a yearly survey conducted on random 1 percent samples of the population (available at https://data.census.gov). When the racial categories used in the census are taken as stable demographic facts, a *highly questionable* move in Puerto Rico because racial identification fluctuates so dramatically over time, census data from 2020 suggest that Puerto Ricans who identify as "Black Alone" are 1.47 times more likely to be incarcerated than Puerto Ricans who identify as "White Alone." The picture gets more complicated when one compares Puerto Ricans who identify as racially mixed: as either "Two or More Races" or "Some Other Race." For racially mixed Puerto Ricans, the reverse pattern seems to be true. Puerto Ricans who identify as "White alone" are 13 times more likely to be incarcerated than those who identify as "Two or More Races," and 7 times more likely to be incarcerated compared to those who identify as "Some Other Race." Some may interpret this as evidence for a kind of "mixed race advantage." Another hypothesis (yet to be tested) is that the surprisingly low incarceration rate of racially mixed Puerto Ricans is itself an artefact of incarceration changing how Puerto Ricans identify racially. By this second hypothesis, the experience of incarceration could be nudging Puerto Ricans into choosing a side (Black or white) at the expense of choosing an intermediary category. Were this to be the case, it would help to explain why some 75 percent of Puerto Rico's general population identified as racially mixed (either "Two or More Races" or "Some Other Race") in 2020, but just 22 percent of the prison population responded this way. Whatever the explanation, this befuddling quantitative portrait highlights the limitations of applying a racial disparities lens to Puerto Rico, where race is an ambiguous and unstable concept.

56. Isar, "Colonial Incongruence at Work."

57. This figure comes from the Puerto Rican Community Survey for 2020. Available at https://data.census.gov/.

58. Local researchers skilled enough to probe through the silencing of race in Puerto Rico have identified various discursive strategies that erase Blackness from Puerto Rican identity. These include "maneuvers of silencing," whereby people avoid using the term *negro* (Black) altogether, instead using euphemisms and comparisons, and "fugitive Blackness," where Blackness is assumed to lie in Haiti, the Dominican Republic, the past, or on the US mainland but never in contemporary Puerto Rico. For many anthropologists and cultural theorists writing in Puerto Rico, the route into seeing Blackness is not primarily through interlocuters' understandings of their own racial identity but through attuning to the semantic erasure of Blackness. See Godreau, "Slippery Semantics"; Isar P. Godreau, "La Semántica Fugitiva: Raza, Color y Vida Cotidiana En Puerto Rico," *Revista de Ciencias Sociales* 9 (2000): 52–71; Hilda I. Lloréns, *Fugitive Blackness: Representations of Race, Art, and Memory in Arroyo, Puerto Rico* (University of Connecticut, 2005); Solsiree Del Moral, "Missing: The Black Girls of Puerto Rico," in *Representations of Afrolatinidad* (forthcoming); Torres, Arlene, *"La Gran Familia Puertorriqueña 'ej Prieta de Beldá": Blackness in Latin America and the Caribbean: Social Dynamics and Cultural Transformations* (Bloomington, IN, 1998).

59. Caroline Mary Parker and Julienne Weegels, "Carceral Citizenship in Latin America and the Caribbean: Exclusion and Belonging in the New Mass Carceral Zone," *European Review of Latin American and Caribbean Studies* 116 (2023): 69–85.

60. Ann Laura Stoler, Carole McGranahan, and Peter C. Perdue, *Imperial Formations* (SAR Press, 2007).

61. According to data from World Prison Brief, available at https://www.prisonstudies.org/country/puerto-rico-usa.

62. LeBrón, *Policing Life and Death.*

63. See Governing, "Police Employment, Officers Per Capita Rates for U.S. Cities," Governing, 2018; Juan Nadal Ferrería, "Colossal Cost of Subsidizing Failure: How the Drug War Impacts Puerto Rico's Budget," *Review Journal of the University of Puerto Rico* 81 (2012): 1139.

64. , Chris Garces, Tomas Martin, and Sacha Darke, "Informal Prison Dynamics in Africa and Latin America: Chris Garces, Tomas Martin and Sacha Darke Contend That Research in Men's Prisons Demands a Widening of Theoretical Perspectives and Methodological Repertoires," *Criminal Justice Matters* 91, no. 1 (2013): 26–27; Sacha Darke, "Surviving in the New Mass Carceral Zone," *Prison Service Journal* 229 (2017): 2–9; Kevin Lewis O'Neill and Anthony W. Fontes, "Making Do: The Practice of Imprisonment in Postwar Guatemala," *Journal of Latin American Geography* 16, no. 2 (2017): 31–48.

65. Darke, "Surviving."

66. Darke, "Informal Prison Dynamics."

67. Chris Garces, "The Cross Politics of Ecuador's Penal State," *Cultural Anthropology* 25, no. 3 (2010): 459–96.

68. Racial data come from the 2017 American Community Survey Data. For the general population in 2017, Puerto Rico was classified as 66 percent "White Alone," 12 percent "Black Alone," and 21 percent as racially mixed (either "Two or More Races" or "Some Other Race"). Data for absolute incarceration rates come from World Prison Brief, "Puerto Rico (USA)," World Prison Brief, 2016.

69. Just 15 of the 132 licensed residential drug treatment centers in operation in 2015 Puerto Rico were for women. See Administración de Servicios de Salud Mental y Contra la Adicción (ASSMCA), "Puerto Rico Mental Health and Addiction Services Administration (ASSMCA), Certification, Licenses and Safety Division, October 2014," 2014.

70. Throughout fieldwork (and six years of graduate school), I worked part-time as graduate research assistant. My introduction to Narcotics Anonymous and Alcoholics Anonymous came through a public health study exploring Dominican men's vulnerability to drug addiction and HIV/AIDS in the Dominican Republic (in Santo Domingo and Boca Chica), and a study of Black men who have sex with men's vulnerability to HIV in New York City. See Mark Padilla et al., "Tourism Labor, Embodied Suffering, and the Deportation Regime in the Dominican Republic," *Medical Anthropology Quarterly* 32, no. 4 (2018): 498–519; Jonathan Garcia et al., "Passing the Baton: Community-Based Ethnography to Design a Randomized Clinical Trial on the Effectiveness of Oral Pre-Exposure Prophylaxis for HIV Prevention among Black Men Who Have Sex with Men," *Contemporary Clinical Trials* 45 (2015): 244–51.

71. Débora Upegui-Hernández and Rafael Torruella, "Humillaciones y Abusos En Centros de Tratamiento Para Uso de Drogas PR," Intercambios Puerto Rico, 2015, https://es.scribd.com/doc/265551445/Humillaciones-y -Abusos-en-Centros-de-Tratamiento-Para-Uso-de-Drogas-PR.

72. Hansen, *Addicted to Christ*; Garces, "Prisons of Charity"; Angela Garcia, "Serenity: Violence, Inequality, and Recovery on the Edge of Mexico City," *Medical Anthropology Quarterly* (2015).

73. Between 2016–2017, I was employed on a mixed-methods study funded by the US National Institute of Drug Abuse, which sought to develop and test a mobile HIV care intervention that would increase access to antiretroviral therapy among homeless injection drug users in San Juan. This part-time job gave me colleagues, company, and work to do during quieter fieldwork moments.

74. I strongly suspect that this was not a satisfying answer for any of my interlocuters, though it was genuinely earnest at the time.

75. See Michael Lapp, "The Rise and Fall of Puerto Rico as a Social Laboratory, 1945–1965," *Social Science History* 19, no. 2 (1995): 169–99.

76. See Proyecto PACTO, Proveyendo Acceso a Cuidado y Tratamiento, available at https://www.iniciativacomunitaria.org/pacto/.

77. Julian H. Steward et al., *The People of Puerto Rico: A Study in Social Anthropology* (University of Illinois, 1956) ; Sidney W. Mintz, "The Culture History of a Puerto Rican Sugar Cane Plantation: 1876–1949," *Hispanic American Historical Review* 33, no. 2 (1957): 224–51; Helen Icken Safa, *The Urban Poor of Puerto Rico: A Study in Development and Inequality* (Holt Rinehart & Winston, 1974).

78. Though written in distinct disciplinary traditions and by a combination of Puerto Rican and mainland US authors, postwar attempts to characterize Puerto Rican personality tended to agree about its essential nature, which was consistently characterized through tropes of dependency, docility, and childishness. See Antonio S. Pedreira, *Insularismo: Ensayos de Interpretación Puertorriqueña* (Biblioteca de Autores Puertorriqueños, 1942); David Landy, *Tropical Childhood: Cultural Transmission and Learning in a Rural Puerto Rican Village* (University of North Carolina Press, 1959); Rene Marques, "El Puertorriqueño Dócil," *Revista de Ciencias Sociales*, no. 1–2 (1963): 35–78. For a review and critique of postwar culture-and-personality studies in Puerto Rico, see Sidney Wilfred Mintz, "Puerto Rico: An Essay in the Definition of a National Culture," in *Status of Puerto Rico: Selected Background Studies*, 339–434 (US Department of Health, Education and Welfare, US Government Printing Office, 1966).

79. In the 1960s, the postwar trope of a "Puerto Rican psyche" was reformulated into Lewis' "culture of poverty" thesis. Lewis attributed Puerto Rican's persistent disadvantage to an inheritable culture of poverty: a series of psychological adaptations to deprivation that provided the poor with a blueprint for living but ultimately led, in Lewis' view, to the inheritance of poverty. Yet the "culture of poverty" Lewis described in was actually intensely characterological, much more akin to a personality or psyche than to a culture. Oscar Lewis, *La Vida: A Puerto Rican Family in the Culture of Poverty* (Random House, 1966). In my own study, I am interested in how persisting and entrenched tropes about the "psyches" and "personalities" of drug users shape re-educados understanding of themselves and each other. But rather than subscribing to these theories analytically, theories about the culture and personality of drug users function in this book as cultural artefacts, not as diagnoses. My approach is deeply influenced by the critical medical anthropology paradigms that Sidney Mintz and his contemporaries inspired, in particular: Philippe Bourgois, *In Search of Respect: Selling Crack in El Barrio* (Cambridge University Press, 2003); Merrill Singer et al., "Why Does Juan Garcia Have a Drinking Problem? The Perspective of Critical Medical Anthropology," *Medical Anthropology* 14, no. 1 (1992): 77–108. Grounded in the political-economy perspectives of classical and neo-Marxist theorists, these authors argued that Puerto Rican poverty were caused not by a nationally "docile" personality or character but instead by global capitalism and its repertoire of structural violence.

80. Hansen, *Addicted to Christ*.

81. Cubist principles have informed my writing. Cubism was prompted by a concern that when a painter imbues a flat surface with an "illusion of space," by making an image *appear* to be three-dimensional, a trickery occurs. The resulting image *looks* a lot like an unbiased window onto reality, but what it really tells us is how the world looks to the painter. Cubists argued that the point of painting should not be to pose as an unbiased window onto reality. Instead, as a flat surface, a painting must behave like one; its jarring collision of perspectives is a reminder of the active work that goes into looking. An equivalent principle, applied to ethnography, is to

avoid writing too naturalistically by writing that partial sightedness and pluralism of perspective into the text itself. See John Berger, "The Moment of Cubism," *New Left Review* 42 (1967): 75.

CHAPTER 1

1. *Hogar* literally means "home" or "hearth," and the Spanish acronym *CREA* stands for *Centro de Re-educación de Adictos* (Center for the Reeducation of Addicts).

2. Chejuán García Ríos was the original founder of Hogar CREA in 1968. I consider his local fame and legacy in the next chapter.

3. This quote comes from a video recording taken by a local journalist, shared with me after the ceremony.

4. By national (US) estimates, 71 percent of people released from prison are rearrested within five years. Formerly incarcerated people are also unemployed at five times the rate of the general population (27% compared to 4%), despite being much more active job seekers. Matthew R. Durose and Leonardo Antenangeli, *Recidivism of Prisoners Released in 34 States in 2012: A 5-Year Follow-Up Period (2012–2017)* (US Department of Justice, Office of Justice Programs, 2021; Prison Policy Initiative, "Out of Prison and Out of Work," 2018, https://www.prisonpolicy.org/reports/outofwork.html. (Note, these figures come from the US mainland as equivalent figures for Puerto Rico specifically are unavailable). The first few weeks following release from a therapeutic community are known to be especially dangerous owing to the elevated risk of overdose mortality. Edle Ravndal and Ellen J. Amundsen, "Mortality among Drug Users after Discharge from Inpatient Treatment: An 8-Year Prospective Study," *Drug and Alcohol Dependence* 108, no 1 (2010): 65–69. As to their clinical outcomes, the only systematic review of therapeutic communities (which drew mostly on US mainland programs, was dogged by poor-quality data sets, and had to exclude most of its sample) indicated a relapse posttreatment rate ranging from 21 percent to 100 percent. Smith et al., "Therapeutic Communities." Given the lousy employment outcomes and risks awaiting these men, the aspirations being stoked up on stage do seem woefully out of touch.

5. I explore Puerto Rican civil commitment law in chapter 4.

6. In government audits of treatment capacity, these men would be classified as "clients" or "service users."

7. For residents ordered into treatment by a civil rather than criminal court, this fee is usually paid by a family member, though this is not always the case (see chapter 4).

8. In government audits of treatment capacity, these men would be classified as "volunteers" as opposed to "service users" or "clients."

9. Set in the abandoned houses of postindustrial Philadelphia, Robert Fairbanks's study of urban poverty describes how "street-level entrepreneurs" devise informal self-help groups that survive by pooling each other's welfare checks. Angela Garcia

offers a similar study of self-help in her account of Mexico's *anexos*, where unregulated and unlicensed self-help groups thrive in a context of medical scarcity and state abandonment. For both authors, "informality" serves to foreground the unwaged, untaxed, and marginal nature of the work performed in self-help networks. But the work performed by re-educados encompasses a broad array of arrangements that transcend the classically informal (unwaged and untaxed) and formal (waged and taxed). For these reasons, I use the construct carceral livelihood, which is agnostic regarding mode of production and captures the variety of new ways of living and making a living that are emerging under and through the expanding and devolving apparatus of the carceral state. See Robert P. Fairbanks, *How It Works: Recovering Citizens in Post-Welfare Philadelphia* (University of Chicago Press, 2009); Garcia, "Serenity."

10. Keith Hart proposed the concept of the informal economy in 1973 to account for income-generating activities of urban migrants in Ghana. Since then, the informal economy has been used to account for wageless work, which is generally understood to be a last resort for those left behind by global capitalism. See Keith Hart, "Informal Income Opportunities and Urban Employment in Ghana" *Journal of Modern African Studies* 11, no. 1 (1973): 61–89; Saskia Sassen, *Informalization in Advanced Market Economies* (Geneva: Development Policies Department, International Labour Office, 1997).

11. Millar, *Reclaiming the Discarded*.

12. Some scholars would argue that the critical distinction should be between "work" and "labor." Within a Marxist tradition, to name one example, labor refers specifically to those activities harnessed by capital for the production of surplus value (profit). By this reading, most of the economically unproductive activities performed by re-educados would not constitute labor. In the present analysis, imposing distinctions such as these is perfectly valid. But focusing only on the productivity or terms and conditions of this work can also ignore its deeper social significance, the significance that indexes the larger whole of which re-educados are just a part. That social significance is about repurposing expulsion into an alternative carceral livelihood: that is, a way of working and a way of living within the confines of the carceral state. Since my primary interest is in what this livelihood brings to re-educados, materially, socially, and existentially, I do not employ this Marxist work-labor distinction, instead I use the terms "work" and "labor" interchangeably.

13. Zatz, "Carceral Labor Continuum."

14. In its contemporary humanitarian sense, volunteer work unusually refers to "freely given labor" performed in the public sphere. See Muehlebach, *The Moral Neoliberal* (University of Chicago, 2012); Mauss, *The Gift: The Form and Reason for Exchange in Archaic Societies* (Routledge, 1954).

15. See, for example, Anita Gibbs, "Probation Service Users as Volunteers in Partnership Projects," *Probation Journal* 43, no. 3 (1996): 142–46; Joe Levenson and Finola Farrant, "Unlocking Potential: Active Citizenship and Volunteering by Prisoners," *Probation Journal* 49, no. 3 (2002): 195–204; Anna Coote, "Help to Work? Britain's Jobless Are Being Forced into Workfare, More Like," *The Guardian*, April 28, 2014; Muehlebach, *Moral Neoliberal*.

16. Though, in theory, this certificate can be "cleaned" via court petition (under Law 34 § 1725a), citizens may only "expunge" a conviction from their record five years after completing a criminal sentence, and only if no further convictions have been acquired in the interim period. Even here, judges hold full discretion to deny petitions. In 2012 (the last year for which data are available), just 14 pardons were granted out of a total of 155 applications filed. In 2011, just 7 petitions were granted. See Restoration of Rights Project, "Puerto Rico: Restoration of Rights & Record Relief."

17. Janine Guzman, "Puerto Rico: Being Charged with a Felony Can Be Just Cause for Dismissal," DLA Piper, May 10, 2019.

18. Uggen et al., *Average Citizen*; Smiley, *Purgatory Citizenship*; Miller and Stuart, "Carceral Citizenship."

19. National Law Center on Homelessness and Poverty and the National Coalition for the Homeless, *Homes Not Handcuffs: The Criminalization of Homelessness in U.S. Cities*, 2009, http://www.nationalhomeless.org/publications/crimreport/CrimzReport_2009.pdf.

20. Legislative Assembly of Puerto Rico, "Ley de la Administración de Servicios de Salud Mental y Contra la Adicción," ley núm. 67 de 7 de agosto de 1993, según enmendada (hereafter Law 67).

21. For a portrait of the legal exclusions facing formerly incarcerated people on the US mainland, see Uggen et al., *Average Citizen*; Smiley, *Purgatory Citizenship*; Miller and Stuart, "Carceral Citizenship."

22. Uggen Christopher et al., "Locked Out 2022: Estimates of People Denied Voting Rights," Sentencing Project, 2022.

23. Ileana I. Diaz, "Malignant Citizenship: Race, Imperialism, and Puerto Rico-United States Entanglements," *Citizenship Studies* 25, no. 3 (2021): 333–52.

24. Lerman and Weaver, *Arresting Citizenship*.

25. Lerman and Weaver, 15–16.

26. Smiley, *Purgatory Citizenship*, 52.

27. Duany draws a distinction between political nationalism and cultural nationalism. Whereas the former entails a desire for political sovereignty, the latter denotes the strong sense of collective "national" identity based on shared language and culture. Crucially, Puerto Rican cultural nationalism is a translocal project, one that unites Puerto Rican islanders to the mainland diaspora through repeating circular migration. Because of this cultural definition of nationality, Duany argues that Puerto Rico is a "nation on the move." Duany, *Nation on the Move*.

28. Duany, *Nation on the Move*, 1–5.

29. Marta I. Cruz-Janzen, "Out of the Closet: Racial Amnesia, Avoidance, and Denial—Racism among Puerto Ricans," *Race, Gender, and Class* 10, no. 3 (2003): 64–81.

30. See Godreau, "Slippery Semantics"; Godreau, "La Semántica Fugitiva"; Lloréns, *Fugitive Blackness*.

31. I frequently encountered Puerto Rican people who, following arrest on the US mainland, were given the option of undergoing compulsory drug treatment in either Puerto Rico or on the US mainland. In fact, one white English-speaking American woman who spoke no Spanish told me she chose to undergo treatment

in Puerto Rico rather than back in Miami. Her connection to Puerto Rico was not via her parents but her husband, himself recovering from a substance use disorder, who was attending a male-only program that had a separate women-only center nearby. In their case, the joint decision to go to Puerto Rico stemmed from being able to maintain proximity to each other.

32. "DSM" is the commonly used shorthand for the American Psychiatric Association's *Diagnostic and Statistical Manual of Mental Disorders*, in this case the fifth edition (V).

33. ATD, "John Maxwell on Leadership," *TD Magazine*, February 8, 2013.

34. The term *vernacular* is especially apt here: unlike *informal* or *lay*, it emphasizes the transfer and syncretic elements of this process. Like the vernacular languages that derived from Latin in Europe, the professional identity being improvised here is influenced by a template: modern images of higher education. See Peggy Levitt and Sally Merry, "Vernacularization on the Ground: Local Uses of Global Women's Rights in Peru, China, India and the United States," *Global Networks* 9, no. 4 (2009): 441–61.

35. These are among the eleven symptoms of substance use disorder listed in DSM-V. See American Psychiatric Association, *Diagnostic and Statistical Manual of Mental Disorders* (American Psychiatric Association, 2013).

36. Claude Lévi-Strauss, *The Savage Mind* (University of Chicago Press, 1966).

37. *Primera Hora*, "Crea Gradúa 30 Almas Libres de Drogas," December 2000.

38. *El Mundo*, "Creando Hombres Nuevos," April 1988.

39. Alba Cabrera, "CREA, Programa Efectivo En Re-Educacion de Adictos," *El Mundo*, January 25, 1969; *El Mundo*, "CREAndo Hombres Nuevos," April 1988; *El Vocero*, "'Calidad de Vida' Chejuan, Un Orgullo de Puerto Rico," July 17, 1987.

40. Karl Ross, "Myths Regarding Founder of Hogar Crea Full of Flaws," *San Juan Star*, September 27, 1995.

41. *El Vocero*, "Hogar CREA 'Buena Cosecha,'" December 6, 2000.

42. Echoing Wool's account of the "economy of patriotism" circulating in US media coverage of injured military soldiers. See Zoë H. Wool, *After War: The Weight of Life at Walter Reed* (Duke University Press, 2015).

43. Centro de Investigaciones Sobre la Adicción (CISLA), *Centro de Investigaciones Sobre La Adicción (CISLA) Boletin Informativo Vol 1. Numero 1. Abril 1964* (1964); Macro Systems, *Drug Treatment and Prevention Programs in the Common Wealth of Puerto Rico*," (San Juan: Archivo Histórico Universitari, 1972).

44. *El Vocero*, "Hogar CREA 'Buena Cosecha,'" December 6, 2000.

45. *El Vocero*, "Hogar CREA."

46. *Primera Hora*, "Crea Gradúa."

CHAPTER 2

1. This is often the argument put forward by nonprofit organizations in the human rights and drug user rights space, with local organizations denouncing therapeutic communities and the re-educados who run them as "former drug users who

do not always possess the moral integrity to fit their roles." See Upegui-Hernández and Torruella, "Humillaciones y Abusos."

2. For US mainland carceral histories, see Alexander, *New Jim Crow*; Wacquant, *Punishing the Poor*; Forman, *Locking Up Our Own*.

3. Sassen, *Expulsions*; Wacquant, *Punishing the Poor*; Gilmore, *Golden Gulag*.

4. Efren Ramirez, "The Mental Health Program of the Commonwealth of Puerto Rico," in *Rehabilitating the Narcotics Addict* (Vocational Rehabilitation Administration, US Department of Health), 2.

5. In 1897 coffee exports accounted for 65.8 percent of Puerto Rico's foreign trade, while sugar accounted for 21.6 percent. By 1901, coffee had declined to 19.6 percent, and sugar had risen to 55 percent of Puerto Rico's exports. See Laird W. Bergad, "Agrarian History of Puerto Rico, 1870–1930," *Latin American Research Review* 13, no. 3 (1978): 63–94.

6. Angel G. Quintero Rivera, "Background to the Emergence of Imperialist Capitalism in Puerto Rico," *Caribbean Studies* 13, no. 3 (1973): 31–63.

7. Sidney W. Mintz, "The Culture History of a Puerto Rican Sugar Cane Plantation: 1876–1949," *Hispanic American Historical Review* 33, no. 2 (1953): 224–51.

8. Bergad, *Agrarian History of Puerto Rico*.

9. Mintz, "Culture History," 248.

10. Gómez Acevedo, *Organización y Reglamentación*.

11. Rocío Zambrana, *Colonial Debts* (Duke University Press, 2021), 10–12.

12. Steward et al., *The People of Puerto Rico*.

13. Picó Fernando, *El día menospensado: historia de los presidiarios en Puerto Rico* (Río Piedras, PR: Ediciones Huracan, 1994).

14. See IPUMS online database (available at https://international.ipums.org/international/).

15. Note, 1910 and 1920 were the only two national censuses in the twentieth century that, in addition to enumerating "race," also specified whether participants were incarcerated or not. For most other decades, censuses either specify race or specify incarceration status but fail to specify both. In 1920, Puerto Rico's general population was categorized as 26.8 percent Black and 73.2 percent white. Duany, "Neither Black or White."

16. This calculation comes from data stored in the IPUMS online database (available at https://international.ipums.org/international/). In Puerto Rico in 1920, the total correctional population (including jails, prisons, camps, and reformatories) amounted to 2,075 people of whom 30.84 percent were Black and 96.16 percent were white. Puerto Rico's general population at the time amounted to 1,356,745 of whom 26.8 percent were Black and 73.2 percent were white. Across the US mainland in 1920, the total correctional population (again including jails, prisons, camps, and reformatories) amounted to 125,389 people, 33.32 percent of whom were Black and 57.68 percent of whom were white. Across the US mainland's general population of 102,611,989, 9.6 percent were Black and 89.4 percent were white.

17. Bergad, Laird W., *The Comparative Histories of Slavery in Brazil, Cuba, and the United States* (New York: Cambridge University Press, 2007), 120, 113.

18. Luis M. Díaz Soler, "Historia de La Esclavitud En Puerto Rico." San Juan, Editorial de La Universidad de Puerto Rico, 1953; Frank Tannenbaum, *Slave and Citizen: The Classic Comparative Study of Race Relations in the Americas*, Beacon Press, 1992.

19. Picó, *El día menospensado*, 56–57.

20. Alongside Catholicism, interdominational Christianity, Evangelicalism, and spiritism all formed part of Oso Blanco's complex religious landscape. See Alberto Ortiz Díaz, *Raising the Living Dead: Rehabilitative Corrections in Puerto Rico and the Caribbean* (University of Chicago Press, 2023), 86–105.

21. Notably, the Federal Medical Center in Lexington, Kentucky, established in 1935. See N. D. Campbell, J. P. Olsen, and Luke Walden, *The Narcotic Farm: The Rise and Fall of America's First Prison for Drug Addicts* (Abrams, 2008).

22. Alberto Ortiz Díaz, "Pathologizing the Jíbaro: Mental and Social Health in Puerto Rico's Oso Blanco (1930s to 1950s)," *The Americas* 77, no. 3 (2020): 409–41.

23. Picó, *El día menospensado*; Díaz, "Pathologizing the Jíbaro."

24. . Díaz, *Raising the Living Dead*.

25. Díaz, x.

26. In fact, prison staff even had a category called "moron-almost-moron," applied to prisoners said to be defined by a "dull-normal intelligence. Díaz, x.

27. Díaz, "Pathologizing the Jíbaro," 428.

28. Díaz, 428.

29. Section 19, Article 6, of the Constitution of the Commonwealth of Puerto Rico (1952) states: "It shall be the public policy of the Commonwealth to . . . regulate its penal institutions in a manner that effectively achieves their purposes and to provide, within the limits of available resources, for adequate treatment of delinquents in order to make possible their moral and social rehabilitation."

30. Federal narcotics laws driving up drug convictions across the United States (including Puerto Rico) during the early twentieth century included, the Harrison Act (1914), the Opium Control Law (1942), the Law of Contraband Narcotics Drugs (1939), and the Narcotics Control Act (1956).

31. It was not until 1980, in DSM-III, that addiction was reclassified as two discrete illnesses, substance abuse and substance dependence.

32. Caroline Jean Acker, *Creating the American Junkie: Addiction Research in the Classic Era of Narcotic Control* (Johns Hopkins University Press, 2002); Lawrence Kolb, "Types and Characteristics of Drug Addicts," *Mental Hygiene* 9 (1925): 300–13.

33. Efren Ramirez, "Puerto Rican Blueprint," in *Narcotics: An American Plan*, ed. Saul Jeffee (P. S. Eriksson, 1966), 112–28; Ramirez, "Mental Health Program."

34. Erikson, Erik H. *Identity and the Life Cycle: Selected Papers* (International Universities Press, 1959).

35. Ramirez, "Puerto Rican Blueprint," 121.

36. Ramirez, "Mental Health Program."

37. Ramirez, 2.

38. Ramirez, 2.

39. Ramirez, 2.

40. Ramirez, "Puerto Rican Blueprint," 118.

41. Ramirez, "Mental Health Program," 2.

42. Macro Systems, *Drug Treatment*, 26.

43. CISLA's stated relapse rate of 5.6 percent (cited in S. Jaffe, *Narcotics—an American Plan* [New York, 1966], 125) was implausible because even opioid substitution therapies, today considered the gold standard for treating opioid addiction, have relapse rates between 40 percent and 60 percent. See National Institute on Drug Abuse, "How Effective Is Drug Addiction Treatment?"

44. Jaffe, *Narcotics*.

45. Peter Fiddick, "Junkie Cure Junkie," *Manchester Guardian Weekly*, February 16, 1967.

46. CISLA's demise was all but assured, some say, by the loss of Ramirez, who was not only highly energetic in his efforts to extract funds from government but was also extremely well connected. (His wife was the daughter of Governor Luis Muñoz Marín.)

47. *Hogar* literally means "home" or "hearth," and the acronym *CREA* stands for Center for the Reeducation of Addicts.

48. Journalists continue to debate the nature and severity of Chejuán's substance use prior to his incarceration; see Cotler Joaquín, "The Rehab Empire Built On Cakes," *Latino USA* (blog), October 16, 2020.

49. Edwin Velez, *Estudio Descriptivo Sobre Los Hogares CREA, INC* (Universidad de Puerto Rico, 1986).

50. Luis Cappa, "Censuran Conducta Efrain Santiago, Comisiones Senado Aprueban $200 Mil Para CREA," *El Mundo*, February 4, 1972.

51. *El Mundo*, "Rehabilitando al Adicto," November 4, 1969.

52. Cabrera, "CREA, Programa Efectivo."

53. Margarita Babb, "Piden Ciudadania Ayude Combatir Los Drogas," *El Mundo*, March 13, 1969.

54. *El Mundo*, "Organizan Comite Pro Hogar CREA," February 16, 1970.

55. *El Mundo*, "Visitaron Hogar CREA," February 19, 1973.

56. Babb, "Piden Ciudadania."

57. Such as Synanon in California; Daytop Village, Odyssey House, and Phoenix House (all in New York City); and Matrix House in Lexington. All shared a programmatic structure based on "addict-led" mutual aid, long-term communalist residence, encounter groups, and a hierarchical work system in which rewards and punishment acted as vehicles for rehabilitation. See Lewis Yablonsky, *The Tunnel Back: Synanon* (Macmillan, 1965); Barry Sugarman, *Daytop Village: A Therapeutic Community* (Holt McDougal, 1974); Judianne Densen-Gerber, *We Mainline Dreams: The Odyssey House Story* (Doubleday Books, 1973); Robert S. Weppner, *The Untherapeutic Community: Organizational Behavior in a Failed Addiction Treatment Program* (University of Nebraska Press, 1983).

58. Macro Systems, "Drug Treatment."

59. Macro Systems, 90.

60. On the contrary, public opinion far more often serves to impede the establishment of drug services, hence the plethora of studies exploring neighborhood

resistance to methadone clinics and so-called NIMBYism, meaning "not in my back-yard"; see Barbara Tempalski et al., "NIMBY Localism and National Inequitable Exclusion Alliances: The Case of Syringe Exchange Programs in the United States" *Geoforum* 38, no. 6 (2007): 1250–63.

61. *El Vocero*, "Calidad de Vida."

62. Ross, "Myths Regarding Founder."

63. Velez, "Estudio Descriptivo."

64. Cited in James Dietz, "Puerto Rico in the 1970s and 1980s: Crisis of the Development Model," *Journal of Economic Issues* 16, no. 2 (1982): 497–506, 497.

65. Henry Wells, "The Modernization of Puerto Rico. A Political Study of Changing Values and Institutions" *VRÜ Verfassung Und Recht in Übersee* 4, no. 2 (1971): 234–35.

66. James L. Dietz, *Economic History of Puerto Rico: Institutional Change and Capitalist Development* (Princeton University Press, 1986).

67. Planning Board of Puerto Rico, *Informe Económico al Gobernador, 1964* [Economic report to the governor], Oficina del Gobernador, Junta de Planificacion, Negociado de Analisis Economico y Social, 1964, http://lcw.lehman.edu/lehman/depts/latinampuertorican/latinoweb/PuertoRico/Bootstrap.htm#_edn9.

68. César J. Ayala, "The Decline of the Plantation Economy and the Puerto Rican Migration of the 1950s," *Latino Studies Journal* 7, no. 1 (1996): 61–90.

69. Helen Safa, "The Transformation of Puerto Rico: The Impact of Modernization Ideology," *Transforming Anthropology* 19, no. 1 (2011): 46–49.

70. Dietz, "Puerto Rico," 501.

71. Dietz, *Economic History*.

72. Richard Weisskoff, *Factories and Food Stamps: The Puerto Rico Model of Development* (Johns Hopkins University Press, 1985).

73. Dietz, *Economic History*; Weisskoff, *Factories and Food Stamps*; Lapp, "Rise and Fall."

74. Helen Safa, *The Myth of the Male Breadwinner: Women and Industrialization in the Caribbean* (Boulder, CO: Westview, 1995).

75. Even though women's income had become crucial to household stability, women continued to be configured by the state as "supplementary wage earners." Safa, *Myth of the Male*. This gendered access to welfare is by no means unique to Puerto Rico. See James Ferguson, *Give a Man a Fish: Reflections on the New Politics of Distribution* (Duke University Press, 2015).

76. Another way of understanding this is as an "abeyance mechanism." See Ephraim Harold Mizruchi, *Regulating Society: Marginality and Social Control in Historical Perspective* (New York: Free Press, 1983); Kim Hopper and Jim Baumohl, "Held in Abeyance: Rethinking Homelessness and Advocacy," *American Behavioral Scientist* 37 no. 4 (1994): 522–52.

77. World Prison Brief, "Puerto Rico."

78. LeBrón, *Policing Life and Death*; World Prison Brief, "Puerto Rico."

79. Salvador Santiago-Negrón and Carmen E. Albizu-García, "Guerra Contra Las Drogas o Guerra Contra La Salud? Los Retos Para La Salud Pública de La Política de Drogas de Puerto Rico," *Puerto Rico Health Sciences Journal* 22, no. 1 (2003).

80. Departamento de Justicia, *Departamento de Justicia Explicación Del Prepuesto Funcional Año Fiscal 1985–1986* (Departamento de Justicia, Biblioteca Legislativa de Puerto Rico, 1986). Departamento de Justicia, *Departamento de Justicia Memorial Explicativo Año Fiscal 1991–1992* (Departamento de Justicia, Biblioteca Legislativa de Puerto Rico, 1992).

81. Macro Systems, *Drug Treatment*, 53.

82. LeeAnn O'Neill and Jennifer Gumbrewicz, "Our Forgotten Colony: Puerto Rico and the War on Drugs," *Modern American* 1 (2005): 8–11.

83. Velez, "Between Two Courts."

84. Michael Wright, "Puerto Rican Prisons 'Ready to Explode' Despite Reform Effort," *New York Times*, November 19, 1982.

85. Civil Rights Litigation Clearinghouse, "Feliciano v. Parole Board of the Commonwealth of Puerto Rico," Civil Rights Litigation Clearinghouse, 1990.

86. *Seattle Times*, "Puerto Ricans Struggle over Once-Grisly Oso Blanco Prison," May 17, 2014.

87. Wright, "Puerto Rican Prisons."

88. Department of Correction and Rehabilitation, *Intermediate Sanctions Plan* (Departamento de Corrección y Rehabilitación, Biblioteca Legislativa de Puerto Rico, 1994).

89. Departamento de Justicia, *Departamento de Justicia Memorial.*

90. In 2016 this per diem was $25, substantially lower than the equivalent incarceration cost of $100 per day. See Alice Speri, "Puerto Rico Wants to Cut the Cost of Incarcerating People by Shipping Them off the Island," *The Intercept* (blog), March 23, 2018. During the 1970s and 1980s, the figure was likely considerably lower.

91. Departamento de Servicios Contra la Adicción, *Informe Anual: 1985–86* (Estado Libre Asociado de Puerto Rico, 1986).

92. A legal title that in the United States designates a private nonprofit organization that is "representative of" and "provides services to the community." "20 U.S. Code § 7011—Definitions," Cornell Law School, Legal Information Institute, 2021.

93. *El Mundo*, "Es Un Exito Casa CREA Juncos," May 2, 1970; *El Mundo*, "Senador Colon Alaba Labor Centro Rehabilitacion Adictos," April 1970.

94. This was the argument famously put forward by Michelle Alexander, who characterized mass incarceration in the United States as a direct continuation of the earlier Jim Crow system of racial segregation and, before that, slavery. See Alexander, *New Jim Crow*. When looked at from a certain angle, the mass criminalization of Puerto Ricans could be read in this light. It undoubtedly does perform important work in maintaining white supremacy. But it is a mistake to ignore the distinct Iberian racial legacies and particular political-economic dynamics of carceral expansions as they differentially play out across Caribbean and Latin American contexts, as scholars of Puerto Rico and southern criminologists have pointed out. See Díaz, *Raising the Living Dead*; Kerry Carrington, Russell Hogg, and Máximo Sozzo, "Southern Criminology," *British Journal of Criminology* 56, no. 1 (2016): 1–20; A. Aliverti, H. Carvalho, and A. Chamberlen, *Decolonizing the Criminal Question: Rethinking the Legacies, Epistemologies and Geographies of Criminal Justice* (Oxford: Oxford University Press, 2022).

95. W. E. B. Du Bois, *Black Reconstruction* (Harcourt, Brace and Howe, 1935); Eric Foner, *Reconstruction: America's Unfinished Revolution, 1863–1877*, updated ed. (Harper Perennial, 2015).

96. Alex Lichtenstein, *Twice the Work of Free Labor: The Political Economy of Convict Labor in the New South* (Verso, 1996).

97. Douglas A. Blackmon, *Slavery by Another Name: The Re-enslavement of Black Americans from the Civil War to World War II* (Anchor, 2009).

98. In its visibility, the chain gang exemplifies a point was made a long time ago by Karl Marx, who wrote that "the criminal produces an impression now moral, now tragic, and renders a 'service' by arousing the moral and aesthetic sentiments of the public." Karl Marx, *Collected Works, Vol. 31, 1861–1863* (1989), 360–61.

99. Therapeutic community directors could forfeit their positions in a variety of ways, as described in the previous chapter, including by being caught using drugs or incurring another criminal conviction.

100. Labor union leaders came out to support Hogar CREA during the organization's "crusades of faith and hope." See *El Mundo*, "Cruzada de Fe y Esperanza," May 26, 1989; *El Mundo*, "Cierra Manana La Cruzada de Hogares CREA," August 31, 1990. The catchphrase "CREAndo Hombres Nuevos" came from an article in *El Mundo*. See *El Mundo*, "CREAndo Hombres Nuevos."

101. *El Vocero*, "Hogar CREA 'Buena Cosecha.'"

102. Arys Rodríguez, "Como Liberarse de La Droga: Expertos y Ex Adictos Analizan La Rehabilitación," *Primera Hora*, March 15, 2010.

103. *El Vocero*, "Hogar CREA 'Buena Cosecha.'"

104. *El Mundo*, "Cruzada de Fe y Esperanza"; Ross, "Myths Regarding Founder."

105. *El Mundo*, "Cruzada de Fe y Esperanza."

106. Capitolio is the home of the bicameral Legislative Assembly and is modeled on the Capitol in Washington, DC.

107. *El Mundo*, "Cierra Manana La Cruzada de Hogares CREA."

108. Muehlebach, *Moral Neoliberal*.

109. Departamento de Servicios Contra la Adicción, *Informe Anual*, 30–31.

110. Velez, "Estudio Descriptivo."

111. Unpaid prison labor in the United States has sometimes threatened to undermine the labor power of working-class workers in the United States. According to Thompson, this was one of the key reasons that the white working class came to oppose convict labor in the 1970s. Heather Ann Thompson, "Rethinking Working-Class Struggle through the Lens of the Carceral State: Toward a Labor History of Inmates and Guards," *Labor* 8, no. 3 (2011): 15–45.

112. Reuben Jonathan Miller and Gwendolyn Purifoye, "Carceral Devolution and the Transformation of Urban America," in *The Voluntary Sector in Prisons* (Springer, 2016), 195–213.

113. These letters were personally shared with me by the late Efren Ramirez, who had cosigned them along with Juan José García Ríos (Chejuán), and who had kept an extended record of therapeutic community communications and publications in his home. Ramirez passed away in 2018.

114. Within four years, DSCA became the lead provider of addiction treatments in Puerto Rico, accounting for nearly half of all total treatment capacity in 1977. Close behind was Hogar CREA, accounting for 44 percent of those enrolled in treatment. Small proportions were also treated through state correction and other therapeutic community or private programs. See Caroline M. Parker, "From Treatment to Containment to Enterprise: An Ethno-History of Therapeutic Communities in Puerto Rico, 1961–1993," *Culture, Medicine, and Psychiatry* 44, no. 1 (2020): 135–57.

115. Wilda Rodriguez, "CREA Le Responde a Sila Nazario," *El Nuevo Dia*, June 15, 1978.

116. *El Reportero*, "Teen Challenge Contra Metadona," January 1981. Departamento de Servicios Contra la Adicción, *Los Programas de Mantenimiento Con Metadona* (Estado Libre Asociado de Puerto Rico, 1975).

117. J. Porter, "The Street/Treatment Barrier: Treatment Experiences of Puerto Rican Injection Drug Users," *Substance Use and Misuse* 34, no. 14 (1999): 1951–75.

118. Jessica M. Mulligan, *Unmanageable Care: An Ethnography of Health Care Privatization in Puerto Rico* (NYU Press, 2014).

119. Invited Responses to Law 67 of 1993, Legislative Library, San Juan, Puerto Rico.

120. Invited Responses to Law 67 of 1993, Legislative Library, San Juan, Puerto Rico.

121. Hansen, *Addicted to Christ*.

122. Both the exemption clause and the special recognition were the result of direct lobbying efforts on the part of therapeutic communities. In letters to the Senate, a congress of community organizations including representatives from Hogar CREA, Teen Challenge, and the Assembly of God argued that forcing communities to employ clinicians would be a "death sentence" to the nonprofit sector. In the letter, they explicitly recommended an article be added that would exempt them. They also implored the government to make greater effort to recognize the contribution of ex-addicts to handling the drug problem and called on the state to extend its support beyond "medical psychiatric approaches," to include diverse "spiritual" and "traditional" approaches. See Legislative Assembly of Puerto Rico, "Ley de Salud Mental de Puerto Rico," ley núm. 408 de 2 de octubre de 2000, según enmendada (hereafter Law 408).

123. Kolb, "Types and Characteristics."

124. In her account of liberal multiculturalism in the context of Australian Indigenous social life, Povinelli argues that liberal forms of multiculturalism perpetuate inequality not by demanding that Indigenous people identify with and live according to the same standards of their colonizers but rather by requiring Indigenous people to live up to an impossible standard of authentic traditional culture. Analogously, carceral citizenship perpetuates the exclusion of its members by encouraging its members to measure each other's worth through the same stigmatizing stereotypes of criminality and pathology that they have experienced and been the victims of themselves. See Elizabeth A. Povinelli, *The Cunning of Recognition: Indigenous Alterities and the Making of Australian Multiculturalism* (Durham, NC: Duke University Press, 2002).

125. Karl Ross, "Crea Rehabilitation Claim of 87 percent Unsubstantiated," *San Juan Star*, September 26, 1995; Upegui-Hernández, "Humillaciones y Abusos."

CHAPTER 3

1. In Spanish: "Te doy mi mano, pongo a latir mi corazón al compás del tuyo y por ti y por mí, me comprometo frente a Dios. Me comprometo y te comprometo a honrar la vida." Translation by Ana Negrón.

2. See, for example, Luigi Esposito and Fernando M. Perez, "Neoliberalism and the Commodification of Mental Health," *Humanity and Society* 38, no. 4 (2014): 414–42; Jarrett Zigon, *"HIV Is God's Blessing": Rehabilitating Morality in Neoliberal Russia* (University of California Press, 2010); Joel Tupper Braslow, "The Manufacture of Recovery," *Annual Review of Clinical Psychology* 9 (2013): 781–809; Singer et al., "Why Does Juan."

3. E. P. Thompson introduced the concept of "time-discipline" to capture the social transformations in the perceptions of and uses of time that came about in response to the rise of industrial capitalism. Thompson argued that industrialization and the demands of capitalism brought about a fundamental change in how people experienced time. In preindustrial societies, time was often measured by natural events, and human activities were guided by seasonal rhythms and natural cycles. With the advent of industrial capitalism, there was a significant shift. Time became a commodity; labor had to be disciplined and regulated to match the requirements of the factory system. Workers were expected to adhere to strict schedules, follow the clock, and work fixed hours. See E. P. Thompson, "The Past and Present Society," *Past and Present* 38 (1967): 56–97.

4. Boredom was initially conceived as an affliction of prosperity, yet anthropological work on unemployment in postsocialist Europe, postcolonial Africa, and Indigenous reservations in the United States increasingly identifies boredom as a plight of the most economically vulnerable too. See Marguerite Van den Berg and Bruce O'Neill, "Introduction: Rethinking the Class Politics of Boredom," *Focaal* 78 (2017): 1–8; Craig Jeffrey, "Timepass: Youth, Class, and Time among Unemployed Young Men in India," *American Ethnologist* 37, no. 3 (2010): 465–68; Lori L. Jervis, Paul Spicer, and Spero M. Manson, "Boredom, Trouble, and the Realities of Postcolonial Reservation Life," *Ethos* (2003).

5. Campbell, *Narcotic Farm*.

6. Kaye, *Enforcing Freedom*.

7. Zigon, *HIV Is God's Blessing*.

8. See Kaye, *Enforcing Freedom*, 167; Zigon, 3.

9. Muehlebach, *Moral Neoliberal*, 62.

10. Dietz, *Economic History*; Weisskoff, *Factories and Food Stamps*.

11. Safa, *Myth of the Male*.

12. Hansen, *Addicted to Christ*.

13. See, for example, Muehlmann, *When I Wear*; Edward Flores, *God's Gangs: Barrio Ministry, Masculinity, and Gang Recovery* (NYU Press, 2014); Millar, *Reclaiming the Discarded*; Philippe Bourgois, *In Search of Respect*.

14. Hansen, *Addicted to Christ*, 290.

15. Anthropological inquiry into contemporary religion has critiqued the notion that religion is waning in the face of secularization by focusing instead upon the mutual constitution and interaction of religion and secularity. See Talal Asad, *Formations of the Secular: Christianity, Islam, Modernity* (Stanford, CA: Stanford University Press, 2003); Charles Taylor, *A Secular Age* (Cambridge: Belknap, 2007). Channeling these ideas, I approach La Casita's therapeutic practices as "secular-spiritual" to draw attention to how practices that may be described as secular (such as labor therapy and keeping busy) intersect with spiritual practices of monastic prayer and meditation.

16. Alberto Ortíz Díaz, "Puerto Rican Christianities in the United States," in *The Oxford Handbook of Latinx Christianities in the United States*, ed. Kristy Nabhan-Warren, 46 (Oxford University Press, 2022).

17. For Puerto Rico's Evangelical ministries, see Hansen, *Addicted to Christ*.

18. Thompson, "Time, Work-Discipline."

19. Thompson, 91.

20. Erving Goffman, "Asylum," *New York* (Anchor Books, 1961).

21. Idleness is described as an "enemy of the soul" in rule 48.1 of Saint Benedict, *The Rule of St. Benedict* (Sands, 1906). Prayer is described as a "holy art" in *Rule of the Master*, an anonymous sixth-century collection of monastic precepts. See Luke Eberle, trans., *The Rule of the Master* (Cistercian, 1977).

22. Agamben, *Highest Poverty*.

23. John Cassian, *John Cassian: The Institutes* (SUNY Press, 2000), 59.

24. John Cassian, *John Cassian: The Conferences* (Newman, 1997), 101.

25. Hansen, *Addicted to Christ*.

26. Agamben, *Highest Poverty*.

27. Max Weber, *The Protestant Ethic and the Spirit of Capitalism* (Skyros, 2015), 105.

28. Jeffrey, "Timepass"; Jervis, "Boredom, Trouble."

29. Van den Berg and O'Neill, "Introduction."

30. Jeffrey, "Timepass"; Jervis, "Boredom, Trouble"; Mains, "Too Much Time"; Singer et al., "Why Does Juan."

31. Mains, "Too Much Time."

32. Jeffrey, "Timepass," 466.

33. Hansen, *Addicted to Christ*, 105.

34. Van den Berg and O'Neill, "Introduction."

35. Jerome, *Selected Letters*, trans. F. A. Wright (Harvard University Press, 1989), 417.

36. Evagrius Ponticus, *The Praktikos: Chapters on Prayer* (Cistercian, 1970).

37. Andrew Crislip, "The Sin of Sloth or the Illness of the Demons? The Demon of Acedia in Early Christian Monasticism," *Harvard Theological Review* 98, no. 2 (2005): 143–69.

38. Kathleen Norris, *Acedia and Me: A Marriage, Monks, and a Writer's Life* (Penguin, 2008), 6–7.

39. Evagrius Ponticus, *The Praktikos*, 18.

40. Evagrius Ponticus, 29.

41. Evagrius Ponticus, 29.

42. Norris, *Acedia and Me*, 5.

43. This is why the institutional and therapeutic scripting of subjectivity has proved such a fruitful area of inquiry. See Nancy D. Campbell and Susan J. Shaw, "Incitements to Discourse: Illicit Drugs, Harm Reduction, and the Production of Ethnographic Subjects," *Cultural Anthropology* 23, no. 4 (2008): 688–717; Summerson Carr, "Anticipating and Inhabiting Institutional Identities," *American Ethnologist* 36, no. 2 (2009): 317–36; Teresa Gowan, *Hobos, Hustlers, and Backsliders: Homeless in San Francisco* (University of Minnesota Press, 2010).

44. Carr, "Anticipating and Inhabiting."

45. For an insightful discussion of this, see Philippe I. Bourgois and Jeffrey Schonberg, *Righteous Dopefiend* (University of California Press, 2009).

46. Marcel Mauss, *On Prayer*, ed. W. S. F. Pickering and trans. Susan Leslie (Durkheim Press / Berghahn Books, 2003).

47. Andreas Bandak, *The Social Life of Prayers—Introduction* (Taylor & Francis, 2017), 2.

48. Evagrius Ponticus, *The Praktikos*, 24.

49. Reinhart Koselleck, *Futures Past: On the Semantics of Historical Time* (Columbia University Press, 2004).

50. Cassian, *Institutes*, 233.

51. Mains, "Too Much Time,"; Van den Berg and O'Neill, "Introduction,"; Jeffrey, "Timepass"; Noelle J. Molé, *Labor Disorders in Neoliberal Italy: Mobbing, Well-Being, and the Workplace* (Indiana University Press, 2012).

52. Agamben, *Highest Poverty*; Hansen, *Addicted to Christ*.

53. In his study of social welfare in South Africa, James Ferguson describes the rise of basic income grants as a "new politics of distribution" that is reorganizing labor, unemployment, the family, and social payments under neoliberalism. While the most widespread criticism of basic income grants is that they would inculcate economic dependency, Ferguson argues that the real problem is that such payments provide only a "shallow and impersonal sort of dependence, instead of a richly social one." For Ferguson, what is missing from basic income grants is a "thick" social incorporation able to provide a rich basis of social personhood. In this chapter and throughout this book, I have tried to show how carceral livelihoods present yet another reorganization of labor, unemployment, and social life. Carceral livelihoods are certainly more encompassing and "thicker" than basic income grants, yet as I have tried to show, they have social and existential problems of their own. See Ferguson, *Give a Man*, 156–64.

CHAPTER 4

1. As mentioned in this book's introduction, I became acquainted with the families of civilly committed therapeutic community residents over the course

of my long-term observations at several different programs, including those I call Comunidad-Luz, Comunidad de Elevación del Espíritu Humano, Mesón de Dios, and La Casita. Several families opened their homes to me and allowed me to attend the court proceedings of their civilly committed relatives. Several of these programs allowed me to tag along to civil commitment proceedings too, with the permission of residents and their families.

2. In court proceedings, I introduced myself as "a PhD student learning about therapeutic communities and civil commitment" and shared an information sheet with my research certificate and contact details.

3. In Massachusetts, for example, where over 10,000 people were involuntarily committed for substance use in 2018, citizens were reportedly taken into police custody, "hand-cuffed or restrained while in transit to courthouses," and, if a petition was granted, incarcerated in correctional facilities alongside offenders. See Paul P. Christopher, Paul S. Appelbaum, and Michael D. Stein, "Criminalization of Opioid Civil Commitment," *JAMA Psychiatry* 77, no. 2 (2020): 111–12.

4. See Nathaniel P. Morris, "Detention without Data: Public Tracking of Civil Commitment," *Psychiatric Services* 71, no. 7 (2020): 741–44.

5. Technically, most residential drug treatment providers do not have a license to provide care to patients with severe mental health disorders, though programs do sometimes accept such patients in practice. This can create a perverse situation in which residents with mental health disorders risk expulsion from residential programs (and, if civilly committed, imprisonment) if their symptoms become too apparent for directors to ignore.

6. Legislative Assembly of Puerto Rico, Law 408, 51.

7. Foucault insisted throughout *Discipline and Punish*, most forcefully in part 4, that the prison was simply the most concentrated development within a larger "carceral archipelago" of institutions (spanning the almshouse, reformatory, hospital, school, etc.) that, by the late nineteenth century, operated in unison to identify deviance and to correct departures from the norm. Foucault, *Discipline and Punish*, 231–39.

8. See Caroline M. Parker, Oscar E. Miranda-Miller, and Carmen Albizu-García, "Involuntary Civil Commitment for Substance Use Disorders in Puerto Rico: Neglected Rights Violations and Implications for Legal Reform," *Health and Human Rights* 24, no. 2 (2022): 59.

9. When it comes to oversight over drafting legislation, evidence for any suggested modifications to laws (enacted or not) provided by professional and medical bodies can be found in the legislative archive in San Juan, where all policy recommendations submitted to the legislature by stakeholder groups are collated and stored. The process of writing mental health laws tends to include, as part of the policymaking, consultation with medical and professional bodies. Yet the archive shows that as an organic law designed to create a new government agency, Law 67 (and its civil commitment clause) were never overseen by professional or medical bodies.

10. Though introduced in 1993, in design and structure Law 67's procedure for civil commitment is anachronistically akin to the "inebriety" laws that operated

across North America in the late nineteenth and early twentieth centuries. These asylum-era inebriety laws facilitated the institutionalization of thousands of "drunkards" in hospitals and dedicated "inebriate colonies" across the United States between the 1840s and 1940s. See Jim Baumohl, "Inebriate Institutions in North America, 1840–1920," *Addiction* 85, no. 9 (1990): 1187–204. In Puerto Rico specifically, conditions at the state psychiatric hospital seem to have been dire. In 1940, some 200 of the 1,200 patients held there are estimated to have died, mostly from chronic enteritis, dysentery, and tuberculosis. See Robert A. Havlena, *An Exploratory Study of Psychiatric Hospital Effectiveness and Factors Related to Client Aftercare Compliance and Rehospitalization in the Commonwealth of Puerto Rico* (Columbia University Press, 1987). For global histories of civil commitment, see H. Yumi Kim, *Madness in the Family: Women, Care, and Illness in Japan* (Oxford University Press, 2022); Claire E. Edington, *Beyond the Asylum: Mental Illness in French Colonial Vietnam* (Cornell University Press, 2019).

11. Legislative Assembly of Puerto Rico, Law 67.

12. Health in Justice Atlas Lab, "Laws Authorizing Involuntary Commitment for Substance Use," Policy Surveillance Program, 2018.

13. Different ICC statutes use different language. Many US ICC statutes use the term *substance use disorder*, though some, especially those introduced prior to 2013 and the publication of DSM-V, use adjacent terms such as *substance abuse* or *substance dependence*. Puerto Rico's Law 67 uses the lay term "drug addict."

14. Matthew T. Walton and Martin T. Hall, "Involuntary Civil Commitment for Substance Use Disorder: Legal Precedents and Ethical Considerations for Social Workers," *Social Work in Public Health* 32, no. 6 (2017): 382–93.

15. Other legal grounds specified in various pieces of US ICC legislation include but are not limited to "danger to property," "pregnant and abusing," "protection of an unborn child," "prior failed treatment," and "would reasonably benefit from treatment." See Health in Justice Atlas Lab; Christopher, Appelbaum, and Stein, "Criminalization"; John C. Messinger, Daniel J. Ikeda, and Ameet Sarpatwari, "Civil Commitment for Opioid Misuse: Do Short-Term Benefits Outweigh Long-Term Harms?," *Journal of Medical Ethics, Institute of Medical Ethics*, May 2021.

16. Legislative Assembly of Puerto Rico, Law 67.

17. For the US mainland, see Christopher, Appelbaum, and Stein, "Criminalization." For Latin America, see Kevin Lewis O'Neill, *Hunted: Predation and Pentecostalism in Guatemala* (University of Chicago Press, 2019); Claudia Rafful et al., "'Somebody Is Gonna Be Hurt': Involuntary Drug Treatment in Mexico," *Medical Anthropology* 39, no. 2 (2020): 139–52.

18. As I only had access to civilly committed men, I am unsure as to how the law is applied to women.

19. A seventy-year-old pensioner I met in an Evangelical program told me his adult children had used Law 67 to accelerate their inheritance through ridding him from the family home. Similarly, a middle-aged resident who'd lost his eyesight and walked with a stick told me that his brother had used the law against him to settle

a feud. In fairness, I never heard the petitioner's side of the story in either of these cases.

20. I first learned about this through interviews with drug treatment activists, and their stories were corroborated in interviews with one state official and two lawyers.

21. This has been explored elsewhere. See Alfred Lubrano "Puerto Rico's Solution to Heroin Crisis: One-Way Tickets to Philly," Philly.com, November 17, 2016; Rafael Torruella, "¿Allá En Nueva York Todo Es Mejor?: A Qualitative Study on the Relocation of Drug Users from Puerto Rico to the United States" (PhD diss., City University of New York, 2010).

22. Morris, "Detention without Data."

23. Paul P. Christopher et al., "Nature and Utilization of Civil Commitment for Substance Abuse in the United States," *Journal of the American Academy of Psychiatry and the Law* 43, no. 3 (2015): 313–20.

24. Paul P. Christopher et al., "Nature and Utilization."

25. I later learned that the closures were due to austerity measures reducing court opening times, though this was not announced on court websites until much later.

26. The corresponding number for Law 408, which stipulates ICC procedures for *both* substance use disorder and psychiatric cases, was 6503 between 2014 and 2017. Since the court records did not distinguish between substance use disorder and psychiatric cases, it is unclear how many citizens were civilly committed on account of substance use disorders specifically.

27. Prior to 2023, the totality of publications describing Law 67 was as follows: Open Society Foundation, *No Health, No Help: Abuse As Drug Rehabilitation in Latin America and the Caribbean* (2016); LawHelp, "Tratamiento Involuntario Para Adicción y Salud Mental (Ley 67)"; Upegui-Hernández, and Torruella, "Humillaciones y Abusos." This changed in 2022; see Parker, Miranda-Miller, and Albizu-García, "Involuntary Civil Commitment."

28. Officially, Law 67 states that legal counsel is supposed to be assigned to any Law 67 recipient who is unable to pay privately. In practice, this rarely happens.

29. Morris, "Detention without Data."

30. Robert A. Brooks, "US Psychiatrists' Beliefs and Wants about Involuntary Civil Commitment Grounds," *International Journal of Law and Psychiatry* 29, no. 1 (2006): 13–21.

31. Goffman, "Asylum."

32. Alicia W. Peters, "'Things That Involve Sex Are Just Different': US Anti-Trafficking Law and Policy on the Books, in Their Minds, and in Action." *Anthropological Quarterly* 86, no. 1 (2013): 221–55.

33. Legislative Assembly of Puerto Rico, Law 67.

34. Since Law 408 was passed in 2000, DSM-IV was replaced (in 2013) with DSM-V, which replaced the two categories of substance abuse and substance dependence with one diagnostic category, substance use disorders.

35. The right to liberty, which we can also understand as the right to not be institutionalized without consent, is codified in one way or another by various pieces

of Puerto Rican, US, and international law, including the Puerto Rican Law 408, the United States constitution, and the UN Declaration on Human Rights.

36. Legislative Assembly of Puerto Rico, Law 67.

37. Legislative Assembly of Puerto Rico, Law 408.

38. This tends not to be the case in ICC statutes that are drafted as part of penal or welfare codes. See Christopher et al., "Nature and Utilization."

39. Legislative Assembly of Puerto Rico, Law 408, 11–12.

40. Section 15.03 of Law 408 of 2000 ("Institutionalization prohibited") also states that any institution "found to have institutionalized a person . . . who does not . . . present the severity that warrants his/her placement at the level of care where he/she has been kept . . . shall be guilty of a crime, under Article 168 of the Puerto Rico Penal Code [33 L.P.R.A. § 4796]."

41. Robin Respaut, "Why It Can Take Longer than a Year to See a Doctor in Puerto Rico," Reuters, February 5, 2019.

42. Though even here, there are operating costs to consider.

43. Goffman, "Asylum."

44. Garcia, *Pastoral Clinic.*

45. Koselleck, *Futures Past*, 11.

46. Parker, Miranda-Miller, and Albizu-García, "Involuntary Civil Commitment," 59.

CONCLUSION

1. Marie T. Mora, Alberto Davila, and Havidan Rodriguez, "Migration, Geographic Destinations, and Socioeconomic Outcomes of Puerto Ricans during La Crisis Boricua: Implications for Island and Stateside Communities Post-Maria," *CENTRO: Journal of the Center for Puerto Rican Studies* 30, no. 3 (2018): 208–30.

2. Ong, "Cultural Citizenship."

3. Take, for example, the laws preventing nonwhite immigrants from obtaining US citizenship, which have operated for most of the nation's history. Only whites were allowed to "naturalize" (obtain US citizenship) from 1790 through 1870, with naturalization closed to most Asian nationals until 1952. In fact, the national origins quota system of immigration restrictions, which explicitly prevented most Asians and southern Europeans from coming to the United States and becoming permanent residents or citizens because of their original national or ethnicity, was not appealed until 1965. As Smith surmises: "though the specifics changed, denials of access to full citizenship based explicitly on race, ethnicity, or gender always denied large majorities of the world's population opportunities for full U.S. citizenship up to 1965—about 83 percent of the nation's history since the Constitution, 88 percent since the Declaration." Rogers M. Smith, *Civic Ideals: Conflicting Visions of Citizenship in US History* (Yale University Press, 1997), 512.

4. Dred Scott v. Sandford, 19 How. 393, 416 (1857).

5. Wendy Sawyer and Peter Wagner, "Mass Incarceration: The Whole Pie 2023," Prison Policy Initiative, 2023.

6. Prison Policy Initiative, "Correctional Control Extends Far beyond Incarceration," 2020, https://www.prisonpolicy.org/graphs/pie2019_correctional_control.html.

7. Rocío Zambrana, *Colonial Debts*.

· BIBLIOGRAPHY ·

"20 U.S. Code § 7011—Definitions." Cornell Law School, Legal Information Institute, 2021. https://www.law.cornell.edu/uscode/text/20/7011.

Acker, Caroline Jean. *Creating the American Junkie: Addiction Research in the Classic Era of Narcotic Control.* Johns Hopkins University Press, 2002.

Administración de Servicios de Salud Mental y Contra la Adicción (ASSMCA). *Perfil Sociodemográfico Y Epidemiológico Del Programa Corte De Drogas 2007–2008 (Drug Court).* Mental Health and Anti-Addiction Services Administration, 2008.

———. *Puerto Rico Mental Health and Addiction Services Administration (ASSMCA), Certification, Licenses and Safety Division, October 2014.* Mental Health and Anti-Addiction Services Administration, 2014.

———. *Puerto Rico Substance Abuse Needs Assessment Program: 2002 Provider Survey Final Report.* Mental Health and Anti-Addiction Services Administration, 2004.

Agamben, Giorgio. *The Highest Poverty: Monastic Rules and Form-of-Life.* Stanford University Press, 2013.

Alexander, Michelle. *The New Jim Crow: Mass Incarceration in the Age of Colorblindness.* New Press, 2012. Kindle edition.

American Psychiatric Association. *Diagnostic and Statistical Manual of Mental Disorders*, 5th ed. American Psychiatric Association, 2013.

Anderson, Benedict. *Imagined Communities: Reflections on the Origin and Spread of Nationalism.* Verso, 1983.

Anderson, Clare. *A Global History of Convicts and Penal Colonies.* Bloomsbury, 2018.

ATD. "John Maxwell on Leadership." *TD Magazine*, February 8, 2013. https://www.td.org/magazines/td-magazine/john-maxwell-on-leadership.

Ayala, César J. "The Decline of the Plantation Economy and the Puerto Rican Migration of the 1950s." *Latino Studies Journal* 7, no. 1 (1996): 61–90.

Babb, Margarita. "Piden Ciudadania Ayude Combatir Los Drogas" [Citizens asked to help combat drugs]. *El Mundo*, March 13, 1969.

Bandak, Andreas. *The Social Life of Prayers—Introduction*. Taylor & Francis, 2017.

Bauman, Zygmunt. *Wasted Lives: Modernity and Its Outcasts*. John Wiley & Sons, 2013.

Baumohl, Jim. "Inebriate Institutions in North America, 1840–1920." *Addiction* 85, no. 9 (1990): 1187–204.

Beckett, Katherine, and Naomi Murakawa. "Mapping the Shadow Carceral State: Toward an Institutionally Capacious Approach to Punishment." *Theoretical Criminology* 16, no. 2 (2012): 221–44.

Berger, John. "The Moment of Cubism." *New Left Review* 42 (1967): 75.

Berlant, Lauren. *Cruel Optimism*. Duke University Press, 2011.

Binswanger, Ingrid A., Marc F. Stern, Richard A. Deyo, Patrick J. Heagerty, Allen Cheadle, Joann G. Elmore, and Thomas D. Koepsell. "Release from Prison—a High Risk of Death for Former Inmates." *New England Journal of Medicine* 356, no. 2 (2007): 157–65. https://doi.org/10.1056/NEJMsa064115.

Blackmon, Douglas A. *Slavery by Another Name: The Re-enslavement of Black Americans from the Civil War to World War II*. Anchor, 2009.

Bonilla-Silva, Eduardo, and Sarah Mayorga. "On (Not) Belonging: Why Citizenship Does Not Remedy Racial Inequality." In *State of White Supremacy: Racism, Governance, and the United States*, edited by Moon-Kie Jung, João H. Costa Vargas, and Eduardo Bonilla-Silva, 77–90. Stanford University Press, 2020.

Bourgois, Philippe. *In Search of Respect: Selling Crack in El Barrio*. Cambridge University Press, 2003.

Bourgois, Philippe I., and Jeffrey Schonberg. *Righteous Dopefiend*. University of California Press, 2009.

Braslow, Joel Tupper. "The Manufacture of Recovery." *Annual Review of Clinical Psychology* 9 (2013): 781–809.

Brooks, Robert A. "Psychiatrists' Opinions about Involuntary Civil Commitment: Results of a National Survey." *Journal of the American Academy of Psychiatry and the Law Online* 35, no. 2 (2007): 219–28.

Cabranes, José A. *Citizenship and the American Empire: Notes on the Legislative History of the United States Citizenship of Puerto Ricans*. Yale University Press, 1979.

Cabrera, Alba. "Acusan Alcalde SJ Usar Fondos Federales Asignadas Hogar CREA Para Hacer Politica" [Mayor of San Juan accused of using federal funds assigned to Hogar CREA to do politics]. *El Mundo*, 4 April 1973.

———. "CREA, Programa Efectivo En Re-Educacion de Adictos" [CREA, effective program in the re-education of addicts]. *El Mundo*, 25 January 1969.

Campbell, N. D., J. P. Olsen, and Luke Walden. *The Narcotic Farm: The Rise and Fall of America's First Prison for Drug Addicts*. Abrams, 2008.

Campbell, Nancy D., and Susan J. Shaw. "Incitements to Discourse: Illicit Drugs, Harm Reduction, and the Production of Ethnographic Subjects." *Cultural Anthropology* 23, no. 4 (2008): 688–717.

Cappa, Luis. "Censuran Conducta Efrain Santiago, Comisiones Senado Aprueban $200 Mil Para CREA" [Behavior of Efrain Santiago criticized, Senate committee approve $200,000 for CREA]. *El Mundo*, February 4, 1972.

Carr, Summerson. "Anticipating and Inhabiting Institutional Identities." *American Ethnologist* 36, no. 2 (2009): 317–36.

Carrington, Kerry, Russell Hogg, and Máximo Sozzo. "Southern Criminology." *British Journal of Criminology* 56, no. 1 (2016): 1–20.

Carson, E. Ann. 'Prisoners in 2019.' 2020. https://bjs.ojp.gov/content/pub/pdf/p19.pdf.

Cassian, John. *John Cassian*. Translated by O. P. Ramsey. Paulist, 2000.

———. *John Cassian: The Institutes*. SUNY Press, 2000.

———. *John Cassian: The Conferences*. Newman, 1997.

Centro de Investigaciones Sobre la Adicción (CISLA). *Centro de Investigaciones Sobre La Adicción (CISLA) Boletin Informativo*. 1, no. 1 (April 1964).

Christopher, Paul P., Paul S. Appelbaum, and Michael D. Stein. "Criminalization of Opioid Civil Commitment." *JAMA Psychiatry* 77, no. 2 (2020): 111–12. https://doi.org/10.1001/jamapsychiatry.2019.2845.

Christopher, Paul P., Debra A. Pinals, Taylor Stayton, Kellie Sanders, and Lester Blumberg. "Nature and Utilization of Civil Commitment for Substance Abuse in the United States." *Journal of the American Academy of Psychiatry and the Law* 43, no. 3 (2015): 313–20.

Civil Rights Litigation Clearinghouse. "Case: Feliciano v. Parole Board of the Commonwealth of Puerto Rico." Civil Rights Litigation Clearinghouse, last updated July 11, 2023. https://www.clearinghouse.net/detail.php?id=932.

Coote, Anna. "Help to Work? Britain's Jobless Are Being Forced into Workfare, More Like." *The Guardian*, Opinion, April 28, 2014. https://www.theguardian.com/commentisfree/2014/apr/28/help-to-work-britains-jobless-forced-workfare-unemployed.

Courtwright, David T. "A Century of American Narcotic Policy." *Treating Drug Problems* 2 (1992): 1–62.

Creighton, Colin. "The Rise of the Male Breadwinner Family: A Reappraisal." *Comparative Studies in Society and History* 38, no. 2 (1996): 310–37.

Crislip, Andrew. "The Sin of Sloth or the Illness of the Demons? The Demon of Acedia in Early Christian Monasticism." *Harvard Theological Review* 98, no. 2 (2005): 143–69.

Cruz-Janzen, Marta I. "Out of the Closet: Racial Amnesia, Avoidance, and Denial—Racism among Puerto Ricans." *Race, Gender, and Class* 10, no. 3 (2003): 64–81.

Darke, Sacha. "Inmate Governance in Brazilian Prisons." *Howard Journal of Criminal Justice* 52, no. 3 (2013): 272–84.

———. "Surviving in the New Mass Carceral Zone." *Prison Service Journal* 229 (2017): 2–9.

Davis, Elizabeth Anne. *Bad Souls: Madness and Responsibility in Modern Greece.* Duke University Press, 2012.

Dayan, Colin. *The Law Is a White Dog—How Legal Rituals Make and Unmake Persons.* Princeton University Press, 2013.

Densen-Gerber, Judianne. *We Mainline Dreams: The Odyssey House Story.* Doubleday Books, 1973.

Department of Correction and Rehabilitation. *Intermediate Sanctions Plan.* Departamento de Corrección y Rehabilitación, Biblioteca Legislativa de Puerto Rico, 1994.

Departamento de Justicia. *Departamento de Justicia Explicación Del Prepuesto Funcional Año Fiscal 1985–1986.* Departamento de Justicia, Biblioteca Legislativa de Puerto Rico, 1986.

———. *Departamento de Justicia Memorial Explicativo Año Fiscal 1991–1992.* Departamento de Justicia, Biblioteca Legislativa de Puerto Rico, 1992.

Departamento de Servicios Contra la Adicción (DSCA). *Los Programas de Mantenimiento Con Metadona.* Estado Libre Asociado de Puerto Rico, 1975.

———. *Informe Anual: 1985–86.* Estado Libre Asociado de Puerto Rico, 1986.

———. *Memorial Explicativo Para El Prepuesto de Gastos de Funcionamiento y de Mejoras Permanentes Año Fiscal 1985–1986.* Estado Libre Asociado de Puerto Rico, 1986.

Díaz, Alberto Ortiz. "Pathologizing the Jíbaro: Mental and Social Health in Puerto Rico's Oso Blanco (1930s to 1950s)." *The Americas* 77, no. 3 (2020): 409–41.

———. *Raising the Living Dead: Rehabilitative Corrections in Puerto Rico and the Caribbean.* Chicago: University of Chicago Press, 2023

———"Puerto Rican Christianities in the United States," in *The Oxford Handbook of Latinx Christianities in the United States,* edited by Kristy Nabhan-Warren, 46. Oxford University Press, 2022.

Díaz Soler, Luis M. "Historia de La Esclavitud En Puerto Rico." San Juan, Editorial de La Universidad de Puerto Rico, 1953.

Dietz, James L. *Economic History of Puerto Rico: Institutional Change and Capitalist Development.* Princeton University Press, 1986.

———. "Puerto Rico in the 1970s and 1980s: Crisis of the Development Model." *Journal of Economic Issues* 16, no. 2 (1982): 497–506.

Du Bois, W. E. B. *Black Reconstruction.* Harcourt, Brace, and Howe, 1935.

Duany, Jorge. "Neither White nor Black: The Representation of Racial Identity among Puerto Ricans on the Island and in the U.S. Mainland." In *Neither Enemies nor Friends: Latinos, Blacks, Afro-Latinos,* edited by Anani Dzidzienyo and Suzanne Oboler, 173–88. Palgrave Macmillan, 2005.

———. *The Puerto Rican Nation on the Move: Identities on the Island and in the United States.* University of North Carolina Press, 2003.

Durkheim, Emile. *Durkheim: The Division of Labour in Society.* Macmillan International Higher Education, 2013.

Durose, Matthew R., and Leonardo Antenangeli. *Recidivism of Prisoners Released in 34 States in 2012: A 5-Year Follow-Up Period (2012–2017)*. US Department of Justice. Office of Justice Programs, 2021.

Eberle, Luke, trans. *The Rule of the Master*. Cistercian, 1977.

Edin, Kathryn, and Maria Kefalas. *Promises I Can Keep: Why Poor Women Put Motherhood before Marriage*. University of California Press, 2011.

El Mundo. "Cierra Manana La Cruzada de Hogares CREA." August 31, 1990.

———. "Creando Hombres Nuevos" [Creating new men]. April 8, 1988.

———. "Cruzada de Fe y Esperanza." May 26, 1989.

———. "Director Hogares CREA Dice Hay Mas de 50 Mil Adictos a Drogas En Isla" [Director of Hogares CREA says there are more than 50,000 drug addicts across island]. October 18, 1972.

———. "Es Un Exito Casa CREA Juncos" [It's a success CREA House Juncos]. May 2, 1970.

———. "Organizan Comite Pro Hogar CREA" [Committee pro Hogar CREA organized]. February 16, 1970.

———. "Rehabilitando al Adicto" [Rehabilitating the addict]. November 4, 1969.

———. "Senador Colon Alaba Labor Centro Rehabilitacion Adictos" [Senator Colon praises work of addict rehabilitation center]. April 8, 1970.

———. "Visitaron Hogar CREA." February 19, 1973.

El Reportero. "Teen Challenge Contra Metadona." January 1981. http://pciponline .org/.

El Vocero. "'Calidad de Vida' Chejuan, Un Orgullo de Puerto Rico." July 17, 1987.

———. "CREA Contribuye a Reforestación" [CREA contributes to reforestation]. June 24, 1999.

———. "Hogar CREA 'Buena Cosecha'" [Hogar CREA "Good Crop"]. December 6, 2000.

Erikson, Erik H. *Identity and the Life Cycle: Selected Papers*. International Universities Press, 1959.

Evagrius Ponticus. *The Praktikos: Chapters on Prayer*. Translated by John Eudes Bamberger. Cistercian Studies Series 4. Cistercian Publications, 1970.

Fairbanks, Robert P. *How It Works: Recovering Citizens in Post-Welfare Philadelphia*. University of Chicago Press, 2009.

Ferguson, James. *Give a Man a Fish: Reflections on the New Politics of Distribution*. Duke University Press, 2015.

Ferrería, Juan Nadal. "Colossal Cost of Subsidizing Failure: How the Drug War Impacts Puerto Rico's Budget," *Review Journal of the University of Puerto Rico* 81 (2012): 1139.

Fiddick, Peter. "Junkie Cure Junkie." *Manchester Guardian Weekly*, February 16, 1967.

Figueroa, Mabel. "'Chejuan' García: Rehabilitador de Vidas y Sueños." *Primera Hora*, March 18, 2000.

Figueroa-Lazu, Damayra, Jennifer Hinojosa, and Yarimar Bonilla. "Puerto Rico's 2020 Race/Ethnicity Decennial Analysis." CentroPR, October 13, 2021.

https://centropr.hunter.cuny.edu/reports/puerto-ricos-2020-decennial
-analysis-datasheet-series/.

Flores, Edward. *God's Gangs: Barrio Ministry, Masculinity, and Gang Recovery*. NYU Press, 2014.

Folbre, Nancy. "The Unproductive Housewife: Her Evolution in Nineteenth-Century Economic Thought." *Signs: Journal of Women in Culture and Society* 16, no. 3 (1991): 463–84.

Foner, Eric. *Reconstruction: America's Unfinished Revolution, 1863–1877*. Updated ed. Harper Perennial, 2015.

Fontes, Anthony W. *Mortal Doubt: Transnational Gangs and Social Order in Guatemala City*. University of California Press, 2018.

Forman, James, Jr. *Locking Up Our Own: Crime and Punishment in Black America*. Farrar, Straus and Giroux, 2017.

Foucault, Michel. *Discipline and Punish: The Birth of the Prison*. Vintage, 1977.

Garces, Chris. "The Cross Politics of Ecuador's Penal State." *Cultural Anthropology* 25, no. 3 (2010): 459–96.

———. "Prisons of Charity: Christian Exceptionality and Decarceration in Ecuador's Penal State." In *Governing Gifts: Faith, Charity, and the Security State*, edited by Erica Caple James. 2019. https://www.academia.edu/38714742/ Prisons_of_Charity_Christian_Exceptionality_and_Decarceration_in _Ecuadors_Penal_State.

Garces, Chris, Tomas Martin, and Sacha Darke. "Informal Prison Dynamics in Africa and Latin America: Chris Garces, Tomas Martin and Sacha Darke Contend That Research in Men's Prisons Demands a Widening of Theoretical Perspectives and Methodological Repertoires." *Criminal Justice Matters* 91, no. 1 (2013): 26–27.

Garcia, Angela. *The Pastoral Clinic: Addiction and Dispossession along the Rio Grande*. University of California Press, 2010.

———. "Serenity: Violence, Inequality, and Recovery on the Edge of Mexico City." *Medical Anthropology Quarterly* 29, no. 4 (2015). http://onlinelibrary.wiley.com/ doi/10.1111/maq.12208/full.

Garland, David. *Mass Imprisonment: Social Causes and Consequences*. Sage, 2001.

———. *Punishment and Modern Society*. University of Chicago Press, 1990.

Geertz, Clifford. "Thick Description: Toward an Interpretive Theory of Culture." *Turning Points in Qualitative Research: Tying Knots in a Handkerchief* 3 (1973): 143–68.

Gibbs, Anita. "Probation Service Users as Volunteers in Partnership Projects." *Probation Journal* 43, no. 3 (1996): 142–46.

Godreau, Isar, Hilda Lloréns, and Carlos Vargas-Ramos. "Colonial Incongruence at Work: Employing US Census Racial Categories in Puerto Rico." *Anthropology News* 51 (May 2010): 11–12. https://doi.org/10.1111/j.1556-3502.2010.51511.x.

Goffman, Erving. "Asylum." *New York*. Anchor Books, 1961.

Gómez Acevedo, Labor. *Organización y reglamentación del trabajo en el Puerto Rico del siglo 19 (proprietarios y jornaleros)*. San Juan: Instituto de Cultura Puertorriqueña, 1970.

Governing. "Police Employment, Officers per Capita Rates for U.S. Cities." Governing.com, 2018. https://www.governing.com/gov-data/safety-justice/police-officers-per-capita-rates-employment-for-city-departments.html.

Gowan, Teresa. *Hobos, Hustlers, and Backsliders: Homeless in San Francisco*. University of Minnesota Press, 2010.

Greenberg, Joshua R. *Advocating the Man: Masculinity, Organized Labor, and the Household in New York, 1800–1840*. New York: Columbia University Press, 2009.

Guzman, Janine. "Puerto Rico: Being Charged with a Felony Can Be Just Cause for Dismissal." DLA Piper, May 10, 2019. https://www.dlapiper.com/en/us/insights/publications/2019/05/puerto-rico-being-charged/.

Hansen, Helena. *Addicted to Christ: Remaking Men in Puerto Rican Pentecostal Drug Ministries*. University of California Press, 2018.

Hart, Keith. "Informal Income Opportunities and Urban Employment in Ghana." *Journal of Modern African Studies* 11, no. 1 (1973): 61–89.

Havlena, Robert A. *An Exploratory Study of Psychiatric Hospital Effectiveness and Factors Related to Client Aftercare Compliance and Rehospitalization in the Commonwealth of Puerto Rico*. Columbia University Press, 1987.

Health in Justice Atlas Lab. *Laws Authorizing Involuntary Commitment for Substance Use*. Policy Surveillance Program, 2018. https://lawatlas.org/datasets/civil-commitment-for-substance-users.

Hennigan, Brian. "House Broken: Homelessness, Housing First, and Neoliberal Poverty Governance." *Urban Geography* 38, no. 9 (2017): 1418–40.

Hirsch, Jennifer S., Holly Wardlow, Daniel Jordan Smith, Harriet Phinney, Shanti Parikh, and Constance A. Nathanson. "Best, Worst, and Good Enough." *Comparing Cultures: Innovations in Comparative Ethnography* (2020): 155–80.

Holston, James. *Insurgent Citizenship: Disjunctions of Democracy and Modernity in Brazil*. Princeton University Press, 2021.

Hopper, Kim, and Jim Baumohl. "Held in Abeyance: Rethinking Homelessness and Advocacy." *American Behavioral Scientist* 37, no. 4 (1994): 522–52.

Human Rights Watch. "Punishment and Prejudice: Racial Disparities in the War on Drugs." HRW.com, 2022. https://www.hrw.org/legacy/campaigns/drugs/war/key-facts.htm.

Jaffe, S. *Narcotics—an American Plan*. P. S. Ericsson, 1966.

Jeffrey, Craig. "Timepass: Youth, Class, and Time among Unemployed Young Men in India." *American Ethnologist* 37, no. 3 (2010): 465–81.

Jerome. *Selected Letters*. Translated by F. A. Wright. Harvard University Press, 1989.

Jervis, Lori L., Paul Spicer, and Spero M. Manson. "Boredom, Trouble, and the Realities of Postcolonial Reservation Life." *Ethos* (2003). https://psycnet.apa.org/record/2003-08562-002.

Johnson-Hanks, Jennifer. "On the Limits of Life Stages in Ethnography: Toward a Theory of Vital Conjunctures." *American Anthropologist* 104, no. 3 (2002): 865–80.

Joseph, Gilbert M., and Emily S. Rosenberg. *Foreign in a Domestic Sense: Puerto Rico, American Expansion, and the Constitution.* Duke University Press, 2001.

Jung, Moon-Kie, Joao Costa Vargas, and Eduardo Bonilla-Silvam, eds. *State of White Supremacy: Racism, Governance, and the United States.* Stanford University Press, 2011.

Justia US Law. "Feliciano v. Barcelo, 497 F. Supp. 14 (D.P.R. 1979)." Justia US Law, accessed January 11, 2024. https://law.justia.com/cases/federal/district-courts/FSupp/497/14/1614272/.

Kampen, Thomas, Lex Veldboer, and Reinout Kleinhans. "The Obligation to Volunteer as Fair Reciprocity? Welfare Recipients' Perceptions of Giving Back to Society." *VOLUNTAS: International Journal of Voluntary and Nonprofit Organizations* 30, no. 5 (2019): 991–1005. https://doi.org/10.1007/s11266-018-00082-4.

Kaye, Kerwin. *Enforcing Freedom: Drug Courts, Therapeutic Communities, and the Intimacies of the State.* Columbia University Press, 2019.

———. "Rehabilitating the 'Drugs Lifestyle': Criminal Justice, Social Control, and the Cultivation of Agency." *Ethnography* 14, no. 2 (2013): 207–32.

Kelvin A. Santiago-Valles. "Forcing Them to Work and Punishing Whoever Resisted: Servile Labor and Penal Servitude under Colonialism in Nineteenth Century Puerto Rico." In *Birth of the Penitentiary in Latin America*, edited by Ricardo D. Salvatore and Carlos Aguirre, 123–68. University of Texas Press, 1996.

Kolb, Lawrence. "Types and Characteristics of Drug Addicts." *Mental Hygiene* 9 (1925): 300–313.

Koselleck, Reinhart. *Futures Past: On the Semantics of Historical Time.* Columbia University Press, 2004.

Landy, David. Tropical Childhood: Cultural Transmission and Learning in a Rural Puerto Rican Village. University of North Carolina Press, 1959.

La Roche, Claire R., Bennie D. Waller, and Scott A. Wentland. "'Not in My Backyard': The Effect of Substance Abuse Treatment Centers on Property Values." *Journal of Sustainable Real Estate* 6, no. 1 (2014): 63–92.

Lapp, Michael. "The Rise and Fall of Puerto Rico as a Social Laboratory, 1945–1965." *Social Science History* 19, no. 2 (1995): 169–99.

LeBrón, Marisol. *Policing Life and Death: Race, Violence, and Resistance in Puerto Rico.* University of California Press, 2019.

———. "Puerto Rico and the Colonial Circuits of Policing: How Reconsidering the History of Policing in Puerto Rico Complicates Our Understandings of the Island's Colonial Relationship with the United States." *NACLA Report on the Americas* 49, no. 3 (2017): 328–34.

———. "Puerto Rico's War on Its Poor." Boston Review, December 11, 2018. http://bostonreview.net/class-inequality/marisol-lebron-puerto-rico-war-poor.

Legislative Assembly of Puerto Rico. "Ley de la Administración de Servicios de
Salud Mental y Contra la Adicción." Ley núm. 67 de 7 de agosto de 1993, según
enmendada (Contiene enmiendas incorporadas por las siguientes leyes: ley
núm. 2 de 8 de enero de 1994, ley núm. 53 de 13 de agosto de 2005, ley núm.
182 de 6 de agosto de 2008, ley núm. 172 de 16 de agosto de 2012, ley núm. 45
de 21 de septiembre de 2021). 1993. https://docs.pr.gov/files/ASSMCA/
Licenciamiento/Ley%2067-1993.pdf.

———. "Ley de Salud Mental de Puerto Rico." Ley núm. 408 de 2 de octubre de
2000, según enmendada (Contiene enmiendas incorporadas por las siguientes
leyes: ley núm. 183 de 6 de agosto de 2008, ley núm. 88 de 17 de mayo de 2012,
ley núm. 170 de 16 de agosto de 2012, ley núm. 172 de 16 de agosto de 2012, ley
núm. 211 de 25 de agosto de 2012). 2000. https://docs.pr.gov/files/ASSMCA/
Licenciamiento/Ley%20408-2000.pdf.

Lerman, Amy E., and Vesla M. Weaver. *Arresting Citizenship: The Democratic
Consequences of American Crime Control*. University of Chicago Press, 2014.

Levenson, Joe, and Finola Farrant. "Unlocking Potential: Active Citizenship and
Volunteering By Prisoners." *Probation Journal* 49, no. 3 (2002): 195–204.

Lewis, Oscar. *La Vida: A Puerto Rican Family in the Culture of Poverty*. Random
House, 1966.

Lévi-Strauss, Claude. *The Savage Mind*. University of Chicago Press, 1966.

Levitt, Peggy, and Sally Merry. "Vernacularization on the Ground: Local Uses of
Global Women's Rights in Peru, China, India and the United States." *Global
Networks* 9, no. 4 (2009): 441–61.

Lewis, Oscar. *Five Families: Mexcan Case Studies in the Culture of Poverty*. Basic
Books, 1959.

Lichtenstein, Alex. *Twice the Work of Free Labor: The Political Economy of Convict
Labor in the New South*. Verso, 1996.

Looney, Adam, and Nicholas Turner. "Work and Opportunity before and after
Incarceration." *Brookings* (blog), March 14, 2018. https://www.brookings.edu/
research/work-and-opportunity-before-and-after-incarceration/.

Lubrano, Alfred. "Puerto Rico's Solution to Heroin Crisis: One-Way Tickets to
Philly." Philly.com, November 17, 2016. http://www.philly.com/philly/news/
special_packages/Puerto_Ricos_solution_to_heroin_crisis_one-way_tickets
_to_Philly.html.

Macro Systems. *Drug Treatment and Prevention Programs in the Commonwealth of
Puerto Rico*. San Juan: Archivo Histórico Universitario, 1972.

Maddrell, Avril. "Carceral Transitions Experienced through Community Service
Placements in Charity Shops." In *Carceral Mobilities*, edited by Jennifer Turner
and Kimberley Peters, 221–35. Routledge, 2017.

Mains, Daniel. "Neoliberal Times: Progress, Boredom, and Shame among Young
Men in Urban Ethiopia." *American Ethnologist* 34, no. 4 (2007): 659–73.

———. "Too Much Time: Changing Conceptions of Boredom, Progress, and the
Future among Young Men in Urban Ethiopia, 2003–2015." *Focaal* 78 (2017):
38–51.

Manza, Jeff, and Christopher Uggen. *Locked Out: Felon Disenfranchisement and American Democracy*. Oxford University Press, 2008.

Marques, Rene. "El Puertorriqueño Dócil." *Revista de Ciencias Sociales*, no. 1–2 (1963): 35–78.

Marx, Karl. *Theories of Surplus-Value: Volume IV of Capital*. Progress, 1963.

Masquelier, Adeline. "The Scorpion's Sting: Youth, Marriage and the Struggle for Social Maturity in Niger." *Journal of the Royal Anthropological Institute* 11, no. 1 (2005): 59–83.

Mauss, Marcel. *The Gift: The Form and Reason for Exchange in Archaic Societies*. Routledge, 2002.

———. *On Prayer*. Edited by W. S. F. Pickering. Translated by Susan Leslie. Durkheim Press / Berghahn Books, 2003.

McKim, Allison. "Roxanne's Dress: Governing Gender and Marginality through Addiction Treatment." *Signs* 40, no. 1 (2014). http://www.jstor.org/stable/10.1086/673089.

Messinger, John C., Daniel J. Ikeda, and Ameet Sarpatwari. "Civil Commitment for Opioid Misuse: Do Short-Term Benefits Outweigh Long-Term Harms?" *Journal of Medical Ethics*, May 2021. https://doi.org/10.1136/medethics-2020-107160.

Millar, Kathleen. "The Precarious Present: Wageless Labor and Disrupted Life in Rio de Janeiro, Brazil." *Cultural Anthropology* 29, no. 1 (2014): 32–53.

———. *Reclaiming the Discarded: Life and Labor on Rio's Garbage Dump*. Duke University Press, 2018.

Miller, Reuben Jonathan, and Gwendolyn Purifoye. "Carceral Devolution and the Transformation of Urban America." In *The Voluntary Sector in Prisons*, 195–213. Springer, 2016.

Miller, Reuben Jonathan, and Forrest Stuart. "Carceral Citizenship: Race, Rights and Responsibility in the Age of Mass Supervision." *Theoretical Criminology* 21, no. 4 (2017): 532–48.

Mintz, Sidney Wilfred. "Cañamelar: The Contemporary Culture of a Rural Puerto Rican Proletariat." In *The People of Puerto Rico*, 314–417. University of Illinois Press, 1956.

———. "The Culture History of a Puerto Rican Sugar Cane Plantation: 1876–1949." *Hispanic American Historical Review* 33, no. 2 (1957): 224–51.

———. "Puerto Rico: An Essay in the Definition of a National Culture." In *Status of Puerto Rico: Selected Background Studies*, 339–434. US Department of Health, Education and Welfare, US Government Printing Office, 1966.

Mizruchi, Ephraim Harold. *Regulating Society: Marginality and Social Control in Historical Perspective*. New York: Free Press, 1983.

Mora, Marie T., Alberto Davila, and Havidan Rodriguez. "Migration, Geographic Destinations, and Socioeconomic Outcomes of Puerto Ricans during La Crisis Boricua: Implications for Island and Stateside Communities Post-Maria." *CENTRO: Journal of the Center for Puerto Rican Studies* 30, no. 3 (2018): 208–30.

Morris, Nathaniel P. "Detention without Data: Public Tracking of Civil Commitment. *Psychiatric Services* 71, no. 7 (2020): 741–44. https://doi .org/10.1176/appi.ps.202000212.

Muehlebach, Andrea Karin. *The Moral Neoliberal: Welfare State and Ethical Citizenship in Contemporary Italy.* University of Chicago Press, 2012.

Muehlmann, Shaylih. *When I Wear My Alligator Boots: Narco-Culture in the US Mexico Borderlands.* University of California Press, 2013.

Mulligan, Jessica M. *Unmanageable Care: An Ethnography of Health Care Privatization in Puerto Rico.* NYU Press, 2014.

National Employment Law Project. "Ban the Box: U.S. Cities, Counties, and States Adopt Fair Hiring Policies." National Employment Law Project, 2022. https://www.nelp.org/publication/ban-the-box-fair-chance-hiring-state-and -local-guide/.

National Institute on Drug Abuse. *How Effective Is Drug Addiction Treatment?* National Institute on Drug Abuse, 2020.

National Law Center on Homelessness and Poverty and the National Coalition for the Homeless. *Homes Not Handcuffs: The Criminalization of Homelessness in U.S. Cities.* 2009. http://www.nationalhomeless.org/publications/crimreport/ CrimzReport_2009.pdf.

Norris, Kathleen. *Acedia and Me: A Marriage, Monks, and a Writer's Life.* Penguin, 2008.

NPR. "The Rehab Empire Built on Cakes." NPR, December 5, 2018. https:// www.npr.org/2018/12/04/673450332/the-rehab-empire-built-on-cakes.

O'Neill, Bruce. *The Space of Boredom: Homelessness in the Slowing Global Order.* Duke University Press, 2017.

O'Neill, Kevin Lewis. *Hunted: Predation and Pentecostalism in Guatemala.* University of Chicago Press, 2019.

———. *Secure the Soul: Christian Piety and Gang Prevention in Guatemala.* University of California Press, 2015.

O'Neill, Kevin Lewis, and Anthony W. Fontes. "Making Do: The Practice of Imprisonment in Postwar Guatemala." *Journal of Latin American Geography* 16, no. 2 (2017): 31–48.

Ong, Aihwa. "Mutations in Citizenship." *Theory, Culture, and Society* 23, no. 2–3 (2006): 499–505.

Parker, Caroline M. "From Treatment to Containment to Enterprise: An Ethno-History of Therapeutic Communities in Puerto Rico, 1961–1993." *Culture, Medicine, and Psychiatry* 44, no. 1 (2020): 135–57.

Parker, Caroline M., Oscar E. Miranda-Miller, and Carmen Albizu-García. "Involuntary Civil Commitment for Substance Use Disorders in Puerto Rico: Neglected Rights Violations and Implications for Legal Reform." *Health and Human Rights Journal* (blog), September 1, 2022. https://www.hhrjournal .org/2022/08/involuntary-civil-commitment-for-substance-use-disorders-in -puerto-rico-neglected-rights-violations-and-implications-for-legal-reform/.

Parker, Caroline Mary, and Julienne Weegels. "Carceral Citizenship in Latin America and the Caribbean: Exclusion and Belonging in the New Mass Carceral Zone." European Review of Latin American and Caribbean Studies 116 (2023): 69–85.

Pedreira, Antonio S. Insularismo: Ensayos de Interpretación Puertorriqueña. Biblioteca de Autores Puertorriqueños, 1942.

Peters, Alicia W. "'Things That Involve Sex Are Just Different': US Anti-Trafficking Law and Policy on the Books, in Their Minds, and in Action." Anthropological Quarterly 86, no. 1 (2013): 221–55.

Picó, Fernando. El día menospensado: historia de los presidiarios en Puerto Rico. Río Piedras, PR: Ediciones Huracan, 1994.

Planas, Lydia Pena de, Myriam Rodriguez de Lopez, and Carmen Alvarez. El Tratamiento De Adictos A Drogas En Puerto Rico [The treatment of drug addicts in Puerto Rico]. Universidad de Puerto Rico, 1965.

Planning Board of Puerto Rico. Informe Económico al Gobernador, 1964 [Economic report to the governor]. Oficina del Gobernador, Junta de Planificacion, Negociado de Analisis Economico y Social, 1964. http://lcw.lehman.edu/lehman/depts/latinampuertorican/latinoweb/PuertoRico/Bootstrap.htm#_edn9.

Porter, J. "The Street/Treatment Barrier: Treatment Experiences of Puerto Rican Injection Drug Users." Substance Use and Misuse 34, no. 14 (1999): 1951–75. https://doi.org/10.3109/10826089909039434.

Povinelli, Elizabeth A. The Cunning of Recognition: Indigenous Alterities and the Making of Australian Multiculturalism. Illustrated ed. Durham, NC: Duke University Press, 2002.

Preble, Edward, and John J. Casey. "Taking Care of Business—the Heroin User's Life on the Street." Substance Use and Misuse 4, no. 1 (1969): 1–24.

Primera Hora. "Crea Gradúa 30 Almas Libres de Drogas" [CREA graduates 30 souls free from drugs]. Primera Hora, December 2000.

Prison Policy Initiative. Correctional Control Extends Far beyond Incarceration. 2020. https://www.prisonpolicy.org/graphs/pie2019_correctional_control.html.

———. Out of Prison and Out of Work. 2018. https://www.prisonpolicy.org/reports/outofwork.html.

Rafful, Claudia, María Elena Medina-Mora, Patricia González-Zúñiga, Janis H. Jenkins, M. Gudelia Rangel, Steffanie A. Strathdee, and Peter J. Davidson. "'Somebody Is Gonna Be Hurt': Involuntary Drug Treatment in Mexico." Medical Anthropology 39, no. 2 (2020): 139–52. https://doi.org/10.1080/01459740.2019.1609470.

Ramirez, Efren. "The Mental Health Program of the Commonwealth of Puerto Rico." In Rehabilitating the Narcotics Addict. Vocational Rehabilitation Administration, US Department of Health, 1966. http://www.addapr.info/images/Rehabilitating_the_Narcotic_Addict_-_Copy.pdf.

———. "Puerto Rican Blueprint." In Narcotics: An American Plan, edited by Saul Jeffee, 112–28. P. S. Eriksson, 1966.

Ramirez, Efren, and Juan José García Ríos. "Letter from Efren Ramirez and Juan José García Ríos to Governor, Hon. Rafael Hernández Colón." March 19, 1985. Ocean Park Ambulatory Therapeutic Community.

Ravndal, Edle, and Ellen J. Amundsen. "Mortality among Drug Users after Discharge from Inpatient Treatment: An 8-Year Prospective Study." *Drug and Alcohol Dependence* 108, no. 1 (2010): 65–69. https://doi.org/10.1016/j .drugalcdep.2009.11.008.

Respaut, Robin. "Why It Can Take Longer than a Year to See a Doctor in Puerto Rico." Reuters, 2016. http://www.reuters.com/investigates/special-report/ usa-puertorico-healthcare/.

Restoration of Rights Project. *Puerto Rico: Restoration of Rights & Record Relief.* 2020. https://ccresourcecenter.org/state-restoration-profiles/ puerto-rico-restoration-of-rights-pardon-expungement-sealing/.

Rivera, Enrique, Nicolas Cornier, Andres Rivera, and Carmen Cruz. "Análisis de La Situación de La Salud En Puerto Rico, Salud Mental." 2005. http://nesile .tripod.com/analisissaludmental.pdf.

Rivera, Juan Antonio Ocasio. "The Federal Oversight Board for Puerto Rico: A Blatant Act of Colonialism." Latino Rebels, April 13, 2016. http://www .latinorebels.com/2016/04/13/the-federal-oversight-board-for-puerto-rico -a-blatant-act-of-colonialism/.

Rodriguez, Wilda. "CREA Le Responde a Sila Nazario" [CREA responds to Sila Nazario]. *El Nuevo Dia*, June 15, 1978.

Ross, Karl. "Crea Rehabilitation Claim of 87% Unsubstantiated." *San Juan Star*, September 26, 1995.

——. "Myths Regarding Founder of Hogar Crea Full of Flaws." *San Juan Star*, September 27, 1995. http://pciponline.org/.

Safa, Helen. *The Myth of the Male Breadwinner: Women and Industrialization in the Caribbean*. Boulder, CO: Westview, 1995.

——. "The Transformation of Puerto Rico: The Impact of Modernization Ideology." *Transforming Anthropology* 19, no. 1 (2011): 46–49.

——. *The Urban Poor of Puerto Rico: A Study in Development and Inequality*. Holt Rinehart & Winston, 1974.

Saint Benedict. *The Rule of St. Benedict*. Sands, 1906.

Santiago-Negrón, Salvador, and Carmen E. Albizu-García. "Guerra Contra Las Drogas o Guerra Contra La Salud? Los Retos Para La Salud Pública de La Política de Drogas de Puerto Rico" [War on drugs or war against health? The pitfalls for public health of Puerto Rican drug policy]. *Puerto Rico Health Sciences Journal* 22, no. 1 (2003). http://prhsj.rcm.upr.edu/index.php/prhsj/ article/download/740/531.

Sassen, Saskia. *Expulsions*. Harvard University Press, 2014.

——. "The Informal Economy: Between New Developments and Old Regulations." *Yale Law Journal* 103, no. 8 (1994): 2289.

Sawyer, Wendy, and Peter Wagner. "Mass Incarceration: The Whole Pie 2022." Prison Policy Initiative, 2022. https://www.prisonpolicy.org/reports/pie2022.html.

Seattle Times. "Puerto Ricans Struggle over Once-Grisly Oso Blanco Prison." May 17, 2014. http://www.seattletimes.com/nation-world/puerto-ricans-struggle-over-once-grisly-oso-blanco-prison/.

Singer, Merrill, Freddie Valentin, Hans Baer, and Zhongke Jia. "Why Does Juan García Have a Drinking Problem? The Perspective of Critical Medical Anthropology." *Medical Anthropology* 14, no. 1 (1992): 77–108.

Smith, Lesley A., Simon Gates, and David Foxcroft. "Therapeutic Communities for Substance Related Disorder." *Cochrane Library.* http://onlinelibrary.wiley.com/doi/10.1002/14651858.CD005338.pub2/full.

Smith, Rogers M. *Civic Ideals: Conflicting Visions of Citizenship in US History.* Yale University Press, 1997.

Speri, Alice. "Puerto Rico Wants to Cut the Cost of Incarcerating People by Shipping Them Off the Island." *The Intercept* (blog), March 23, 2018. https://theintercept.com/2018/03/23/puerto-rico-prisons-hurricane-maria/.

Stark, David M. "A New Look at the African Slave Trade in Puerto Rico Through the Use of Parish Registers: 1660–1815." *Slavery and Abolition* 30, no. 4 (2009): 491–520. https://doi.org/10.1080/01440390903245083.

Steward, Julian H., Sidney Mintz, Robert Manners, Eric Wolf, Elena Seda, and Raymond Scheele. *The People of Puerto Rico: A Study in Social Anthropology.* University of Illinois Press, 1956.

Sugarman, Barry. *Daytop Village: A Therapeutic Community.* Holt McDougal, 1974.

Summerfield, Penny. *Women Workers in the Second World War: Production and Patriarchy in Conflict.* Routledge, 2013.

Tannenbaum, Frank. *Slave and Citizen: The Classic Comparative Study of Race Relations in the Americas.* Beacon Press, 1992.

Tempalski, Barbara, Risa Friedman, Marie Keem, Hannah Cooper, and Samuel R. Friedman. "NIMBY Localism and National Inequitable Exclusion Alliances: The Case of Syringe Exchange Programs in the United States." *Geoforum* 38, no. 6 (2007): 1250–63.

Thomas, Lorrin. *Puerto Rican Citizen.* University of Chicago Press, 2010.

Thompson, Edward P. "Time, Work-Discipline, and Industrial Capitalism." *Past and Present* 38 (1967): 56–97.

Thompson, Heather Ann. "Rethinking Working-Class Struggle through the Lens of the Carceral State: Toward a Labor History of Inmates and Guards." *Labor* 8, no. 3 (2011): 15–45.

Thompson, Lanny. *Imperial Archipelago: Representation and Rule in the Insular Territories under US Dominion after 1898.* University of Hawaii Press, 2010.

Torres, Arlene. *"La Gran Familia Puertorriqueña 'ej Prieta de Beldá"*: Blackness in Latin America and the Caribbean: Social Dynamics and Cultural Transformations. Bloomington, IN, 1998.

Torruella, Rafael. "¿Allá En Nueva York Todo Es Mejor?: A Qualitative Study on the Relocation of Drug Users from Puerto Rico to the United States." PhD diss., City University of New York, 2011.

Uggen, Christopher, Jeff Manza, and Angela Behrens. "'Less than the Average Citizen': Stigma, Role Transition and the Civic Reintegration of Convicted Felons." In *After Crime and Punishment*, edited by Shadd Maruna and Russ Immarigeon, 279–311. Willan, 2013.

United Nations. *Principles for the Protection of Persons with Mental Illness and the Improvement of Mental Health Care*. 1991. https://www.equalrightstrust.org/sites/default/files/ertdocs//UN_Resolution_on_protection_of_persons_with_mental_illness.pdf.

Upegui-Hernández, Débora, and Rafael Torruella. *Humillaciones y Abusos En Centros de Tratamiento Para Uso de Drogas PR* [Humiliation and abuse in drug treatment centers in Puerto Rico]. Intercambios Puerto Rico, 2015. https://es.scribd.com/doc/265551445/Humillaciones-y-Abusos-en-Centros-de-Tratamiento-Para-Uso-de-Drogas-PR.

Van den Berg, Marguerite, and Bruce O'Neill. "Introduction: Rethinking the Class Politics of Boredom." *Focaal* 78 (2017): 1–8.

Vargas, João H. Costa. "The Black Diaspora as Genocide. Brazil and the United States—a Supranational Geography of Death and Its Alternatives." In *State of White Supremacy: Racism, Governance, and the United States*, edited by Moon-Kie Jung, João Costa Vargas, and Eduardo Bonilla-Silvam, 243–70. Standford University Press, 2011.

Velez, Alexandra Sun. "Between Two Courts: Mass Incarceration and the Prisoner's Rights Movement in Puerto Rico, 1970–1990." PhD diss., University of Georgia, 2021.

Velez, Edwin. *Estudio Descriptivo Sobre Los Hogares CREA, INC* [Descriptive study of Hogares CREA, INC]. Universidad de Puerto Rico, 1986.

Wacquant, Loïc. *Punishing the Poor: The Neoliberal Government of Social Insecurity*. Duke University Press, 2009.

Walmsley, Roy. "World Prison Population, 11th Edition." Institute for Criminal Policy Research, 2016. https://www.prisonstudies.org/sites/default/files/resources/downloads/world_prison_population_list_11th_edition_0.pdf.

Walton, Matthew T., and Martin T. Hall. "Involuntary Civil Commitment for Substance Use Disorder: Legal Precedents and Ethical Considerations for Social Workers." *Social Work in Public Health* 32, no. 6 (2017): 382–93.

Weber, Max. *The Protestant Ethic and the Spirit of Capitalism*. Skyros, 2015.

Weisskoff, Richard. *Factories and Food Stamps: The Puerto Rico Model of Development*. Johns Hopkins University Press, 1985.

Wells, Henry. "The Modernization of Puerto Rico. A Political Study of Changing Values and Institutions." *VRÜ Verfassung Und Recht in Übersee* 4, no. 2 (1971): 234–35.

Weppner, Robert S. *The Untherapeutic Community: Organizational Behavior in a Failed Addiction Treatment Program*. University of Nebraska Press, 1983.

Williamson, John D. "Self-Help and Mutual Aid." In *Today's Priorities in Mental Health: Children and Families—Needs, Rights, and Action*, edited by Stuart

H. Fine, Robert Krell, Tsung-yi Lin, Morton Beiser, David S. Freeman, and Richard Nann, 237–41. Dordrecht, Netherlands: Springer, 1981.

Wool, Zoë H. *After War: The Weight of Life at Walter Reed*. Duke University Press, 2015.

World Prison Brief. "Puerto Rico (USA)." World Prison Brief, 2016. http://www.prisonstudies.org/country/puerto-rico-usa.

———. "United States of America." World Prison Brief, 2020. https://www.prisonstudies.org/country/united-states-america.

Wright, Michael. "Puerto Rican Prisons 'Ready to Explode' Despite Reform Effort." *New York Times*, November 19, 1982. http://www.nytimes.com/1982/11/19/us/puerto-rican-prisons-ready-to-explode-despite-reform-effort.html.

Yablonsky, Lewis. *The Tunnel Back: Synanon*. Macmillan, 1965.

Zatz, Noah. "The Carceral Labor Continuum: Beyond the Prison Labor/Free Labor Divide." 2021. https://escholarship.org/uc/item/2ps7w65b.

Zigon, Jarrett. *"HIV Is God's Blessing": Rehabilitating Morality in Neoliberal Russia*. University of California Press, 2010.

· INDEX ·

blanqueamiento, 13–14, 15, 16–17
boredom, 91, 99, 100–103, 106, 108, 109
bricolage, 50
British colonialism, 14
brotherhood, 5, 7, 55, 56, 137
Brown University, 117–18

Camila, 124–28, 131, 132
campesinos (rural people), 65
Cannon, Joseph, 10
capitalism: and colonialism, 61, 136;
    crisis of, 74; and the displacement of
    young men, 76; and incarceration,
    8; "keeping busy," 90; labor therapy,
    93; late capitalism, 8, 25; subject
    formation, 93, 94; "surplus" labor, 3;
    time management, 98; voluntary work,
    2; wage-scarce capitalism, 94. *See also*
    neoliberalism
"carceral," definition, 8
carceral archipelago, 114, 169n7
carceral circuit, 33
carceral citizenship: animosity toward
    other initiatives, 86; concept, 8,
    10–11, 12, 38, 47; "cunning" of, 86; as
    exclusion, 87–88, 136; history of, 61–
    62; micropractices, 60; and race, 42;
    risk of forfeiture, 137–38
carceral devolution, 83
carceral labor, history of, 38
carceral livelihoods, 8, 12–13, 38, 79, 84, 94
carceral state, 2–3, 13, 61
carceral turn, 3, 19, 61, 76, 88, 136
Carlos, 124–28, 131–32
Carr, Summerson, 105
carta de hogar, 120
Cartagena, 86, 87
case reports, 78, 129–30, 132
"case workers," 36, 37
cash payments, 37
La Casita, 1, 3–5, 21–23, 26–27, 35, 56, 89–
    109, 111, 125–26, 131–32, 134–35
Cassian, John, 98, 108
Catholic church, 22, 52, 53, 64, 95
Cédula de Gracias a Sacar, 14, 15
cell phones, 131
census race categories, 15–16, 17, 63
Center for the Investigation of Addiction
    (Spanish acronym, CISLA), 66–67,
    68, 69

centralized drug treatment services, 84
"certified penitents," 34
certified professionals, 34, 49, 51, 137–38
chain gangs, 79, 80
"characterologically flawed" citizens, 61
characterological theory, 50, 72, 86, 92, 105
character transformation, 4, 70, 72, 130, 135
charismatic leadership, 48, 73
childhood development, disrupted, 67
children, 34, 35
chores, 72, 89–90, 96–103
Christianity: acedia, 102; atonement, 43,
    46, 47, 53; boredom, 101–2; Catholic
    church, 22, 52, 53, 64, 95; center
    rules based on, 45–46; Evangelical
    church, 22, 49, 81, 84, 93–94, 95, 121;
    faith-based residential drug programs,
    22, 85, 129; graduation ceremonies,
    52–53; imminent transformation, 131;
    labor therapy, 93; La Casita, 92, 95;
    monasticism, 94, 99, 102, 106; mutual
    aid, 22–23, 42, 46; penance, 53, 54, 139;
    Pentecostal church, 22, 95; prayer, 48,
    51, 72, 89, 95, 99, 102, 106; Protestant
    missionaries, 95; Protestant work ethic,
    99; redemption, 53, 54, 80, 82, 139;
    rescue, 81; salvation, 109; secular-
    spiritual Christianity, 94–95; training
    sessions, 49
chronicity of addiction, 131
citizenship: ethical citizenship, 82; of
    last resort, 94; and the limits of penal
    confinement, 8–10; naturalization,
    172n3; new modes of, 136; professional
    sense of, 50; racially stratified
    citizenship, 32–33, 41–42; reentry as
    "full" citizen, 137, 139; stratified, 32–33,
    41–42. *See also* carceral citizenship
citizenship pageants, 82
civic duties, 79, 81, 82
civic support, 69, 70, 73, 79
civil commitments, 21, 26, 39–40, 110–33
civil rights movement, 2, 138
Civil War, 64
class-action lawsuits, 77
cleanliness, 22
clinical diagnosis of addiction, 119, 122–23
clinical epistemologies, 50
"clinically expected recurrence," 128–29
clinical treatment of drug addiction, 83

Legislative Assembly, 84
leisure time, 97, 98, 102
Lewis, Oscar, 154n79
liberalism, 9, 41, 136, 139. *See also*
 neoliberalism
libretas, 62–63, 64
licensing, 7, 21, 37, 90, 169n5
Lindsay, John, 68
lived experience, 7, 46–47, 90
"livelihood," definition, 12
Lloréns, Hilda, 42
loans, 7
lobbying, 69, 84, 85, 165n122
local community organization, 69
love, 45, 55
low-paid work, 79
Luis, 56–57

Mains, Daniel, 101
makeshift operations, 22, 92, 96
male breadwinner model, 93
mandatory drug tests, 56
mandatory minimum sentencing, 77
mandatory requirements of release, 39
Mano Dura ("Strong Hand"), 19
Manos a la Obra, 74–75
Manuel, 48–49, 50, 51, 57
manufacturing jobs, 74, 75
marches, 82
market discipline, 93, 108
Marx, Karl, 2, 164n98
Marxist materialism, 25
masculine identity, 51
mass emigration, 75, 134
"mass expulsion," 61
Mauss, Marcel, 38, 106
maximum benefit principle, 127, 128, 131
maximum treatment principle, 123, 124,
 128
Maxwell, John, 49
mayors, 52, 69, 70, 79
meaningfulness, 3, 12–13, 57, 91, 108–9, 137
medals/awards, 43
media coverage, 51–53, 68, 69, 70, 73, 80,
 81, 137
medical insurance, 112, 113, 127
medicalization of drug services, 84
meditation, 98, 106
Mental Health Act of 2000, 85, 115. *See also*
 Law 408 of 2000 (Mental Health Act)

Mental Health and Anti-Addiction Services
 Administration, 7
mental illness, 112–13, 114
Mesón de Dios, 24, 27, 35, 36, 111
mestizaje, 13–14, 16, 18, 42
methadone programs, 84–85, 86
microenterprises, 79
micropractices, 60
middle classes, 33, 34, 55, 69
military power, 54
military veterans, 44, 89
"millennium free of drugs" initiative,
 80–81
Miller, Reuben Jonathan, 11
minimum wage, 37
Mintz, Sidney, 62, 149n41
modernization, 74, 76
modern slavery, 79–80
monitoring, 123
moral character education, 7, 58–59, 70, 72.
 See also character transformation
moral culpability, 46
moral debt, 34, 53, 54, 57
moral obligations, 45, 46, 130
moral rehabilitation, 66
"moral therapy," 93
moral worth, 33
Muehlebach, Andrea, 82
multiculturalism, 165n134
multiple graduations, 55–56. *See also*
 cycling between *internado* and
 re-educado
municipal codes, 39–40
Muñoz Marín, Luis, 16, 74, 75
mutual aid, 22, 42, 46
mutual obligation, 9

Narcotics Anonymous, 21, 30, 39
national anthems, 31
national duty, 32
national identity, 16, 18, 41, 54
national service, 54
nation-states, 9, 11
negro identification, 15, 16, 17
neoliberalism, 2, 82, 85, 90, 93, 97, 139
New York, 19, 25, 68
noncompliance leading to incarceration,
 38, 116
non-prison incarceration, 8. *See also* civil
 commitments